United States and China in Power Transition

Attention Authors

'We Convert Fighters into Writers'. That's the motto of Manas Publications since more than four decades. Our message to the world is that India can win the battle not only by the bullet but also by the pen. There is no dearth of intellectuals in our country, but their knowledge is confined to them only. No sincere effort has been made by any other publisher to channelise their knowledge in national interest. That is why the talent of a large number of intellectuals remains latent. An author transforms his knowledge into a manuscript, and it is our job to spread his/her knowledge by converting it into a beautiful book. For over four decades, Manas has been motivating the intellectuals by publishing their manuscripts and would like to publish your manuscript too. If you or your colleagues have any manuscript ready for publication or are working on it, kindly contact us with detailed synopsis and list of contents. We will transform your work into a valuable publication. If you wish, we can also suggest you the suitable subjects for writing the books related to your area of expertise. Manas is known for its publishing quality and commitments. We take utmost care in production and give wide publicity to the book as well as its author through our national and international distribution network.

United States and China in Power Transition

David Lai
Research Professor,
Strategic Studies Institute, USA

Manas Publications
(We Convert Fighters into Writers)
New Delhi-110002 (INDIA)

MANAS PUBLICATIONS
(We Convert Fighters into Writers)
(Publishers, Library Suppliers, Importers & Exporters)
4402/5-A, Ansari Road (Opp HDFC Bank)
Darya Ganj, New Delhi-110 002 (India)
Off. ✆ 23260783, 23265523, Fax: 011-23272766
E-mail: manaspublications@vsnl.com
manaspublications@gmail.com

Strategic Studies Institute, USA

2013

ISBN 978-81-7049-441-6
₹ 695/-

Designed at
Manas Publications

Printed in India at
HS Offsets, Delhi
and published by Mrs Suman Lata for
Manas Publications, 4402/5-A,
Ansari Road (Opp HDFC Bank),
Darya Ganj, New Delhi-110002 (INDIA)

CONTENTS

Foreword

The United States and China have experienced many changes in their relations in the past 30 years. Some international security experts posit that the most profound one has begun—an apparent power transition between the two nations. This potentially titanic change, it is argued, was set in motion by China's genuine and phenomenal economic development over the past decade, or so. Clearly, China's impact on the United States and the US-led international system has been growing steadily.

Historically, most great power transitions were consummated by war. Can China and the United States avoid a deadly contest and spare the world another catastrophe? The good news is that the two nations expressed goodwill in the mid-2000s, with China's promise of peaceful development and the US call for China to become a responsible stakeholder in the extant international system. The bad news is that China and the United States still have many unsettled issues, some of which directly involve the two nations' core interests and others indirectly entangled with China's neighbors. Those issues can lead to the two nations stumbling into unintended clashes, hence triggering a repeat of the great power tragedies of the past.

Some scholars predict that over the next 30 years and beyond, this apparent power transition process will continue to be a defining factor in the US-China relationship. What can we expect from China and the United States with respect to the future of international relations? As China's economic, political, cultural, and military influences continue to grow globally, what kind of a global power will China become? What kind of a relationship will China develop with the United States? How does the United States maintain its leadership in world affairs and develop a working relationship with China that encourages it to join hands with the United States to shape the world in constructive ways?

In this monograph, Dr. David Lai offers an engaging discussion of these questions and others. His analysis addresses issues that trouble US as well as Chinese leaders. Dr Lai has taken painstaking care to put the conflicting positions in perspective, most notably presenting the origins of the conflicts, highlighting the conflicting parties' key opposing positions (by citing their primary or original sources), and pointing out the stalemates. His intent is to remind US, as well as Chinese, leaders of the complicated nature of US-China relations, during a power transition and to encourage them to look at the existing conflicts in this new light. He also intends for the analysis to help the two nations' leaders look beyond their parochial positions and take constructive measures to manage this complicated process—one that will affect future international relations in seminal ways.

The Strategic Studies Institute is pleased to offer this monograph as a contribution to the discussion of this important issue.

DOUGLAS C. LOVELACE, JR.
Director
Strategic Studies Institute

Summary

This analysis discusses the nature of US-China relations in the context of an ongoing power transition between these two great powers, the rise of China and its impact, China's tortuous experience during its transition to modernity, US-China conflicts over the two nations' core interests, and the future of the US-China power transition.

Main Arguments

This analysis holds the following propositions. First, as a result of its genuine development and the impact of its expanding influence on the international system, China and the United States are inescapably engaged in a power transition process, which is, on top of all other issues, about the future of international relations.

Second, the history of power transition is filled with bloodshed; yet China and the United States are willing to blaze a new path out of this deadly contest.

Third, although China and the United States have exchanged goodwill for a peaceful future, the two nations nevertheless have many contentious and unsettled conflicts of interest that are further complicated by the power transition process and, if not properly managed, can force the two to stumble into unintended war against each other, hence repeating the history of power transition tragedy.

Finally, the next 30 years will be a crucial stage for China's development and the evolution of the US-China power transition.

Unfortunately, these titanic changes are overshadowed by the inherently conflicting relations between China and the United States. It will take these two great powers extraordinary efforts to come to terms with the emerging new realities.

Policy Recommendations

This analysis covers a wide range of issues related to and complicated by the ongoing US-China power transition. It has made an effort to put these issues in perspective. The intent is to remind US, as well as Chinese, leaders of the complicated nature of US-China relations under the condition of this power transition and to encourage them to look at the existing conflicts in this new light. It is also intended to persuade the two nations' leaders to look beyond their parochial positions and take constructive measures to manage this complicated process. The following are some key policy recommendations derived from this analysis.

- While the United States and China have always had conflict since the founding of the People's Republic of China (PRC) in 1949, US and Chinese leaders should always bear in mind that since China embarked on its genuine economic revolution in 1978, the defining character of the US-China relationship has become known as a power transition. The two nations' policies and interactions therefore must take this factor into account.
- Power transition is about the future of international relations. Historically, systematic changes were settled on battlefields. In the current situation, the United States and China have exchanged goodwill to blaze a new path for a peaceful transition. However, this is just the first step in the right direction; as the power transition process unfolds, there will be new and unexpected challenges. The US and Chinese leaders therefore need to do more to find ways to adjust to the new situations and reassure each other from time to time to avoid war.
- Power transition is also about titanic changes in great power relations. The most critical one is between the

United States and China. The US and Chinese leaders should gain a good understanding of what the two nations can or cannot do with respect to the changes. Both nations' leaders should guard against the temptation to do the impossible, which will be a recipe for disaster and war.

- As China continues to grow and expand, it will find it more difficult to compromise, but will be increasingly capable of taking stronger stands on matters involving its extant and expanding national interests. China should guard against the tendency to initiate premature confrontation with the United States.
- The United States should bear in mind that a rising China will naturally "ask for more," even if Chinese leaders try to make China's expansion less demanding. The United States should therefore guard against the tendency to overreact to China's moves.
- The struggle for the fate of Taiwan is no doubt the most explosive issue between China and the United States. The two great powers have many conflicts. However, the conflict over the fate of Taiwan is the only one overshadowed by the "dictate of the gun"—China's determination to use force if peaceful means fails to bring about unification and the US commitment to "resist any resort to force or other forms of coercion that would jeopardize the security, or the social or economic system, of the people on Taiwan" (US Public Law 96-8, The Taiwan Relations Act of 1979). This outstanding issue is now further complicated by the power transition process. It is not an exaggeration to say that if the US-China power transition were to catch fire, the fight over the fate of Taiwan would be the most likely trigger. That said, we should see that the current "stabilizer" in the Taiwan Strait is a US-defined status quo. Specifically, the United States opposes any unilateral attempt to change the status of Taiwan; it holds China against the temptation of a forceful unification with Taiwan; and at the same time, warns Taiwan not to provoke China by pushing forward the independence agenda. This US balancing act rests on the backing of US military power. However, as China

continues to modernize its military power, the power balance over the Taiwan Strait will change. This analysis suggests that although the use of force is a dangerous component of the Taiwan issue, it is in the interest of both the United States and China to guard against the temptation to look at the Taiwan issue in purely military terms and run a deadly military contest on this issue. In the meantime, China should guard against the temptation to upset this status quo prematurely.

- At present, the US policy of measured arms sales to Taiwan is a point of repeated contention between China and the United States. Several times in the last two decades, the conflict over arms sales to Taiwan has led to deep and abrupt downturns in the two nations' relations, especially the military relations. In the years ahead, while the United States should find ways to make the decisions to provide Taiwan with needed defensive weapons less provoking to China, China should modify its reactions and avoid suspending the US-China military-to-military (mil-to-mil) contacts, which are most needed at times of tension and conflict.
- In the past three decades, the United States and China have developed a highly interconnected and interdependent relationship. However, the two nations' military relations remain tenuous, and at times confrontational. In the years ahead, while the two nations will follow their own strategy to maintain the leading edge (in the case of the United States) and develop the needed capability (in the case of China) of their military power to counter-balance each other, it is in the two nations' interest to develop an effective, reliable, and sustainable contact between the two militaries. In the last two decades, the United States and China have established a few high-level military contacts. However, these contacts are rather superficial. They cannot be used to help reduce tension when the two nations are in conflict. As some Chinese analysts put it, when China and the United States come

to blows over their core interests, their superficial mil-to-mil contacts are the first to be cut; but when the relations between the two nations rebound, the mil-to-mil contacts are the last to resume.[1] This is really dangerous for the two nations that are trying to prevent unintended wars. This analysis suggests that the United States and China consider exchanging resident students (military officers) in each other's military schools at all levels as a long-term remedy to this problem. As the United States and China continue to agonize over the power transition in the years ahead, this "grass-roots" effort and investment will allow the two militaries to learn about each other's principles and operational codes; it will pay valuable dividends that the current *ad hoc* and on-and-off mil-to-mil contacts can never produce.

- Although China is one of the oldest civilizations in the world, it is still a developing nation and has many unsettled "nation-building" issues, such as its avowed mission to reunite with Taiwan, settlement of the East and South China Sea disputed territories and ocean interests, and harmonizing its relations with the people of Tibet and Xinjiang inside and outside of China. This analysis has shown that the United States does not see eye-to-eye with the Chinese leaders on these so-called Chinese core interests; however, it also suggests that the United States should maintain its role as a keeper of order and justice in the Western Pacific and try to avoid becoming a directly-involved disputing party to China's claimed core interests. This is especially the case with respect to China's territorial dispute with Japan in the East China Sea and disputes with the Southeast Asia nations in the South China Sea.
- In addition to the above, the United States and China also have a thorny issue in the Korean Peninsula. For decades, the United States has mostly treated the North Korea problem as a military issue and responded to many

of North Korea's provocative acts with military countermeasures. China, however, while ostensibly trying to persuade North Korea to control its provocative acts, adamantly opposes the US military posturing in the Korean Peninsula, charging that the real intent of the intensified US military activities in Northeast Asia is a US attempt to deter China. As recently as June 2011, China solicited Russia's support to issue a joint statement openly denouncing the US approach: "the two countries pledged support for each other on a wide range of issues, including Russia's security challenges from the United States and Europe as well as US pressure on China in the Asia-Pacific regions."[2] US political and military leaders should see that, with China and Russia standing in the way, a military solution to the North Korea problem is not an option. Hasty military reactions to the North Korea problem are increasingly becoming a point of contention between China and the United States. This is dangerous to the power transition process.

- In the light of this situation, the US repositioning and reduction of military forces in South Korea appeared to be proper policy adjustments. In the years ahead, the United States should gradually turn the remaining US military forces in the Korean Peninsula from the decades-long tactical operations into a strategic deterrence presence. This adjustment is consistent with the Nixon Doctrine that expects our allies and friendly nations in Asia to bear the primary responsibility for their security interests, while the United States provides needed military, economic, and political support. In the meantime, the United States should take China's advice to replace the Korean War Armistice with a peace treaty and normalize US relations with North Korea. This act should relieve the United States from a hostile problem that has cost the United States blood and treasure for well over six decades. With the removal of hostility, North Korea has no more excuse to develop nuclear weapons. The United States is no longer part of the problem. The eventual denuclearization in North Korea, which is a China-led principle and initiative, will be an issue of the Northeast Asia nations. The United States can reengage in this issue as an "off-shore balancer"[3] with much strategic flexibility.

- In the next 30 years, the gap between the US and Chinese comprehensive national power will continue to exist, but it will become smaller. The power transition theory believes that the risk of war will become bigger when the two nations' national power approaches parity. The US and Chinese leaders must pay more attention to the changes coming out of the power transition in the years ahead and make more efforts to manage the changes accordingly.

Endnotes

1. Dong Feng "What Is the Matter with the US-China Military Relations?" *World Affairs*, No. 13, 2010.
2. Wu Jiao, "New Era for Sino-Russian Ties: Joint Declaration Pledges Mutual Support on Key Security Issues," *China Daily*, June 17, 2011.
3. See Christopher Lane's works for the idea of the United States as an off-shore balancer.

Chapter - 1

Introduction

We can't predict with certainty what the future will bring, but we can be certain about the issues that will define our times. And we also know this: The relationship between the United States and China will shape the 21st century....[1]

President Barak Obama

This is quite a calculated statement of the US-China relationship. On the one hand, the President signals that the United States can no longer shape the world solely in its image or with US unilateral efforts; but has to invite China to help with the mission. On the other, the President's remarks express concern for the tenuous nature of the US-China relationship. Indeed, there are many unsettled issues in this relationship, most of which are about the prospect of China's projected rise and its impact on the United States and the US-led international order. Can China continue with success in its reforms and reach the goals set by its modernization plan (projected well into the mid-century)? While many aspects of China, most notably its economy, have been integrated into the international system, its authoritarian government still insists on going its own way, most likely for a long time to come.

Can Chinese leaders continue to muddle through China's changes without embracing genuine political modernization? Moreover, although China is the world's longest-surviving nation, its nation building is still unfinished. Can China consolidate its national unity with Taiwan, Tibet, and Xinjiang, and settle the disputed territories in the East and South China Seas in peaceful ways? In addition to these so-called nation-building imperatives, China also has growing external interests in global economic, political, cultural, and military affairs. What are China's intentions? What kind of a global power will China become? What kind of a relationship will China develop with the United States? How does the United States maintain its leadership in world affairs and develop a working relationship with China so that China can join hands with the United States to shape the world in constructive ways?

These are, in essence, questions pertaining to a power transition ostensibly taking place between the United States and China. Given that the United States and China are two of the most powerful nations in the world, these issues, as Obama rightly puts it, define our times. A clear understanding of the power transition, and especially China's part in this process, is essential for the leaders of these two great nations. This analysis holds the following propositions. First, as a result of its genuine development and the impact of its expanding influence on the international system, China and the United States are inescapably engaged in a power transition process.

Second, the history of power transition is filled with bloodshed; yet China and the United States are willing to blaze a new path out of this deadly contest.

Third, although China and the United States have exchanged goodwill for a peaceful future, the two nations have nevertheless many difficult conflicts of interest that are being further complicated by the power transition process and, if not properly managed, can force the two to wage unwanted war against each other, hence repeating the history of power transition tragedy.

Finally, the next 30 years will be a crucial stage for China's development and the evolution of the US-China power transition.

Unfortunately, these titanic changes are overshadowed by the inherently conflicting relations between China and the United States. It will take these two great powers extraordinary efforts to come to terms with the emerging new realities.

Endnotes

1. Opening remarks by President Barak Obama at the first US-China Strategic and Economic Dialogue, Washington, DC, July 27, 2009.

Chapter - 2

The Power Transition Theory

Power transition is a business among powerful nations. The term comes from Kenneth Organski's classic work, *World Politics*.[1] It refers to several important aspects of international relations. First, it is about a significant increase of national power in a big nation (in terms of its territorial and demographic sizes) as a result of its genuine and rapid economic development. Second, it is the impact of this growing power on the international system, especially on the hegemonic position of the dominant nation in this international system. Throughout history, changes in the balance of power and efforts to keep or alter the international order have led to struggles among the big nations and set the stage for great power wars.[2] These confrontations usually result in changes of international leadership and the rearrangement of international systems.

In a world of independent sovereign nations, there is always an uneven distribution of power—some nations are more powerful than others, differentiated by their sheer size and level of development. Over the ages, big nations have sought dominance in the international system. As Organski observes, "at any given moment the single most powerful nation on earth heads an international order which includes also some other major powers of secondary importance and some minor nations and dependencies as well".

There is peace and stability as long as the dominant nation and its powerful allies maintain firm control of the international order of this system (the political, economic, and security institutions and rules of conduct).[3] However, international relations are always in flux, so is great power status due to changes in national power. Challenge to the system will emerge if one or a few of the second-ranked big nations that are also dissatisfied with the existing international order experience significant increase in their national power. This occurred in the industrial age through industrialization. With their newfound power, rising nations typically make efforts to alter the international order to better serve their interests.

Robert Gilpin adds to this line of thought with his classic work, *War and Change in World Politics*, in which he states that the expanding nations' efforts necessarily bring them to confront the dominant nation and its allies about the rules governing the existing international system, the division of the spheres of influence, and even territorial boundaries. War will break out between the dominant power and the challenger(s) if they cannot settle their differences in peaceful ways. Gilpin calls this "hegemonic war". It is the primary means great powers use to resolve the differences in their relations or to create a new international order. Unfortunately, "[e]very international system that the world has known has been a consequence of the territorial, economic, and diplomatic realignments that have followed such hegemonic struggles".[4]

At the initial stage when the hegemonic nation enjoys a substantial edge over the rest, particularly the potential contender, the international system is in a state free of great-power war. The potential contender does not have the capability to challenge the dominant nation or overthrow the international order. Under these circumstances, the strong need not fight, and the weak dare not try.

As a general rule, mature nations maintain a moderate and steady growth rate. An expanding contender, however, will experience exponential growth in its national power, due largely to its rapid internal economic development. In absolute terms, the dominant nation is still advancing; but in a relative sense, it is losing ground to the rising power. The change of power balance brings the great-power relations into a war-prone zone. Organski and Jacek Kugler argue that shifts in the distribution of power create the conditions for great-power conflict; and war looms when a contender's national power narrows its gap with that of the dominant nation.[5] One probable course of action is that the dominant nation preempts the upstart before the latter gets a chance to challenge the status quo. The other possibility is that the contender, believing that the dominant power is bent on making efforts to prevent its rise and that its newfound power allows it to rival or surpass the dominant nation, initiates a fight, forcing the dominant nation to a military showdown.[6] If the contender wins the fight and overtakes the dominant nation to become the new and most powerful state in the system, it will usher the world into a new international order.

History is full of stories of bloody contests for systemic dominance. The classic case of power transition and hegemonic war took place between the ancient Greek states of Athens and Sparta in 431 BC. Athens was an expanding state. It gained its hegemonic power first by consolidating numerous small Greek city-states into the Delian League under Athenian leadership to fight against Persian invasions and, following the victory over the Persians, collecting the wealth from the subject city-states to build up an Athenian Empire. This expanding Athenian empire went on to challenge the Peloponnesian League led by Sparta. Athens and Sparta subsequently fought the protracted Peloponnesian War to settle the hegemonic control of the ancient Greek world. Thucydides, an Athenian historian of the time, took note of this 27-year-long war and observed succinctly the reason for this deadly contest: "the real cause for this war was the growth of the Athenian power and the fear generated in the minds of the Spartans that made the war inevitable".[7]

Just about the time when the ancient Greeks and Persians fought for supremacy along the northern Mediterranean Sea and Asia Minor, the ancient Chinese in East Asia were waging wars to settle their contention for hegemony over the Chinese states. From 720 to 470 BC, a period called Spring and Autumn[8] in Chinese history, five hegemonic powers took turns to impose order among a large number of widespread and fragmented Chinese enfeoffed states (over 200 in number). The rise and fall of these hegemonic powers all took place with the use of force. The small Chinese states fell victim to the great power conflict during those 250 years and subsequently were conquered or annexed by the hegemonic powers.

By the time the Chinese states entered the Warring States era (471-221 BC)[9], the number of states was reduced to seven. These seven major powers contended for supremacy in the Chinese heartland. Constant warfare was the hallmark of this era of 250 years. Finally, the state of Qin defeated the rest and founded a centralized Middle Kingdom known as the Qin Dynasty in 221 BC. For the next 2,000 years, this insulated Middle Kingdom (protected by the Himalaya mountain plateau, the Gobi desert, and the Pacific Ocean) had no "peer competitor". Although the Middle Kingdom suffered cyclical dynastic rise and fall over the centuries, periodic internal breakups and warfare, and invasion from outsiders such as the Mongols and Manchurians as well, the Chinese were able to retain the Middle Kingdom, assimilate the outsiders into the Chinese fold, and continue the China-centered international order in East Asia.

That is not the case in the Eurasian landmass. The last 2,000 and more years witnessed the rise and fall of many great powers (the Persian Empire, Roman Empire, and the Arab Empires, to name a few of the early hegemonic powers). Some of the empires simply vanished. Since the 1500s, hegemonic reach took on a global scale. The Portuguese Empire, Spanish Empire, Dutch Empire, Russian Empire, French Empire, British Empire, German Empire, and so on, took turns to impose colonial rule in different parts of the world. The rise and fall of these empires and subsequent change of international order all took place with the use of force. Hegemonic competition eventually took a heavy toll on the contending empires in World War I and World War II. The destruction of imperial Germany and Japan and the decline of the British Empire are textbook examples of the "tragedy of great power struggle".[10]

In 1816, Great Britain was the most powerful nation on earth, commanding about a third of the world's material capabilities. Riding on the wave of its Industrial Revolution, Great Britain developed a dominant navy, became the financial and trading center of the world, and expanded its imperial reach (colonial control) to every continent, hence as the saying goes, the sun never set on the British Empire. As a systemic hegemony, Great Britain, in concert with the other great powers in Europe, established a system of political, economic, and security order commonly known as the *Pax Britannica* and preserved more than half of a century of relative peace and stability in Europe.

However, British power gradually declined. In the latter part of the 19th century, the United States and Germany rapidly rose up, following their internal consolidation (the US Civil War and German Unification, respectively) and economic development. By the time World War I broke out in 1914, Great Britain did not have the capacity to dictate peace and stability in the international system.

At the conclusion of World War I, the United States became a powerful nation in the world. President Woodrow Wilson believed that the time had come for the United States to lead the world. Through his famous "Fourteen Points," Wilson put forward a plan to construct a new world order. Unfortunately, the European powers were skeptical of Wilson's vision, and the American people were not prepared to follow the President and accomplish his mission. The US Congress did not endorse the President's plan. The United States shied away from world leadership and retreated to isolation.

Without a dominant power and strong leadership, the world of great powers remained in a state of turmoil during the 1920s and 1930s. Shifts of power set the stage for another great power conflict. The Great Depression added a severe blow to this chaotic situation. Germany, in the meantime, recovered from its defeat and gathered strength to make another attempt to gain control of the international system. The great power struggle eventually led to the outbreak of World War II.

Another Power Transition in the Making?

The power transition theory provides a very useful perspective for the understanding of great power relations. The change of power distribution and the associated peace and war periods in the 19th century and the first half of the 20th century lend support to the central claim of the power transition theory that preponderance of power maintains international order and peace and the lack of it breeds great-power war.

This theory is useful again for world leaders at the turn of the 21st century, as the international system is undergoing profound changes. The turning point is perhaps best set at the end of the Cold War in 1991. With the collapse of the Soviet Union, the United States stood as the lone superpower. Political commentators celebrated the eventual arrival of the "unipolar world"[12] and the "end of history".[13] Indeed, as their arguments go, the Cold War was the last contest between US/Western liberalism and other ideologies. The Western ideal has prevailed; there is no credible challenge on the horizon; the history of ideological struggle has come to an end; henceforth, all the nations in the world would, in one way or another and sooner or later, turn to democratic government and market capitalism. The United States was urged to take advantage of this historic opportunity to consolidate the *Pax Americana* and facilitate the world's rush to its destiny.

However, as Henry Kissinger puts it, three times in the last 100 years, the United States had opportunities to "tower over the international stage" and "recast the world in its image," but it met with frustration at all three occasions.[14] The first opportunity came in the aftermath of World War I. President Woodrow Wilson put forward the American vision of a new world order to the warring states of the "Old World (Europe)": "the United States possessed the world's best system of government, and that the rest of mankind could attain peace and prosperity by abandoning traditional diplomacy and adopting America's reverence for international law and democracy".[15] Unfortunately, Wilson was confronted with skepticism in the Old World and constrained by isolationism at home. His plan for the new US-led international order slipped away.

The second opportunity came at the end of World War II. The United States was more powerful and mature this time. It almost single-handedly established a new world order that included the United Nations (UN), an improvement on President Woodrow Wilson's idea for the League of Nations, the Breton Woods system of international monetary management, and the General Agreement on Tariffs and Trade (GATT) for international trade. Unfortunately, while this new world order was still in its infancy, the Soviet Union came to challenge the American design. It carved out its own sphere of influence (the communist camp), put in place the communist way of government and economics, and staged a Cold War against the United States. The confrontation between the two superpowers practically put the American dream on hold for the next four decades.

The Cold War eventually came to an end. With the disappearance of its arch enemy, the United States for the third time saw the opportunity to reform the world based on its values. Regrettably, as Kissinger writes, while the United States was the most powerful nation in the world, it could not prevent the titanic shift of power from the Atlantic to the Asia-Pacific and the "diffusion of power" to a large group of second-ranked nations. The United States found itself in "a world which bears many similarities to the European state system of the 18th and 19th centuries," and in which the United States had to negotiate rather than dictate business with peers.[16]

The most telling factor is the steady decline of the US power, from the overwhelming 36.4 percent of the world power share at the end of World War II down to below 15 percent in the 1980s. The other revealing factor is the rise and fall of the Soviet power. In the early 1970s, the Soviet power share surpassed that of the United States. But the Soviet edge was not overwhelming. The national power balance between the two superpowers was right in the "war-prone zone" from the early 1960s to the fall of the Soviet Union.

In retrospect, we can make the argument that the Cold War was in essence the manifestation of the deadly power transition between the Soviet Union and the United States. The inability of either superpower to gain an overwhelming advantage over the other could have been a main factor in making the Cold War such a protracted one. The mutually assured nuclear destruction could have been a key factor in preventing the Cold War from turning hot.[17]

The Cold War came to an abrupt end with the disintegration of the Soviet Union in 1991. The sharp drop of Soviet power is well-registered in this plot. Its successor, Russia, was reduced to the second-rank category afterwards.

Following the fall of the Soviet Union, the United States was back on top of the world. However, contrary to the views of many who celebrated the return of the almighty superpower, but consistent with Kissinger's assessment, the US edge over the other great powers was much smaller. The erosion of the US dominant position is evident.

Right below the two superpowers, one cannot miss China. China has such a big power potential that even before it embarked on its modernization mission in 1978, it had a power base greater than all the other second-ranked major powers.

China's population may have been a major factor in making its big power base. However, India's population size does not seem to have the same effect here. The difference between China and India in the chart is big and informative—both have potentials, but China is way ahead of India.

The COW National Material Capabilities data used in this plot are updated to 2001 (version 3.02). There could be questions about the validity of these measures in the 1990s and beyond, given the changes of national power in the information age and under conditions of globalization (in fact, version 4.0 is already available; it is updated to 2007). But for this analysis, an argument can be made that the measures still hold and provide us a good sense of the positional standing and reversals of the great nations in the past.

Organski has it right that power transition is a long process. For instance, it took Germany more than 70 years to catch up with Great Britain. The transition of system leadership from Britain to the United States also took more than half of a century. Looking at the changes of great power standing, we can say that the conditions of another power transition have been taking shape over the last 20 to 30 years; it is likely to take another 20 to 30 years to reach the point where a new "pecking order" of great powers becomes established. The specter of another power transition is casting a long shadow over the American dream of the *Pax Americana*.

Who is the Contender?

If two or more second-ranked big nations rise at the same time, how would a dominant nation identify its challenger? For example, the United States and Germany both expanded their national power in the second half of the 19th century and surpassed Great Britain at the turn of the 20th century. The US rise was even more spectacular. Why did Great Britain only single out Germany?[18] Today, we are witnessing the rise of China, India, and Brazil. The European Union (EU) is also becoming a formidable actor on the world stage. In addition, one has to take a resurgent Russia into account. Finally, a "normalized" Japan (presumably so with expected modifications to its government and military apparatus) will be a full-fledged great power in international security and political affairs. If we accept that the post-Cold War international system is like the one with the United States at the top of the pyramid, how do we see, and how does the United States determine, which one of these rising great powers is a serious contender?

Organski thought about this issue 50 years ago and offered some answers to this question. Some of his thoughts are definitional; others, situational. They nevertheless offer us a starting point to make sense of the currently changing great power relations.

The power transition theory provides that a contender must be first, one of the *second-ranked* nations in geographic and demographic measures (small nations thus have no such capacity or potential), and second, a *dissatisfied* second-ranked nation. These two basic requirements make sure that given the opportunity, this dissatisfied second-ranked nation has the will and capability to change the existing international order and its acts will bring it to confront the dominant power.

Dissatisfaction is a subjective term. Organski has provided two objective ways to deal with this concept. One, a dissatisfied rising power is not an ally of the dominant nation; and the other, it has no part in the creation of the existing international order. As such, this rising great power presumably does not share the fundamental values of the system and typically finds the existing international order working against its interests. When it becomes more powerful, a dissatisfied rising power will make an effort to change the international order.

In addition, power transition, as defined by Organski, should be an act between an international system leader and a contender, and involving the change or creation of an international system/order. One should not confuse power transition with inter-state rivalries, for the latter may or may not involve contention for the control of an international system/order.

These qualifications are undoubtedly incomplete; yet they offer us a first-step filter to separate the obvious non-contenders from the potential challengers. For instance, we can comfortably exclude the European great powers and Japan from the pool of possible contenders.

Great Britain has long relinquished its hegemonic position and become a "loyal lieutenant" to the United States. France has also long lost its hegemonic status. Since the creation of the US-led international order, France has often been a strong critic of the United States; yet it is only a "loyal dissident" in the US-led camp. The EU is a community of states that are mostly allies of the United States and by definition satisfied supporters of the US-led international order. The EU is a friendly competitor, but there is no sense of threat from its formation and development. Germany and Japan have both been transformed and have become firm supporters of the US-led international order. They are significant and influential great powers, but they do not have the desire to contend with the United States for world leadership.

Japan's case deserves a few more words here. Japan's initial imperial ambition before and during World War II was to establish a regional order in East and Southeast Asia under Japan's rule. A case can be made that Japan's rise and contention for the control of East Asia created a power transition between Japan and China. For centuries, China as the Middle Kingdom was the dominant power in East Asia without peers. The Middle Kingdom maintained a tributary system with its surrounding neighbors, including Japan, as vassal states. When Japan rose up in power through its industrialization drive, it used force to defeat China and tried to replace the Chinese system with its "Greater East Asia Co-Prosperity Sphere" covering Manchukuo, Korea, and Southeast Asia, stretching all the way to Singapore. During its conquering course, however, Japan joined hands with Nazi Germany to contend for world dominance. To a large extent, this move was a key factor in bringing Japan to the World War II showdown with the British/US-led allies in the Pacific.

Today, Japan and China are in a very special situation. For the first time in their history, the two nations are both strong powers. There is tension between the two regarding which one leads in East Asia. It appears that with its bigger potentials, China would enjoy an upper hand over Japan in East Asia, and the world as well. But the Japan-China competition will only be a rivalry sideshow. China's focus is on the United States. Japan is a US ally, and its dealing with China will be unavoidably subsumed under the US strategic design.

The above screening is straightforward. However, it is not so with the following second-ranked nations: Brazil, Russia, India, and China (the BRIC countries). This "gang of four" came to the spotlight of international attention in 2001 through a study by the high-powered American Goldman Sachs Group, Inc., titled *Dreaming with BRICs: The Path to 2050.* The report argues that these four countries occupy more than a quarter of the world's landmass, hold more than 40 percent of the world's population, and are all experiencing rapid economic development; their combined economies could eclipse the economies of the current richest countries (the G-7 powers of the United States, Germany, Japan, Great Britain, France, Italy, and Canada).

Which one of the BRICs is a contender for the next world leader? Or will the four collectively pursue the throne? Indeed, the heads of the BRICs have already held their first summit in

Yekaterinburg, Russia, on June 16, 2009 and issued a declaration calling for the establishment of a multipolar world order.[19] In April 2010, the heads of the four nations held their second summit in Brazil, focusing on issues such as reforming the global financial system and climate change. Since 2006, BRIC foreign ministers have met annually. Their financial ministers and heads of central banks have also held frequent meetings.[20]

Although the power transition theory will not rule out such a possibility, it really is a stretch at this point to expect the BRICs to take the global lead. There are, after all, good reasons to disqualify Russia and exclude India and Brazil as serious contenders for world leadership.

Russia (through its predecessor, the Soviet Union) fought and lost the Cold War with the United States. Unfortunately, the United States and the West have not been able to transform Russia into a genuine friend and supporter of the US-led international order. By many accounts, Russia is a dissatisfied second-ranked nation. Its transition to democracy is still tenuous. The United States and the West still hold apprehension over a resurgent Russia. Indeed, suspicion of the Russian Bear is a key factor in the US-led drive for repeated North Atlantic Treaty Organization (NATO) expansion. Russia is not happy with its treatment by the United States and the West. It is determined to and eventually will restore its great power status. However, although Russia will be a formidable power to be reckoned with, it can no longer be a contender for world leadership—with Soviet-style communism down the drain, Russia simply has no viable political, economic, or cultural alternatives to offer the world. It could follow Germany's footsteps to make another try, but it would be doomed to disaster.[21]

India will not be a likely contender for world leadership, either. Although the founder of contemporary India, Jawaharlal Nehru, claimed that India "must be a sound great power or disappear,"[22] India has some insurmountable roadblocks preventing it from reaching that potential. One is its fragmented internal makeup. Ethnic and religious fragmentation will keep India as a weak actor in world politics. Another obstacle is the conflict with its "separate-at-birth brother," Pakistan. And the most difficult barrier is China.

As the teaching of its ancient sage, Kautilya, informs us, India and China are immediate neighbors and they are natural enemies.[23] vill need to get distant friends such as Russia, Japan, and the United States to counter-balance China (my enemy's enemy is a friend). That also makes India a ready candidate for the United States to recruit in its struggle with China in the power transition. India's problem is with China, but China's problem is with the United States. India's problem with China is bilateral. China's problem with the United States is global. In the long run, as Fareed Zakaria puts it, India will be "a check on China's rising ambitions, and a natural ally of the United States".[24] India is not a contender for global leadership.

Brazil is blessed with an abundance of natural resources, a sizeable but manageable population (as compared to the oversized populations of its fellow BRICs, China and India), a vast homeland free of territorial disputes, and a functioning economic and political system. Although it has 10 neighbors around its borders, Brazil has no implacable enemy or insurmountable barrier on its way to prominence (although its Portuguese heritage requires it to work harder in the Spanish-speaking neighborhood). Brazil has everything it needs to become the preeminent power in South America. Its economic development is pushing it toward this end.

Brazil's rise to preeminence in South America challenges the US position in the Western Hemisphere. However, Brazil has a good chance to negotiate its way up. First, Brazil does not have the ambition to challenge the United States for world leadership, although its rise will contribute to the relative decline of the US global position. Brazil qualifies as a satisfied member of the second-ranked powers by virtue of being a member of the Organization of American States. Brazil wants to "reach its deserved spot in the world"[25] as one of the second ranked great powers but not to overtake the United States. Given that the United States has more challenging interests elsewhere in the world, it has good reasons to accept Brazil's rise, especially if US interests are protected and if Brazil does it right. The United States can promote Brazil to become a responsible stakeholder and help preserve peace and stability in the southern part of the Western Hemisphere.

Now we have narrowed down the pool of possible contenders to the lone country of China. By many accounts, China is a well-qualified contender. It is a dissatisfied second-ranked power. It is not a US ally and played no part in the establishment of the current international order. The United States did not even recognize the Beijing government when it was established in 1949, and for 30 years after that kept China out of the US-led international community. China, for its part, once denounced the US-led international order and pushed for its destruction. China is now experiencing rapid economic development. Given the favorable conditions created through economic reform and the Chinese government's well-planned strategy to continue China's modernization, Robert Fogel, a Nobel laureate in economics, predicts that by 2040, the "Chinese economy will reach $123 trillion, or nearly three times the economic output of the entire globe in 2000. . . . China's share of global GDP [gross domestic product]—40 percent—will dwarf that of the United States (14 percent) and the European Union (5 percent) 30 years from now".[26] In addition, the impact of China's economic growth and expansion on the international system is already discernible. Finally, China believes that it has political, economic, and cultural alternatives to offer the world. Chinese leaders have always had views and concerns for the world. Assuming the position of world leadership will be natural when the time comes. The question now is not whether China is a contender in this power transition, but how China manages its rise and the power transition with the United States.

Endnotes

1. AFK Organski, *World Politics*. New York: Alfred A. Knopf, 1969, 2nd Ed. References to Organski in this monograph are all from this work.

2. There are different definitions of great power and great power war. This analysis takes its definitions from Jack S. Levy's classic work, *War in the Modern Great Power System, 1495-1975*, Lexington, KY: The University Press of Kentucky, 1983. Specifically, a "great power" is "a state that plays a major role in international politics with respect to security-related issues. The great power states can be differentiated from other states by

their military power, their interests, their behavior in general and interactions with other powers, and other powers' perceptions of them, and some formal criteria". See Levy's book for the details.

3. See also Charles Kindleberger, *The World in Depression, 1929-1939*, Berkley, CA: University of California Press, 1973; and *World Economic Primacy*, New York: Oxford University Press, 1996; Robert Keohane, *Theory of Hegemonic Stability and Changes in International Regimes, 1967-1977*, Ole Holsti, eds., *Changes in the International System*, Boulder, CO: Westview Press, 1980.

4. Robert Gilpin, *War and Change in World Politics*, London, UK: Cambridge University Press, 1981.

5. A F K Organski and Jacek Kugler, *The War Ledger*, Chicago, IL: The University of Chicago Press, 1980, pp. 4, 8. References to Organski and Kugler are all from this book.

6. There is a classic debate in the field of international relations studies about this situation. The "Balance of Power School" holds that relative parity of power among a group of great powers, say, five or seven (the odd one is usually a balancer or tie breaker), is conducive to peace in the system (the peace may not be just; it only refers to the absence of great-power war). The reason is that since no one power has an assured capability to win a fight and dominate the system; there is no incentive for the great powers to fight. The "Preponderance of Power School," whose thoughts are the underpinning of the power transition theory, argues that the opposite is true—in the parity-of-power system, there is greater danger of war because the conditions encourage gambling. Only in a system where a dominant nation and its allies hold a preponderant superiority over the rest can peace and stability be assured. Clarity of the "pecking order" promotes peace whereas relative parity breeds uncertainty and, hence, war. Bruce Bueno de Mesquita points out that the two schools may have missed the key point—it is not the distribution of power, but the national decision-makers' take on certainty/uncertainty that determines the course of action. See Bruce Bueno de Mesquita, "Risk, Power Distribution, and the Likelihood of War," *International Studies Quarterly*, December 1981; and *The War Trap*, New Haven, CT: Yale University Press, 1980. The debate, however, is not settled.

For the power transition theory, Organski points out that in theory, the dominant power is more likely to preempt the challenger, but in reality, the latter is responsible for most of the power-transition wars in the past. Steve Chan disputes Organski's view by providing analysis that in theory and in reality, the dominant power initiates the fight. See Steve Chan, *China, the US, and the Power-Transition Theory*, New York: Routledge, 2008.

7. Thucydides, *The History of the Peloponnesian War*, New York: Penguin Books, 1954, emphasis added.

8. Spring and autumn is the Chinese way of characterizing the change of seasons and time. Confucius used this term as the title of a chronicle of the State of Lu, Confucius' home state, and one of the great powers of the time, and its relations with the other states between 722 and 481 BC. This period is subsequently named after this work.

9. The name Warring States came from the *Record of the Warring States*, a work compiled early in the Han Dynasty (202 BC-220 AD), covering mostly warfare and interstate relations among the Chinese states from 476 BC to the unification of China by the Qin in 221 BC.

10. This term is from John J. Mearsheimer, *The Tragedy of Great Power Politics*, New York: Norton, 2001.

11. For a comprehensive discussion of the Correlates of War project and the datasets, see the following publications: J. David Singer, Stuart Bremer, and John Stuckey, "Capability Distribution, Uncertainty, and Major Power War, 1820-1965," in Bruce Russett, eds., *Peace, War, and Numbers*, Beverly Hills, CA: Sage, pp. 19-48. J. David Singer, "Reconstructing the Correlates of War Dataset on Material Capabilities of States, 1816-1985," *International Interactions*, Vol. 14, pp. 115-132; Correlates of War Project, 2008, "State System Membership List, v 2008.1," available from, *correlatesofwar.org*. J. David Singer and Melvin Small, CORRELATES OF WAR PROJECT: INTERNATIONAL AND CIVIL WAR DATA, 1816-1992 (Computer file), Ann Arbor, MI: J. David Singer and Melvin Small (producers), 1993, Ann Arbor, MI: Inter-university Consortium for Political and Social Research (distributor), 1994, DOI:10.3886/ICPSR09905.

12. Charles Krauthammer, "The Unipolar Moment," *Foreign Affairs*, 1990/91.
13. Francis Fukuyama, "The End of History?" *National Interest*, Summer 1989.
14. Henry Kissinger, *Diplomacy*, New York: Simon & Schuster, 1994, p. 805.
15. *Ibid.*, p. 18.
16. *Ibid.*, p. 805.
17. There is a sizeable literature about this point in international relations studies.
18. It is beyond the scope of this analysis to provide a full discussion of this issue. For a debate, see Zhiqun Zhu, *US-China Relations in the 21st Century: Power Transition and Peace*, New York: Routledge, 2006; and Steve Chan, *China, the US, and the Power-Transition Theory*, New York: Routledge, 2008.
19. Tony Halpin, "Brazil, Russia, India and China Form Bloc to Challenge US Dominance," *The Times*, June 17, 2009 available from *www.timesonline.co.uk/tol/news/world/us_and_americas/article6514737.ece*.
20. "The BRICs: Trillion-Dollar Club," *The Economist*, April 15, 2010; "Second Summit Meeting of the BRIC Leaders in Brasilia," *People's Daily Online*, Xinhua News Agency, April 16, 2010.
21. See a recent analysis of Russia as a "mediocre power" by John W. Parker, "Russia's Revival: Ambitions, Limitations, and Opportunities for the United States," The National Defense University Institute for National Strategic Studies, *Strategic Perspective*, Vol. 3, January 2011.
22. Jawaharlal Nehru, *The Discovery of India*, New York: The John Day Company, 1946.
23. Kautilya, *The Arthasastra*, L. N. Rangarajan, ed., rearranged, trans., New Delhi, India: Penguin Books, 1992, particularly Part X, "Foreign Policy," and Part XI, "Defense and War".
24. Fareed Zakaria, "The Prize Is India," *Newsweek*, November 30, 2009.

25. Ministry of Defense, Federative Republic of Brazil, *National Strategy of Defense*, December 18, 2008, p. 8.
26. Robert Fogel, "$123,000,000,000,000 China's Estimated Economy by the Year 2040. Be Warned," *Foreign Policy*, Vol. 7, January 2010.

Chapter - 3

US-China Power Transition: From Potential to Reality

Napoleon Bonaparte is probably the first Western statesman to characterize the geostrategic significance of China. "Let China sleep, for when she wakes up, she will shake the world," said the Emperor of France. No one knew precisely what prompted Napoleon to make this warning, but no one seemed to care, either. Indeed, in the early 1840s, about two decades after the passing of the French strongman, the European colonial powers forced their way into China. They used advanced warships and firearms to "wake up" the Chinese. The pre-modern China under the corrupt and close-minded Qing rulers was no match to the Western powers. They easily carved up China into their spheres of influence, pressed China to open up its port cities to foreign trade, and quickly set up commercial, manufacturing, and many other modern operations in China.

The Western powers ostensibly intended to turn China into their overseas production and supply base; yet they had nevertheless brought China into the modern world. This sudden and forceful change threw China into a situation of confronting some strong enemies in the words of Li Hongzhang, a prominent statesman of the late Qing Dynasty, "not seen in thousands of years of the Chinese history".[1] This centuries-old feudal and agrarian society was pressed disgracefully to confront modernity. Its fundamental values, operating rules, and practically all aspects of its way of life were under pressure for change.

In the face of these daunting challenges, many concerned Chinese stepped forward to advocate ways to cope with change. However, to China's disappointment and the Western powers' fortune, the initial Chinese efforts had largely failed. The awakened China did not come to shake the world.

In retrospect, the Chinese failed to do so not because Napoleon was wrong about China's potentials, but because they had taken questionable approaches towards modernity. This reflection finds strong support from the example of China's fellow Asian nation, Japan. With arguably much smaller potentials and under very similar internal and external conditions,[2] Japan was able to transform itself into a powerful modern state, replace China as the leading nation in East Asia for much of the 20th century, and become an economic superpower of the world, notwithstanding its devastating loss in World War II. Many other factors aside, one can reasonably argue that the different approaches these two nations took towards modernization most likely set them apart.[3]

By many accounts, the questions of what kind of a modern state an agrarian nation should become and how to pursue modernization are the basic issues confronting developing nations when they are brought to the modernization process. Japan settled these issues squarely in 1860 when it launched the Meiji Reformation and moved on. China unfortunately has been struggling with these issues since it was brought to confront them in the mid-19th century. In many ways, China's inability to settle these issues has made its transition to modernity a painful and difficult experience. It has also kept China at odds with the dominant powers that set the course of the world's modernization process. It is not unreasonable to argue that until China puts these issues behind, it will not be able to reach its full potential and turn itself into a truly modernized great power in the years to come.[4]

China's Tortuous Transition to Modernity

There are several key features in China's long road to modernity. First, like many other agrarian societies, China got on the modernization process through a push from the Western powers. Although China had been a civilized nation for centuries, the Chinese did not seem to have the intellectual impulse to initiate adventurous scientific inventions. The Chinese way of thinking and inquiry as conceived by Confucius, Lao Tzu, and other classical political thinkers and the ensuing Chinese political, economic, and cultural traditions are not conducive to scientific development. That is largely the reason why the Chinese had maintained the same way of life for centuries prior to the arrival of the Western powers.[5]

Second, also like the case of many other agrarian societies, the push for change came in the way of Western invasion and humiliation. Indeed, the disgraceful defeat in the Opium Wars of the mid-19th century and subsequent war defeats and concessions to foreign intrusions in China's sovereign rights marked the beginning of China's modern history. Although a bad beginning like this does not necessarily doom the modernization course to failure, with Japan as a success case, these insulting early encounters with the modern world did cast a dark shadow over China's subsequent quest for modernity, which has always contained the calls of anti-West, learning to subdue the West, and eventually overtaking or even defeating the West. This sentiment runs deep and has got the Chinese into a state of contradiction that on the one hand, they must learn from the West to modernize China, but on the other, they have to reject, resist, or hold reservations about aspects of modernization, especially the cultural aspects and the methods of government. Chinese learning from the West therefore has always been selective at best, and distorted or misguided at its worst. It is with this contradiction that China has agonized with its modernization process since 1840.

1840-1910: From Misguided Development to Revolution

"*Yangwu*": *Foreign Affairs and Business Promotion.*[6] Although the First Opium War of 1840 launched by Great Britain against

China marked the beginning of China's modern history, it did not push start China's modernization process right away. In fact, only a handful of concerned Chinese, most notably Lin Zexu, the commanding officer who lost the opium war to the British; provincial high officials such as Zeng Guofan, Li Hongzhang, Zuo Zongtang, and Zhang Zhidong; and gentry scholars such as Wei Yuan and Feng Guifen, took it as a wakeup call, investigated the significance of this humiliating encounter with a Western power, and "opened their eyes to see the outside world" (Wei's influential work, *The Illustrated Treatise of the Maritime Kingdoms*, was one of China's first books on foreign nations).[7] Most of the corrupt Qing rulers continued to dismiss the outside world, paid no attention to the challenges China was facing, and made no effort to improve China's deteriorating economic and security conditions that had been going on for decades prior to the arrival of the Western powers. Their poor conduct made China all the more vulnerable to colonial advance. In 1856, China was to lose the Second Opium War to the combined forces of Great Britain and France.

The humiliating defeat in the Second Opium War finally got the Qing rulers to see that the fate of the Middle Kingdom was at stake. They were forced to take measures to save the nation. By that time, there was a consensus among most Qing high officials that the Western powers were more advanced and stronger than China, but China could learn from the West to restore its supremacy, because they believed that the Western intruders were merely superior in their fighting capability but still inferior culturally and politically to the Chinese civilization.[8] Wei Yuan put it categorically, the West had three advantages: warships, firearms, and military training; China could learn and acquire these advanced capabilities and skills from the West and use them to check the West. With endorsement from key high officials, Wei's observation was to become the rallying call for China's 30-plus years of guarded opening to the outside world (*Yangwu*) and self-strengthening movement from 1860 to the mid 1890s.

It is also possible that those prochange officials "*Yangwu* officials" made this case as a roundabout effort to get the Qing rulers to allow learning and imports from the West. They knew that the Qing rulers cared mostly about the preservation of their dynastic rule of China. By placing the reform movement under the principle of "Chinese learning as the fundamentals, Western learning for practical use[9] they excluded learning of political and cultural practices from the West and made the changes to China appear non-threatening to the ruling class—it was portrayed as an improvement of the Chinese system but not an all-around revolution.

Whatever the case, the *Yangwu* had the blessing from the Qing rulers and brought some marked developments to China's military affairs, commerce, industries, shipbuilding, railroad transportation, coal and mineral mining, postal and telegraph communications, medical service, and education. Young Chinese students were also sent to the United States, Europe, and Japan, and many of these later returned to China and became key figures in China's subsequent modernization process.[10]

Of note is the development of China's naval capabilities during this time. Through their own construction, and also through purchase from the West, the *Yangwu* officials established four formidable modern fleets. By the late 1880s, the newly established Chinese navy had more than 80 advanced warships, ranking No. 6 in the world and the largest in Asia.[11]

However, these controlled developments were soon to expose their flaws in a war fought, ironically, not against the Western powers but against a fellow developing nation, Japan. China suffered a catastrophic defeat. Among the heavy losses on land and at sea, its entire elite Northern Fleet had vanished.

This defeat was even more humiliating because for centuries, the Chinese had looked down upon the Japanese. Thus when the news came that the Qing government had conceded to the disgraceful Treaty of Shimonoseki of 1895, agreeing to cede Taiwan and pay a huge amount of indemnity to Japan, a public uproar erupted in China.

The One-Hundred-Day Reform Movement. Riding the wave of this national anger, a group of radical reformers under the leadership of Kang Youwei and Liang Qichao came to advocate political change in China. They argued that learning from the West must include the Western fundamentals, not just the practical matters; if China were to modernize and become powerful, it must adopt the Western way of government, business, military affairs, education, and so on; and make revolutionary changes in China accordingly. These changes would preferably turn China into a constitutional monarchy. They highly regarded Japan as an example but claimed that China could do better with the radical reforms.

Those radical calls eventually reached the Qing rulers. Emperor Guangxu was persuaded by the radical reformers' arguments and put Kang Youwei in charge of the reform movement. On June 11,1898, with Kang's recommendations, the emperor issued his imperial edict for reform. In the next three months, numerous imperial decrees, mostly recommended by the radical reformers, were promulgated to direct the changes.[12] The most significant calls were to: 1) abolish the 1,300-year old imperial examination system, replacing it with modern schools and introducing the teaching of science and technology into the classrooms; 2) promote industrialization; 3) introduce capitalist ideas and practice into China's economy; 4) encourage the growth of private business in an attempt to downscale the state and official-run operations put in place in the past 30 years; 5) transform the military; and, 6) reform the government and allow the spread of political freedom, such as the freedom of the press and the right to criticize the government.[13]

These were sweeping changes, and the radical reformers wanted their implementation immediately.

Unfortunately, the emperor and the radical reformers went too fast and too far beyond what they were allowed by the paramount ruler of the Qing, Empress Dowager Cixi, who was the young 17-year-old Emperor's aunt and the "ruler behind the curtains" for much of the time since 1861,[14] "supervising" the Emperor since he was put on the throne at the age of four. Empress Dowager Cixi confined the Emperor under house arrest, resumed her rule behind the curtains, and purged the radical reformers (Kang Youwei and

Liang Qichao learned about the Empress Dowager's plot and fled to Japan, but six other key radical reformers were captured and beheaded in the streets of Beijing).

The Revolution of 1911. Although Empress Dowager Cixi purged the radical reformers, she did not kill the reform measures. She simply did not like the way the young emperor and the radical reformers handled the reform movement; and she apparently took the action to pre-empt the radical reformers' plot to remove her from power (taking her life if necessary). Indeed, in the following years, the Empress Dowager implemented many of the proposed changes. She also ostensibly followed the radical reformers' suggestions to prepare for a change of the political system in China.

While in exile, Liang Qichao had become a leading advocate for China to become a constitutional monarchy; he suggested a 6-step approach toward this goal. The Qing rulers were to: 1) issue an intent to establish constitutional monarchy; 2) send senior officials to visit key Western countries and study their constitutions and political designs; 3) create an agency to handle the translation of foreign constitutions and related studies and propose a draft constitution; 4) let the nation debate this draft for 5 to 10 years; and finally, 5) adopt a constitution and change the nation into a constitutional monarchy).[15]

Empress Dowager Cixi apparently followed these prescriptions. She dispatched two groups of special envoys abroad to study foreign governments in 1905 and 1906. Upon their return, all recommended constitutional monarchy to her. On August 27, 1908, Cixi issued an imperial edict (in the name of the defunct Emperor Guangxu) for constitutional reform and scheduled the transition to take place in 9 years.

Cixi may have believed that the proposed constitutional monarchy would turn the Qing ruler into a royal figure similar to the British King/Queen or the Japanese Emperor and preserve the privileges of her Manchu clan that had ruled the Middle Kingdom since 1644. However, her decision came too late and would not work for China. Empress Dowager Cixi and Emperor Guangxu died 3 months after the issuance of this reform order, leaving the

Dynasty in the hands of 3-year old baby emperor, Pu Yi, the last Qing emperor, whom the Empress Dowager had installed the day before her death. No one in this falling dynasty was able to carry out the reform.

The more fundamental problem with this reform was that the Qing rulers were foreigners to the Han Chinese; they had no cultural mandate to claim divine rule or perpetual monarchy in China. In fact, by this time, calls for overthrowing the Qing Dynasty and expulsion of the Manchu clan had already emerged in China. Sun Yat-sen, the leading revolutionary and later the founding father of the Republic of China (ROC), made this a rallying call for his followers. Reform of the Qing had no appeal to the Chinese any more. In the meantime, armed uprisings against the Qing started to rock the dynasty from below. On October 10, 1911, the revolutionaries in central China staged the Wuchang Armed Uprising, proclaiming the end of Qing and the beginning of the ROC, setting off a chain defection of the provinces from the Qing. October 10 is observed in mainland China as the beginning of the ROC; it is the National Day in Taiwan because the ROC government is still there. (Taiwan and cross-Taiwan Strait relations will be discussed in later sections).

On January 1, 1912, an ROC interim government was established in Nanjing. Sun Yat-sen was elected its provisional president. One month later, the Qing Emperor abdicated its rule. The Qing Dynasty was history.

1911-1949: Deadly Contests for the Fate of China

With the downfall of the Qing Dynasty and China's 2,000-plus-year-old dynastic order, the Chinese leaders had an opportunity to start China's modernization mission anew. Unfortunately, they consumed much of their energy through "in-house" fights —fighting among the Chinese themselves for the control of China.[16] The opportunity for China's modernization slipped away.

The key stumbling block was the failure to establish a functioning modern government and consolidate the nation to work for modernization. Sun Yat-sen initially wanted to build a new China as a federalist union like the United States.[17]

Yet his interim government did not have the power to command the warlord-divided nation to act as directed. And only a few weeks into his presidency, Sun also had to give up his presidency and turn it over to Yuan Shikai, a military strong man who controlled much of the northern parts of China, as a negotiated compromise to solicit cooperation from Yuan to consolidate victory over the Qing. This political deal got what it bargained for. However, Yuan soon betrayed the revolutionaries. He disrupted the newly established government, turned it into an authoritarian regime, and even tried to restore dynastic rule in China. Following the death of Yuan, shortly after his failed attempt to become an emperor in 1916, the warlords took turns to control the defunct government and plunged China into more than 10 years of bloody internal warfare.[18]

Sun Yat-sen had to mobilize the nation again to fight against those narrow-minded warlords. Unfortunately, he died untimely of liver cancer in 1925. Fortunately, however, Sun left behind a well-defined political party, the Kuomintang (KMT); a set of well-articulated principles for governance, the "Three People's Principles" of nationalism, democracy, and economic prosperity;[19] and a 3-step approach for the KMT to pursue reunification, rejuvenation, and modernization of China: 1) using military force to unify China; 2) imposing authoritarian rule to develop China; and 3) applying constitutional rule to keep peace and prosperity in China.[20] Moreover, Sun also left behind a growing military force that could support the KMT's mission. Fortunately as well, the head of this military force, Chiang Kaishek, was a determined successor of Sun and a professed follower of Sun's principles. Following Sun's death, Chiang quickly consolidated his leadership in the KMT and continued Sun's fight against the warlords. In 1926, Chiang launched the Northern Expedition to attack the strongest of all warlords. In 3 years, Chiang finally brought the fragmented China under his control.[40]

In October 1928, the ROC government proclaimed its unification of China. Chiang Kai-shek assumed the presidency and delivered his directive that the KMT was to become an unchallenged ruling party of the ROC and exercise authoritarian rule in China until its political, economic, and social conditions were ripe for constitutional rule.

Yet by this time, the Chinese Communist Party (CCP), founded in 1921, had become a formidable challenger to the KMT and Chiang. The Chinese Communists, as one of the founders of the CCP and its eventual leader Mao Zedong puts it, learned about Communism through the Bolshevik Revolution of October 1917.[21] They believed that Communism would make a better future for China and were determined to turn it into reality.

Chiang Kai-shek had no desire for the Communist idea and the Soviet model. He got a bad taste of them during his "study trip" to the Soviet Union in 1923. (He was dispatched by Sun Yat-sen and is believed to have seen the dark side of Soviet communism). He opposed Sun Yat-sen's decision to join hands with the Communists to fight for the new China and reluctantly let the Communists participate in the KMT's Whampoa Military Academy, KMT party affairs, and the Northern Expedition. With the passing of Sun and shortly before the conclusion of the Northern Expedition, Chiang made a "bloody split" with the Communists, killing many of them (the controversial "Purifying of the Party" in the KMT's terms, and the "April 12 Tragedy of 1927" in the CCP version). He subsequently launched a campaign to purge the Communists everywhere (in violent ways).

Following this setback, the Communists accepted Mao Zedong's call that "political power grows out of the barrel of a gun" and decided to pursue their cause with resort to arms.[22] Between 1927 and 1937, the Communists and the Nationalists (the English term for the KMT and its followers) waged the First KMT-CCP Civil War.

The Japanese invasion of China, begun in 1931 and flaming into full-scale warfare in 1937, forced the two sides to put their fight on hold and join hands again to deal with a common enemy. But as soon as the Anti-Japanese War was over in 1945, the two quickly resumed their deadly contest and waged the Second KMT-CCP Civil War. In 1949, the Communists defeated the Nationalists. The triumphant Communists renamed the nation the People's Republic of China (PRC). The defeated KMT and Chiang

Kai-shek sought shelter in Taiwan and restored the ROC government on the island. The two sides continued their fight during the Cold War (in all forms short of full-scale armed invasion of each other). A divided China has continued to this date.

1949-1978: False Start of Modernization and Self-Destruction

With a new China under their firm control, the CCP had a golden opportunity to modernize this war-torn nation and turn it into a great power. In all fairness, the CCP under the leadership of Mao Zedong was committed to this mission. At this moment, the CCP enjoyed overwhelming support from the Chinese people who in the previous 20 years had been mobilized by Mao's forces and inspired by his vision for a new China.[23] With the CCP's success in land reform, initial economic restructuring, and a defiant war against the United States in Korea, the 500 million Chinese[24] were confident and eager to unleash their production power to turn China around.

Organski, while working on his power transition theory, took note of the Chinese upward movement and believed that China had entered the stage of transitional growth. He also noted that some in the West already suggested that the world make room for this awakened and soon-to-expand China.[25] However, the Chinese move soon turned out to be a misguided false start. Once again, the Chinese leaders had taken some very questionable measures. In almost three decades, instead of making China great, they brought this nation to ruins.

The most questionable measure was still about government. Like its Qing predecessors, the CCP rejected the Western democratic way of government. Yet for blind-minded ideology as well as ill-advised practical reasons, it chose to replicate the Soviet dictatorship in China.[26] In so doing, the CCP created a "modern" government that ironically retained the fundamental flaws of past Chinese governments—it was a government ruled by man but not by law, without checks and balances, and good on political repression. Thus although the CCP claimed to have broken from China's dynastic tradition, this political system would soon make it a ruling party no different from those of the past and was also largely responsible for its paramount leader Mao Zedong's abuse of power and much of the catastrophic destruction he brought to China during his reign.

Mao might be a great revolutionary and war fighter; but he was no good on economic development. He used political rather than economic approaches to run the nation. In 1957, Mao launched the first of his many political movements in the PRC. It was the senseless "Anti-Rightists Movement" in which over half a million individuals were repressed for what the CCP later claimed was the "wrong doing of a handful of anti-CCP conspirators.[27]" Most of the so-called "rightists" were intellectuals who answered Mao's call to "help the CCP improve its governance". Their criticism of the CCP and suggestions for the betterment of China apparently were too harsh for Mao. The result was devastating. Almost a whole generation of talented people who would otherwise have been valuable assets for China's modernization was laid to waste in jail, reform camps, demoted positions, or simply in political and psychological trauma for decades.

While the Anti-Rightist purge spun out of control (ib'YS in the CCP's later admission), Mao would make the situation even more fanatic—he charged the nation to make a "Great Leap Forward" in economic development. Mao claimed that with his, and presumably the Chinese people's, unmatched political will and courage, China's development could catch up with that of Great Britain in 15 years and the United States in 20 to 30 years.[28] But in 3 years (1958-60), this misguided movement became a laughing stock, with people fabricating forged productivity reports everywhere. China did not make any leap in its modernization. Its economy had instead moved backward. The misconduct of these political movements brought 3 years of severe economic disasters to the people nationwide.[29]

In the aftermath of these disastrous political movements, some level-headed CCP leaders, Liu Shaoqi and Deng Xiaoping most notably, took measures to bring China back on track to develop its economy in realistic but not fanatic ways. But in a few years, Mao could not stand their efforts, accused them of leading China astray to capitalism, and launched the infamous "Cultural Revolution" in 1966 to remove those so-called "leaders of capitalism promoters"and to "purify" the Chinese people. In the next 10 years, this political movement turned China upside down. The destruction of China in all aspects was utterly beyond words.

1978-2008: Yangwu All Over Again

Mao passed away in September 1976. He left behind a China with a dysfunctional and backward economy and a nation with over 900 million people exhausted in repeated political movements and constant preparation for war against the United States, the Soviet Union, and hostile neighbors. The prospect of China's modernization was as remote as ever.

This situation was to change in 2 years. Deng Xiaoping, a legendary figure who went through dramatic ups and downs in his political career under Mao's dictatorial rule, emerged a winner in the post-Mao CCP leadership power struggle. He subsequently led the CCP leaders to put a stop to Mao's fantasies and launched the economic reform in China in 1978.

Initially, few had expected Deng to make anything spectacular. Yet by the late 1980s, his development policy started to turn China around. The CCP followed the footsteps of Japan, South Korea, Taiwan, Hong Kong, and Singapore to pursue wealth through a relentless export-oriented policy. Foreign investment and joint ventures flooded China. China was soon to become the factory of the world. By the mid 1990s, China-made consumer products started to fill department stores all over the world. By its 30th anniversary, Chinese economic development had made phenomenal progress. In three vital measures of national wealth and viability, gross domestic product (GDP), trade, and energy consumption, China ranks second after the United States. China overtook Germany to become the second largest trading nation in 2008; it surpassed Japan in GDP size in 2010. In iron and steel production, China is the largest in the world. China is also the largest consumer of iron and steel, a reflection of its massive construction everywhere.[30]

Moreover, China is also a record-holder of most foreign direct investment (FDI) in the last several decades, the most attractive place for foreign investment since September 2001 (as the previous most attractive place, the United States, has been under constant threat of terrorist attack), and so on and so forth.[31]

However, behind these glittering figures, one can see a China still struggling with the same old problem of modernization that this section has recounted. Indeed, the current Chinese economic reform bears remarkable similarities to the *Yangwu* movement of 150 years ago. First, both were openings to the outside world from a closed society. The Qing Dynasty had its self-imposed isolation for over 200 years. The PRC was shut out of the post-World War II international system for 30 years. In both situations, the Chinese people were tightly controlled inside this dictatorial kingdom with little knowledge of the outside world.

Second, both reforms were preceded by extremely poor economic situations in China. Both economic systems had run into dead ends. Economic reform and development were desperate necessities. Both governments had no way out but to launch economic reform.

Third, and most importantly, both ran a guarded reform. The *Yangwu* reformers were clear about what they wanted from the West: technology and modern products. They did not want anything to interfere with the dynastic rule in China. The current Chinese economic reform is meant to be China's modernization drive. However, it is for four specific areas only: modernizations in agriculture, industry, science and technology, and national defense.[32] There is no mention of the "fifth modernization," that is, socio-political system modernization (although the CCP had made some reluctant political changes to accommodate economic development in the last 30 years). Sound familiar? It is like *Yangwu* all over again. Thus for all the years since 1860 when the *Yangwu* started, China's modernization has been marching in place. Genuine progress is yet to come.

The current economic reform, however, is much more difficult than the *Yangwu* movement 150 years ago. Unlike their *Yangwu* predecessors, the PRC reformers carried a heavy ideological burden—every reform measure must be set to improve, but not to undermine socialism and the CCP's rule of China. This was almost a mission impossible, for the defining character of China's opening and economic reform was to attract foreign capital, technology, and management skills and to turn the dysfunctional command economy (the mainstay of socialism) into capitalist market economic operations. The CCP leaders knew it well from their ideological prescriptions (i.e., Marxism) that there is a law-like relationship between the economic foundation and its corresponding political superstructure, i.e., democracy is associated with market economy, and communism is defined by command economy, respectively. How could the CCP carry out the economic reform but still preserve socialism and its legitimate rule of China?

The answer was a tricky one. Early in the reform drives, the CCP passed a Party resolution to designate China as a socialist state at its early stage and promised to use whatever means to turn it into a prosperous socialism. This resolution may sound simple, but it had many implications. First, it made China's economic backwardness and other shortcomings excusable. Second, the promise to improve the Chinese people's standard of living gave the CCP legitimacy for its continued rule of China. Third, since socialism was supposed to be a higher stage of development than capitalism (according to the Marxist teaching), it was all right for China to make up the lessons of capitalism that it was unable to take during the war-torn years prior to 1949 and ill-advised to skip in the first 30 years of the PRC. Finally, the CCP also claimed that this early stage would be a long one (in the Chinese philosophical sense, that is, open ended). This means that the CCP can practice capitalism in China under a socialist cover as long as it deems necessary. All of the above were covered under the disguise of socialism with Chinese characteristics.

This "breakthrough" helped the CCP get the economic reform started. But its ideological requirement continued to demand that every reform measure be politically correct. Notwithstanding Deng Xiaoping's pragmatic "Cat Theory—it does not matter whether the cat is white or black, it is a good cat if it catches mice,"

Chinese reformers had to tell whether their intended reform measures were for "Mr. S (Socialism)" or "Mr. C (Capitalism)". Indeed, to this date, China still has to put a label on its much-changed economy and greatly-developed private business—it is called a "*socialist* market economy".

John King Fairbank has long ago pointed out that the *Yangwu* officials' "halfway Westernization," in tools but not in values, was a fallacy. Chinese scholar Luo Rongqü also has a highly respected and widely quoted (by Chinese analysts) observation that modernization is a worldwide historical process in which industrialization pushes traditional and agrarian societies towards modern industrial societies, penetrating into economics, politics, culture, and many other areas, generating profound changes in these areas. China pays a heavy price for its leaders' refusal to heed these valuable observations.

The China Threat

In addition to making its modernization drive cumbersome, China's uneasy transition to modernity has external consequences as well. The biggest problem is perhaps the perpetuation of China as an outsider to the US/Westled international system. Although China's economy and many other aspects of the nation have been gradually integrated with those of the outside world, its way of government is still out of place with the prevailing democratic institutions in this international system. This outsider problem keeps China in the dissatisfied group of the international system, largely because Chinese leaders do not share their core political values with their counterparts in the world's leading states. Thus when China started its upward development, it automatically became a threat to the US/Westled international system.

The United States has been watching closely and with great concern about the changes in China. Interestingly, the United States was instrumental in bringing about China's initial changes. Forty years ago (with President Richard Nixon's historic visit to China in 1972), the United States brought China out of its self-imposed isolation, and in subsequent years helped with China's economic development (by way of substantial American business investment in China and providing Chinese business the critical access to the US and worldwide markets along the way). The motivation behind this US engagement policy was manifold. One, as President Nixon put it, was to "stop the 700 million Chinese from nurturing their hatred against the Americans". (The United States and China were bitter enemies back then, and the United States did not recognize the regime in Beijing as a legitimate government for 30 years prior to the reconciliation in 1979).[33] The other was to use China as a counter-balance against the Soviet Union. The third, and a long-term goal, was that over time, economic development in China would bring about political changes and eventually turn China into a democratic state. By virtue of being a democracy, China would have shared fundamental values with the United States and a prosperous China would be a US friend rather than an enemy.

This engagement policy served US interests well until the turn of the 1990s when the Cold War ended. As the United States led many in the world to celebrate the fall of Communism and the advance of democracy, Chinese leaders survived the shock and reemerged from China's internal political turmoil, the Tiananmen Square student movement, to defiantly reaffirm their determination to continue communist rule in China and resist US heavy pressure for political change. This defiant act effectively recast China's relationship with the United States as an unfinished business of the Cold War. It also restored the ideological divide between the two nations that had been set aside in the previous decade for the strategic reasons mentioned above.

This change was significant. It cast a dark shadow over China's subsequent rise. Complicating this change of perception, China and the United States inadvertently found themselves in a show of force over the Taiwan Strait crisis of 1995-96.

Just as the world was experiencing great political changes at the turn of the 1990s, Taiwan made its transition to democracy. The "engineer" of Taiwan's democratic change, President Lee Teng-hui, was also pushing Taiwan toward *de jure* independence from mainland China. (Since its separation from mainland China in 1949 following China's Civil War of 1946-49, Taiwan has maintained a *de facto* independence). Lee's move had alerted the mainland Chinese leaders who maintain that Taiwan is part of China and promise to keep it that way at all costs, including the use of force. In March 1996, Taiwan held its first-ever direct presidential election and the call for Taiwan independence was a divisive issue in this election. In an attempt to deter Taiwan's pro-independence forces, China fired missiles near Taiwan (landing in waters off the northern and southern tips of the island).

The United States has been involved in the China-Taiwan dispute since its beginning in 1949 and has made commitments to the defense of Taiwan first through the Mutual Defense Treaty of 1954 (when the United States held the ROC government in Taiwan as the legitimate government for the entire country of China) and then the Taiwan Relations Act of 1979 (when the United States switched diplomatic recognition of China from Taipei to Beijing). In an effort to prevent the Taiwan Strait crisis from escalating into a large-scale military confrontation, the United States sent two aircraft carrier battle groups to the troubled waters, staging the largest show of US combat forces in the Western Pacific since the end of World War II and invoking for the first time two of the US commitments made in the Taiwan Relations Act (TRA) of 1979.[34]

The crisis faded away, yet the consequences continued to impact US-China relations. The most serious one was China's subsequent move to build up a military deterrence against Taiwan and accelerate China's overall military modernization.[35] Chinese leaders had no doubt that in order to keep Taiwan in the fold, they had to hold possible US intervention in check. This was a huge undertaking, taking into account the then US Defense Secretary William Perry's reminder in the aftermath of the crisis: "Beijing should know—and this (the reinforced US fleet) will remind them—that, while they are a great military power, that the premier, the strongest military power, in the Western Pacific is the United States".[36] A military buildup to accomplish this mission thus made China all the more threatening.

In the meantime, signs of a power transition between China and the United States had come to the surface. The most significant one was China's economic takeoff.[37] In fairness, this economic development was good to the Chinese. Unfortunately, against the backdrop of its long-unsettled and recently-turned-confrontational relations with the United States and the West, this rising China generated fear on the other side of the Pacific. Indeed, a "China threat" debate quickly emerged to dominate US and Western discussion of international politics and policy considerations toward China.

Over the last 15 years, much has been written about the China threat.[38] Three books are of particular interest: *The Coming Conflict with China* by Richard Bernstein and Ross H. Munro, *The Tragedy of Great Power Politics* by John J. Mearsheimer, and *The Clash of Civilizations and the Remaking of World Order* by Samuel P. Huntington.

The Coming Conflict with China was the first book on the China threat. It brought the first wave of China threat debate to a high point in 1997. Bernstein and Munro made the following controversial observations:

China's economic development was unstoppable;

- It had the potential to become the largest economy in the world;
- Unlike the Soviet Union, which was a powerful military founded on a weak economy, China had a powerful economy creating a credible military force;
- A more powerful China would be more assertive on its national interests, many of which were still in dispute;
- China is an unsatisfied and ambitious power whose goal is to dominate Asia;
- China's deep-seated historic sense of itself, its basic material and human conditions, and its own assessment of its national interests combine to make a Chinese move toward Asian hegemony virtually inevitable.
- A hegemonic China would upset Asia's balance of power that the United States established and has maintained since the end of World War II;
- China and the United States had opposing and irreconcilable goals;

- China took the United States as its arch enemy; the two were locked in a collision course;
- The Taiwan issue could be a trigger to get China and the United States to an armed conflict.[41]

Bernstein and Munro are two well-versed journalists with extensive experience in China and Asia. Their account of the China threat easily made a stir in the American public. "China rising" and "China threat" quickly became synonymic buzzwords in the US media, academic, and policy circles.

Mearsheimer's work came just in time to support Bernstein and Munro's views by providing a theoretical explanation as to why China would be expected to do the above-mentioned acts. The basic character of the international system dictates that great powers behave the way they do. In international politics, the first requirement for a state is survival. In an international system where states operate under anarchy (without a higher authority above them) and each possesses offensive capability and holds unpredictable intentions, a state's best bet for survival is to maximize its national power. Great powers by nature have a higher order of needs. Their need for survival is not merely to be more powerful than their neighbor next door. There is a natural tendency for them to strive to be the most powerful nation in their own regions. The quest for power has no end. Regional hegemons will naturally aim for global hegemony. No regional hegemony likes to see rival great powers dominate other regions, or to have peers. The drive for global hegemony necessitates a competition among the great powers. The most common way for them to win is to increase their own power base on the one hand, and to do everything possible to prevent or undermine the development of other regional hegemons on the other.[42]

Following this logic, Mearsheimer argued that an increasingly powerful China would try to dominate Asia in much the same way the United States did in the Western Hemisphere, and China's next move must be to push the United States out of Asia. Mearsheimer would not blame China for having its own version of the Monroe Doctrine directed at the United States—that is what hegemonic powers do to each other. Indeed, as Bernstein and Munro put it, from the Chinese point of view, the era of American domination in Asia, which was an undesirable accident in the first place, should be coming to an end. China's leaders are [already] asking themselves: Why should distant, flawed, self-interested America be the hegemony in a part of the world where for the better part of two millennia China reigned supreme? As far as we can tell, the entire leadership in Beijing has by now been swept into the view represented by that question.[43]

By the same token, the United States will do everything it can to prevent China from gaining its hegemonic position in Asia. Mearsheimer said that his theory did not have any normative or ideological bias; it was an offensive realist's account of the brutal nature of great power politics. In October 2003, Mearsheimer made a 12-day visit to China (his first), giving his uncompromising talks to people at China's prestigious universities, high-profile policy think tanks, and even the Chinese Foreign Ministry. He reassured his hosts everywhere: his talks were nothing personal; he had nothing against the Chinese people; but the fear of a China threat was just a natural reaction from the United States.[44]

Huntington, however, framed the China threat in an entirely different way. First, he rejected the universal state envisioned by the West and articulated by successive American leaders, and more forcefully by Francis Fukuyama in his "The End of History" essay.[45] Huntington argued that Western culture and civilization were also historical phenomena; their assertions followed the material success and failure of the United States and the West, which happened to have been in undisputed relative decline for quite some time; as the US/West's primacy eroded, other power centers rose up; and the shift in power among civilizations was leading to the revival and increased cultural assertiveness of non-Western societies and to their increasing rejection of Western culture.

Second, Huntington pointed out that China's economic development had given much self-confidence and assertiveness to the Chinese, who also "believed that wealth, like power, is proof of virtue, a demonstration of moral and cultural superiority; as it became more successful economically, China would not hesitate to emphasize the distinctiveness of its culture and to trumpet the superiority of its values and way of life compared to those of the West and other societies".[46]

However, few, if any, Chinese acknowledged Huntington's complement. Most dismissed his remarks about the China threat. As Huntington saw it, culture and cultural identities were shaping the pattern of cohesion, disintegration, and conflict in the post-Cold War world; and "the dominant division [would be] between 'the West and the rest, ' with the most intense conflicts occurring between Muslim and Asian societies on the one hand, and the West on the other".[47] Of the two principal opponents, China was the more dangerous one, for the Muslim world did not have a core state to lead the fragmented Muslim nations to defy the West, but a unified, powerful, and assertive China could.

China as a Responsible Stakeholder

The Chinese were understandably upset with the China threat allegations. They argued that the whole perception of the China threat was a racist act that had a long tradition with the Europeans in general (the fear of the "Yellow Peril," for instance)[48] and the United States in particular (the Chinese Exclusion Act of 1882 and other past discriminatory acts against the Chinese in the United States).[49] In addition, the Chinese argued that the China threat charges were reflections of the US/West's selfishness—they simply did not want the Chinese to share with them the resources for a better life (read as the American/Western life style). That was why there were so many concerns about the China threats such as those in food supply (*Who Will Feed China?*[50]), in energy consumption (Who will fuel China?), in environmental impact (Who will clean up China?), and many others. But emotions aside, most Chinese argued that the China threat perceptions were a result of the US/West Cold War thinking—the United States needed an enemy to sustain its military spending and give meaning to the "American Empire".[51]

As the China-threat debate waged on, Chinese also came to see that a power transition process was complicating the already precarious US-China relations. However, Chinese analysts argued that power transition was a problem based on Western experience.[52] They insisted that China had been a Confucian society for over 2, 000 years; Chinese followed Confucius's teaching to pursue harmony; they had never been aggressive; and they fought only in response to invasions.[53] These counter-arguments, however, had not been effective. After all, most of the Chinese counterarguments over-blew the "harmonious" aspects of the Chinese culture while brushing aside the negative and conflict sides of the Chinese society. In addition, throughout history, Chinese had fought no fewer wars than the Westerners. As a matter of fact, a People's Liberation Army (PLA) task group publication has showed that from 2200 BC (the beginning of the Chinese civilization) to 1911 (when the dynastic history came to an end), China had experienced 3,766 wars, almost one war per year.[54] Moreover, in ancient as well as contemporary Chinese writings about past Chinese warfare, slaughtering of enemy soldiers in tens of thousands was commonplace. The contemporary KMT-CCP civil wars were very brutal as well.

In the face of the unabated China threat concerns, the CCP charged its Central Cadre School, the intellectual center of the CCP's political and ideological works, to find more effective counterar-guments. In 2003, the researchers at the Party school came up with the idea of "China's peaceful rise" (later modified as peaceful development).[55] This call took the key issues of great power transition into account and proposed China's positions. Zheng Bijian, the mastermind behind this project and a long-time advisor to President Hu Jintao (Zheng was also the Vice President of the CCP Central Cadre School), took the international stage to promote this Chinese initiative. In his various high-profile speeches, Zheng reaffirmed China's focus on its mission of modernization and then declared the following:

- China will not repeat past great powers' mistakes of colonial and imperial expansion.
- China will not use force to plunder resources. Instead, China is learning to use market means to obtain what it needs for its development and consumption.56 China is fortunate to have the march of economic globalization going hand

in hand with its economic takeoff. Globalization makes it easier for China to obtain resources peacefully.

- China rejects the old way of relying on force to wreck the existing international system. It is now willingly to become a member of the current international system. China does not hide its intention to promote changes from within the system, but it will do so within its reach and in a non-confrontational way.[57]

Chinese President Hu Jintao and Premier Wen Jiabao subsequently promoted this idea at high-profile international forums and during their official visits to the United States.[58] Zheng Bijian even unprecedentedly published his thoughts in the influential *Foreign Affairs* magazine and candidly asked the United States to accept China's goodwill call.[59]

Americans took the Chinese initiative with mixed assessments. Some, like Mearsheimer, rejected it flatly.[60] Others took this peaceful development initiative as an application of the Chinese strategy of *tao-guang yang-hui*, a strategy Deng Xiaoping initially put together for the Chinese leaders to deal with the changes following the end of the Cold War, and subsequently guided them to manage China's rise in the face of heavy pressure from the United States and the West. The Pentagon has highlighted this Chinese strategy in its annual reports to Congress on the military power of the PRC since 2002. It goes as follows: "observe the situation calmly, hold the positions securely, cope with matters cool-headedly, hide the capabilities and bide the time, practice solid defense, never assume international leadership, but strive to make measured moves". Putting China's peaceful development initiative against this "28-character maxim," one cannot but hold reservations on the true intention of the Chinese peaceful development call.

The George W. Bush administration, however, gave China a well-measured answer. Deputy Secretary of State Robert B. Zoellick delivered the US response through his now-famous speech to the New York-based National Committee on US-China Relations on September 21, 2005. Zoellick welcomed China's forthcoming initiative. He commended China for its impressive economic development, accrediting it to the US policy of integration that started with President Nixon's historic visit to China in 1972 and continued by successive US Presidents (with understandable setbacks and modifications due to the changing nature of international politics and US-China relations). Zoellick did not join those who regretted that US integration policy turned China into a threatening "800-pound gorrilla". Instead, he quoted Secretary of State Condolezza Rice as saying that "the United States welcomes a confident, peaceful, and prosperous China, one that appreciates that its growth and development depends on constructive connections with the rest of the world". At the same time, he urged China to become a *responsible stakeholder* in this system.

Zoellick pointed out that China's quest for peaceful development had internal and external requirements. Internally, although the Chinese leaders' priority was understandably economic development, they must take measures to modernize China's political system, without which China could not have a sustainable peaceful condition for its ambitious mission. Externally, China must work with the United States and other leading nations to create and maintain an environment for all to develop peacefully. This cooperation would require that China share common interests, and more importantly, fundamental values with the United States and the other leading nations. Cooperation on a coincidence of interests is a matter of convenience. But "[r]elationships built on shared interest and values are deep and lasting. We can cooperate with the emerging China of today, even as we work for the democratic China of tomorrow".[61] China's peaceful rise would be possible only with its genuine internal transformation and external cooperation.

The Chinese took the US response with much caution. On the one hand, they believed that it was a reluctant acceptance of China's growing power and international influence. On the other, the Chinese saw that the "responsible stakeholder" designation had many hidden agendas and trappings against China. First, it was a US hegemonic design to incorporate China into the US "orbit". The United States would expect China to follow the rules set by the United States and the West. The latter would be the judge for China's acts. Second, the range of responsibilities would be beyond China's ability. Third, it was an attempt to get China to share the US hegemonic burdens, many of which were against China's moral principles and national interests. Fourth, it was a different way to blame China for those China-threat problems such as rising costs for energy and other national resources, environmental degradation, climate change, and many others, and asked China to bear more responsibility for those global problems.[62]

Chinese analysts nevertheless noted the positive side of the US response—it was one that sought cooperation rather than confrontation. However, they all called for the Chinese leaders to stand firm on China's long-held independent foreign policy, take on responsibilities according to China's ability, moral principles, and national interests, even if they were in conflict with those of the United States and the West. China would be responsible to the world, they argued, but not just to the United States and the West alone. They also pointed out that although the responsible stake-holder designation suggested that the United States welcomed China into the "club of great powers," China would still be treated differently; it would be *an insider in name* but *an outsider in fact* for a long time to come. China would be better served to continue its *tao-guang yang-hui* and focus on its development.[63]

Endnotes

1. Li Hongzhang ("On Coastal Defense"), (*Complete Works of Li Hongzhang*), Tianjin, China: Baihua Wenyi Chubanshe, 2000.

2. Similar to the isolated Qing Dynasty, Japan had a "Closed Country Edict" prohibiting Japanese contact with the outside world during the Tokugawa period from 1836 to 1860 when the Meiji Reformation was launched. Also similar to the forced opening of Qing China, Japan encountered the US intruder, Commodore Matthew C. Perry, and his Black Ships in 1853. The Americans demanded the opening of Japan to foreign trade and commerce.

3. See *China Modernization Report, 2008*, Beijing, China: Beijing University Press, 2008. Specifically, the Report notes that Japan positively pursued learning from the West and transformation in

an all-round way whereas China held reservations especially on the socio-political aspects of change and lost the opportunity to modernize properly (p. iv). See also Barrington Moore's classic discussion in *Social Origins of Dictatorship and Democracy: Lord and Peasant in the Making of the Modern World*, Boston, MA: Beacon Press, 1966.

4. President George W. Bush's *National Security Strategy of 2006* was right on the mark to make the same point.

5. There are numerous Chinese studies about the difference between Chinese and Western thinking and the inability of the Chinese way of thinking to encourage scientific inquiry. Richard E. Nisbett, *The Geography of Thought: How Asians and Westerners Think Differently and Why*, New York: Free Press, 2003, is a good book to start.

6. Chinese use "Westernization Movement" for "*Yangwu* Movement". The translation is not very satisfactory, for *Yangwu* includes a wide range of activities such as foreign affairs, treaty negotiation, purchase of European/Western-made weaponry, and establishing business and manufactory operations.

7. There were about 30 other influential individuals, most of them Qing high officials or gentry scholars, making similar efforts around that time to introduce the outside world to China. Wei Yuan's work is the most influential one. See Yu Heping, Ma Yong, and Su Shaozhi, (*The Course of Modernization in China*), Nanjing, China: Jiangsu People's Publishing, 2001, Vol. 1, pp. 109-112, for a list of these individuals and their works.

8. The most outspoken one is perhaps by Zhang Zhidong in his writing (*On Learning*), Beijing, China: Zhonghua Shuju, 1991, in which he argued that Confucianism had been the core ethical and virtual code for China; its teaching was close to perfect and allowed no revision; this Chinese core value was unshakable; China did not need to learn from any other nation; what China needed was the means to manufacture, which the West could provide; China should make use of the West's technology on the basis of preserving the Chinese fundamentals.

9. Key reform-minded officials Feng Guifen and Shen Shoukang were the first ones to put forward this concept. Zhang Zhidong provided a comprehensive explanation of this concept in his

influential book (*On Learning*). See Wang Zhaoxiang ("Chinese Learning as Fundamental and Western Learning for Practice Reconsidered"), (*Guangxi Social Sciences*), No. 8, 2008.

10. See Yu Heping, Ma Yong, and Su Shaozhi, -(*The Course of Modernization in China*), Nanjing, China: Jiangsu People's Publishing, 2001, Vol. I, for a comprehensive and detailed account of the early modernization developments in China.

11. Wang Zhaohui, ("Military Industrial Strategy and Contemporary Chinese Military Affairs Modernization in the Late Qing Era"), (*Journal of Hunan Science and Technology College*), Vol. 29, No. 3, 2008.

12. The number of decrees varies from 40 (see John King Fairbank and Merle Goldman, *China: A New History*, 2nd Enlarged Ed., Cambridge, MA: Harvard University Press, 2006) to 300 (see Xiao Gongqin (*Transformation in Crisis: Radicals and Conservatives in the Late Qing Politics*), Guangdong, China: Guangdong People's Publishing, 2011).

13. See Yang Tianshi, ("Wuxu Reform: a Relatively Complete Reform Movement"), (*Beijing Daily*), January 12, 2009, for a discussion of these six aspects.

14. Feudal China was a male-dominated society. However, many times in its history, premature boys were put on the throne and their mothers or empresses assumed regency over those young or baby emperors. To avoid direct contact between the male officials and the empress, a semi-transparent curtain was set up to separate them. Ruling behind the curtains has also become a Chinese proverb to refer to situations where an unofficial but powerful ruler or leader controls politics behind the scene.

15. See Liang Qichao ("On Constitutional Monarchy"), Vol. 81, 1901.

16. "In-house" fight is arguably one of China's "national characteristics". The most critical writings about this issue are perhaps the ones by Bo Yang, (*The Ugly Chinese*). Taipei, Taiwan: Lin Bai Chubanshe, 1985; and his other works.

17. See Sun's writings. (*Collection of Sun Yat-sen Vols. 1-11*). Beijing, China: Zhonghua Publishing, 1981-86.

18. Warlords such as Feng Guozhang, Xu Shichang, Cao Kun, Duan Qirui, to name a few.

19. The "Three People's Principles" are Sun's learning from Abraham Lincoln. They are in essence the "government of the people, by the people, and for the people". But in the Chinese context, the first principle refers to nationalism as an identity for the Chinese encompassing the five major groups of Han, Mongol, Tibetan, Manchu, and Muslim, and contains elements of anti-imperialism, and the third principle also means the people's welfare and ownership of land property.

20. The "3-Step Approach" is often translated as the "3-Stage Approach"—military rule, political tutelage, and constitutional rule. See Fairbank and Goldman, *China*, p. 286.

21. Mao Zedong, "On People's Democratic Dictatorship (1949)," *Selected Works of Mao Zedong*, Vol. IV, Beijing, China: Remin Publishing, 1952-60.

22. Chinese Communist Party (CCP) resolution at the emergency meeting held on August 7,1927 (the CCP's landmark meeting of August 7).

23. Many overseas Chinese with good education and expertise were also inspired. According to one study, 1,144 overseas talents returned to China between 1949 and 1951 from the United States, Japan, Great Britain, France, and other Western countries. See Li Tao (*History of Chinese Study Abroad*), Beijing, China: Higher Education Press, 2000.

24. There is no accurate number for China's population between 1949 and 1953. China's first population census was conducted in 1953 and reported a total population of 594 million ("China's Five National Population Censuses," the National Population and Family Planning Commission of P.R. China, available from *www.chinapop.gov.cn*). China experienced a population boom following the founding of the PRC in 1949. An addition of 94 million in 5 years is possible.

25. AFK Organski, *World Politics*. New York: Alfred A. Knopf, 1968, p. 342.

26. Recent studies show that Mao was interested in the US model when he was a young revolutionary. But as soon as he learned

about Marxism and Leninism, he started to dismiss the United States as part of the European imperialist aggressors who had ill-designs for China. Mao showed interest in the United States again during the Anti-Japanese War and shortly before the 2nd KMT-CCP Civil War broke out in the late 1940s, but it was Mao's attempt to solicit support from the United States against first the Japanese and then the Nationalists. It was a matter of strategy but not genuine interest. As the United States openly supported the KMT during the KMT-CCP war, Mao believed that the United States had showed its true colors—it was a bitter enemy of China. As his view of the United States turned from bad to worse and the Cold War was heating up, Mao decided to take the "leaning to one side" approach to form an alliance with the Soviet Union and to build China after the Soviet model in practically every aspect. See Tang Zhouyan (*Mao Zedong's Views on the United States*), Xian, China: Shaanxi People's Publishing, 2009; and many other recent writings about this topic.

27. The CCP sources admit that about 550,000 were "capped as rightists". But recent studies estimate that the number may well be over a million.

28. See "New Year's Day Editorial," *People Daily*, 1958.

29. The CCP calls these 3 years the "difficult period" and admitted that human errors rather than natural disasters were responsible for the problems. See (*Selected Works of Liu Shaoqi*), Beijing, China: Renmin Press, 1985. There is speculation that about 30 million Chinese people died of starvation in those 3 years from 1959 to 1961. But the CCP has never released any reliable information on this matter. A recent study by Yang Jisheng is rather telling. "The Fatal Politics of the PRC's Great Leap Famine: the Preface to Tombstone," *Journal of Contemporary China*, Vol. 19, No. 66, September 2010. See also Frank Dikotter, *Mao's Great Famine: the History of China's Most Devastating Catastrophe, 1958-1962*, New York: Walker & Co., 2010.

30. Energy consumption and iron and steel production are the key indicators in the COW National Material Capabilities dataset.

31. See, for example, the United Nations Conference on Trade and Development (UNTAD), annual World Investment Prospects Survey.

32. CCP resolutions unequivocally stress that China will learn from other nations, especially the Western advanced nations, for their advanced science and technology and government management skills. But there is no discussion of learning their political system. See CCP guideline on constructing socialist spiritual civilization September 18, 1986.

33. Fairbank and Goldman, *China*, pp. 217-218.

34. Luo Rongqu(*A New Analysis of Modernization—Modernization Advances in the World and China*), Beijing, China: Shangwu Press, p. 17.

35. See Richard Nixon's article "Asia after Vietnam," *Foreign Affairs*, October 1967.

36. The two provisions in the Taiwan Relations Act (TRA) are: "It is the policy of the United States . . . (4) to consider any effort to determine the future of Taiwan by other than peaceful means, including by boycotts or embargoes, a threat to the peace and security of the Western Pacific area and of grave concern to the United States; . . . (6) to maintain the capacity of the United States to resist any resort to force or other forms of coercion that would jeopardize the security, or the social or economic system, of the people on Taiwan".

37. When Deng Xiaoping launched China's economic reform and the four modernization drives, he gave priority to economic developments such as agriculture, industry, and scientific advance while putting defense modernization on the back burner. He figured that when the economy had advanced, China would have more money to modernize its military. The Taiwan Strait crisis of 1995-96 putatively got the Chinese to start China's defense modernization ahead of schedule. But in retrospect, China's economy was already making impressive progress; it had the funds to set defense modernization in motion anyway. See Pentagon Annual Report to Congress on the Military Power of the People's Liberation Army (PLA) of the People's Republic of China (PRC); and David Shambaugh, *Modernizing China's Military: Progress, Problems, and Prospects*. Berkeley, CA: University of California Press, 2004.

38. Steven Erlanger, "Christopher to Meet His Chinese Counterpart," *The New York Times*, March 20, 1996.

39. See WW Rostow, *The Stages of Economic Growth: a Non-Communist Manifesto*, Cambridge, MA: Cambridge University Press, 2nd Ed., 1971, for a discussion of the take-off stage of a nation's economic development. China's economic takeoff started around 1993.

40. See Herbert Yee and Ian Storey, eds. *The China Threat: Perceptions, Myths, and Reality*. London, UK: RoutledgeCurzon, 2002; Denny Roy, "The 'China Threat' Issue: Major Arguments," *Asian Survey*, Vol. 36, No. 8, 1996; and Khalid R. Al-Rodhan, "A Critique of the China Threat Theory: A Systematic Analysis," *Asian Perspective*, Vol. 31, Issue 3, 2007.

41. Richard Bernstein and Ross H. Munro, *The Coming Conflict with China*, New York: Alfred A. Knopf, 1997.

42. John J. Mearsheimer, *The Tragedy of Great Power Politics*, New York: Norton, 2001.

43. Bernstein and Munro, *The Coming Conflict with China*, p. 31.

44. See Mearsheimer's writings, "The Future of the American Pacifier," *Foreign Affairs*, September/October 2001; "Clash of the Titans: (Debate between Zbigniew Brzezinski and John J. Mearsheimer)," *Foreign Policy*, January/February 2005; and "China's Unpeaceful Rise," *Current History*, April 2006. Also see Chinese reflection on Mearsheimer's visit to China and analysis of his theory in Xiao Bo ("Mearsheimer: There Is No God in International Politics"), (*East China Morning Post*), November 25, 2003. ("Face to Face with 'Offensive Realism': on John Mearsheimer's Presentation at Shanghai Fudan University"), (*World Watch*), No. 3, 2004; Ren Xiao, ("Words from a Realist Theorist"), (*Studies of International Politics*), No. 2, 2003.

45. Francis Fukuyama, "The End of History?" *National Interest*, Summer 1989. Fukuyama later turned his article into his book, *The End of History and the Last Man*, New York: Free Press, 2006.

46. Samuel P. Huntington, *The Clash of Civilizations and the Remaking of World Order*, New York: Simon & Schuster, 1996, p. 103.

47. *Ibid.*, p. 183.

48. Fang Xuhong and Jiang Taoyong, "The 'Yellow Peril' Allegation on International Relations Perspective", *Journal of Hefei University of Technology*, Vol. 20, No. 5, 2006; Duan Bing and Zhao Xinggang, "Contemporary Fabrications of 'Yellow Peril' and 'China Threat'", *Shanxi Youth Management College Journal*, Vol. 13, No. 3, 2000; Yao Benzhong "On the 'Yellow Peril' 'China Threat' and 'China Collapse'", *Journal of Huzhou Vocational and Technological College*, No. 4, 2004; Xue Xiantian "The History and Essense of 'Yellow Peril' and 'China Threat' Allegations", *Hundred Year Tide*, No. 1, 2007; Liu Bin, "More on the "China Threat" Allegations", *The World Today*, No. 7, 2007.

49. Liu Zhuo ('RSS) and Shen Xiaopeng, ("Racism in US Immigration Policy and the 'Chinese Exclusion Act'"), (*Journal of Liaoming University*), Vol. 32, No. 4, 2004, Ma Yongjie ("What Do We Learn from the Wen-ho Lee Case?"), (*National Security Bulletin*), No. 11, 1999. But some studies show that the Chinese Exclusion Act was not mainly based on racial discrimination. It was based more on economic and employment considerations. See Pi Chaoxia ("An Analysis of the US Century-Old Chinese Exclusion Movement"), Xnno (*Xiang Chao*), No. 8, 2008, Yuan Peng and Lin Yan, ("On the Origins of the US Chinese Exclusion Policy"), (*Japan Studies Forum*), No. 3, 1996, Chen Xiaoyan ("An Analysis on the Fundamental Reasons for the Contemporary US Chinese Exclusion Acts"), (*Journal of Huangzhou University*), Vol. 28, No. 3, 1998.

50. Lester Brown, *Who Will Feed China?* New York: WW Norton & Company, 1995.

51. See Li Cheng (Ngb), (*An Analysis of the US "China threat" Allegations*), Master's Thesis, Beijing College of Foreign Affairs, 2007.

52. Zhu Feng argues that if China's rise succeeds, it will not only pose a major problem for the century-old Western great power politics, but also a fatal blow to the international relations theory, which is largely based on Western understanding and experience. ("China's Rise' and 'China Threat"), (*American Studies*), No. 3, 2005.

53. There have been numerous Chinese writings along these lines and reinforcing each other.
54. (Chinese Military Task Group), (*Chronology of War in Chinese History*). Beijing, China: PLA Publishing House, 2003.
55. Shortly after the call, Chinese leaders realized that the term "rise" could be too aggressive. They quickly replaced it with a more neutral term "development".
56. See a recent cover article in *Fortune* magazine by Bill Powell, "China Buys the World," October 26, 2009, for the scale of China's purchase activities.
57. Zheng Bijian, "China's New Path of Development and Peaceful Rise," Speech at the 30th Annual World Forum, Lake Como, Italy. (*Xuexi Shibao*), Beijing, China, November 22, 2004.
58. Chinese Premier Wen Jiabao delivered the peaceful rise call in his speech at Harvard University during his visit to the United States in December 2003. Chinese President Hu Jintao embraced China's peaceful rise in his speech commemorating the 110th anniversary of the birth of Mao Zedong on December 26, 2003, in Beijing.
59. China later modified the call to become China's peaceful *development* in an attempt to avoid some unnecessary controversies. There are many Chinese writings about this change. See Bonnie S. Glaser and Evan S. Medeiros, "The Changing Ecology of Foreign Policy-making in China: the Ascension and Demise of the Theory of 'Peaceful Rise,'" *The China Quarterly*, June 2007, for a good analysis.
60. See John J. Mearsheimer, "'Clash of the Titans,' A Debate with Zbigniew Brzezinski on the Rise of China," *Foreign Policy*, No. 146, January-February 2005; and "China's Unpeaceful Rise," *Current History*, April 2006.
61. This 28-character maxim is made up of seven 4-character phrases. The 4-character phrase is a very traditional Chinese way of expression. Most of the Chinese proverbs are composed this way. Deng Xiaoping handed down these 4-character strategies to his successors in different occasions. Chinese leaders and officials scholars pieced them together and called this strategy "*tao-guang yang-hui*". There are also many versions of translation for these 28 characters. The current one is mine.

62. Robert B. Zoellick, "Wither China: From Membership to Responsibility?" Remarks to the National Committee on US-China Relations, September 21, 2005, New York City. The 2006 US National Security Strategy endorsed Zoellick's designation of China as a "responsible stakeholder" and reiterated the key points Zoellick made in his speech.

63. See the numerous writings on these issues.

64. The Chinese response to the US "responsible stakeholder" call and the policy recommendations to the Chinese leaders are taken from a few of a large number of Chinese reflections and analyses. Chinese analysts nowadays have more freedom to express their opinions. However, they still tend to sing the same tune and reinforce each other's views, especially on matters of national interests and importance. See Liu Jianfei, ("Who Would the Responsible Great Power Be Responsible to?"), (*Global Times*), January 3, 2007; ("'China as Responsible Stakeholder': Challenge or Opportunity?"), wg (*Outlook*), June 4, 2007; Lin Fengchun, ("Fortune or Misfortune? An Analysis of China as a Responsible Stakeholder"), (*International Issues*), No. 4, 2006; Liu Ming ("On China's International Responsibility"), (*Studies on Mao Zedong and Deng Xiaoping*), No. 1, 2008; Niu Haibin ("On 'China as a Responsible Stakeholder'), (*Contemporary International Relations*), No. 3, 2007; Wang Yiwei, ("The United States Wants to Reduce Its Hegemonic Burden"), (*Huanqiu Times*), June 7, 2006. Wang Lianhe, ("New Thinking in the US China Policy?") (*International Observer*), No. 1, 2006; Xie Lijiao and Tang Yanlin ("The US View on 'China as a Responsible Stakeholder' and US-China Relations"), (*The Journal of Changchun Normal University*), No. 4, 2006; Yuan Peng, ("On US Attitude toward China: From China Threat to China as a Responsible Stakeholder"), (*East China Morning Post*), December 22, 2005; Gong Li, ("Responsible Stakeholder and Constructive Cooperator: Thoughts on Defining US-China Relations in the New Century"), (*Journal of Shanghai Administration Institute*), Vol. 9, No. 2, March 2008; Ma Zhengang ("China's Responsibility and 'China as a Responsible Stakeholder'"), (*International Issues Studies*), April 2007; Lin Limin, ("A Careful Analysis of the Call

'China as Responsible Stakeholder'"), (*People's Forum*), No. 6, 2007; Ni Feng ("From 'Responsible Stakeholder' to 'Constructive Cooperator': President Hu Jintao's Visit to the United States and US-China Relations"), (*Contemporary World*), No. 6, 2006.

Chapter - 4

The Future of US-China Power Transition

In spite of the gulf of distrust between the two sides of the Pacific, China's peaceful development initiative and the US responsible stakeholder response have nonetheless become an unprecedented goodwill exchange between the two great powers in question. This was probably the first time in the history of international relations that a rising power openly addressed the key issues in a power transition process with the dominating nation in this system and pledged to avoid the mistakes that led past great powers to use force against each other to settle their differences over the emerging international order.

This goodwill exchange also brought closure to a long and uneasy time between the two nations struggling over their complicated relations and ushered the two onto a new stage where they would try to figure out how to play their new roles as responsible stakeholders.

In many ways, this US-China power transition resembles a childbearing process, which, after all, is about the making of a new international order. By reasonable measures, we can set the beginning of this process in 1978, the year China embarked on its modernization mission.[1] We can also take the China-US goodwill exchange of 2003-05 and the 2008 Beijing Summer Olympics as "baby shower parties" marking the passage of the "first trimester" of the US-China power transition.

Power transition does not take place overnight. National development takes time. Indeed, it took Germany 70 years to catch up with Great Britain. The rise of the United States also spanned well over half a century following its Civil War in the 1860s. China has a broader base (population in particular) but less developed economic conditions than most past great powers. It is reasonable that China has to take more time to reach its full potential. The first 30 years of its development and its uneasy interaction with the United States fit remarkably well with the pattern of the first trimester of the childbearing process.[2]

Since the end of the Cold War, much has changed in the international system. Along with the rise of China, we have also witnessed the emergence of other great powers (discussed in the earlier section of this analysis). Some argued that the US-led "unipolar moment" would not last long and predicted an eventual transition either to a multipolar world with China being one of the power centers[3] or a change of guard with China at the helm.[4] Others disputed China's qualification as a contender to the US-led international system and held doubts about the validity of a power transition between China and the United States.[5] Many simply took the US-China power transition for granted and discussed various aspects of the US-China relationship under the influence of power transition.

This analysis contends that the development of the other great powers has collectively made the relative share of the US world power smaller, but the ups and downs of those other great powers are arguably sideshows of the evolving international order. China's rise is by far the most conspicuous one.

More importantly, China is the one with the potential and ambitions to become the next No. 1 nation in the world and has made unremitting efforts to shape a new international order for the future, although Chinese leaders have repeatedly denied and downplayed the significance of their ambitions.[6] China may not be able to change the current world single-handedly as the United States did to an extraordinary degree to the previous one, but it will be the nation most instrumental in molding the next international order. China's rise has global significance. Although much of the interaction is between China and the United States, their interactions transcend bilateral rivalries in international politics (China-Japan or China-India rivalries, for example).[7] US-China power transition is about the future of international relations. It was one of the defining characteristics of the changing international relations in the past 30 years and will continue to be so in the years ahead.

Indeed, the next 30 to 40 years of international relations may very well be remembered also as the "second trimester" of the US-China power transition. It is not just for a symmetric measure to predict another 30 years for this period. Chinese leaders are in fact looking to the year 2050 to turn China into a true great power.[8] Their goal is to raise China's per capita income, a better measurement of a nation's wealth and standing than the sheer size of its gross domestic product (GDP), from the current low ranking of No. 96 out of 192 nations in the world of 2009 to within the top 50 or possibly the top 20 ranking by 2050.[9] Chinese leaders worked carefully to create a war-free environment for China's economic reform and development in the past 30 years (avoiding premature confrontation with the United States and mending fences with its neighbors, for the record). They are working hard to ensure that the next 30 to 40 years will be another window of opportunity for China to bring its modernization to fruition.

By 2050, China's comprehensive national power (CNP)[10] is expected to further narrow its gap with that of the United States. China's GDP surpassed that of Japan in August 2010, making China the second largest economy in the world. But, the gap between China and the United States is still substantial. In the years ahead, China has a good chance to become the leader in alternative energy, in science and technology innovation, and in many other fields. In certain aspects, Chinese power can surpass that of the United States. Its overall GDP, for instance, can be bigger than the US GDP. However, the two nations' CNP is still not in parity.

Looking at this unstoppable China, many cannot help but ask: What are we to expect for the US-China power transition in its second trimester and beyond? What are China's intentions? What would China do with its growing power? Would China follow Mearsheimer's prescriptions to push the United States out of Asia? Would China replace the United States to become the next superpower of the world, and along the way, replace the US/West-based political, economic, security, and cultural institutions with Chinese ones? On the flip side of these concerns, one can also ask the following questions: Can the United States stay on top? Can the United States and the West sustain the extant international order and turn China into a satisfied stakeholder? Finally, in a mutual sense, can the two sides blaze a new path for great power politics?

In many ways, the answers to these questions hinge on what China will become and do in the next 20 to 30 years. A better understanding of China's possible choices will help Chinese and Americans to avoid overstepping on each other's interest and overreacting to each other's moves.

Possible Outcomes for the US-China Power Transition

From past experience of power transitions and the current state of the US-China relations, we can discuss three possible outcomes: a deadly contest for change, a peaceful change of guard, or a reluctant accommodation. By many accounts, the last one will be the most likely scenario for the second stage of the US-China power transition.

Deadly Contest for Change?

Deadly contest has been the rule of power transition in the past. However, there are good reasons that this will not be the case for the US-China power transition. First, China and the United States are both aware of the power transition and agree to take measures to manage this evolving process. The goodwill exchange, no matter how questionable at this point, is a step in the right direction.

Second, following this goodwill exchange, the United States and China have established regular high-level communications. The George W. Bush administration and the Chinese government initiated high-level strategic and economic dialogues in 2005.

In 5 years, the two sides held six strategic and five economic annual dialogues.[11] In 2009, the Barack Obama administration and its Chinese counterpart combined the two separate meetings into one annual dialogue between the two governments. The First Round of US-China Strategic and Economic Dialogue took place in July 2009. China sent a delegation of more than 150 ministerial-level officials, the largest ever, to Washington. In May 2010, Secretary of State Hillary Clinton and Treasury Secretary Timothy Geithner reciprocated with a 200-plus-member high-level official delegation, also the largest-ever US official delegation, to Beijing.[12]

These unprecedented high-level dialogues turned out to be innovative measures for the two nations to address a broad range of controversial issues of mutual and global concerns. At the first round, for instance, the key agenda items were climate change, energy cooperation, global financial crisis, arms control, security for Chinese-held US treasury bonds, Chinese currency exchange rate, international economic and financial system reform, and market access. At the second round meetings, the two sides discussed the overall, strategic, and long-term aspects of US-China relations and reached agreements on 26 specific agendas such as energy, environment, science and technology, customs, health, and law enforcement cooperation.[13] In addition to these high-level dialogues, China and the United States have also established more than 60 other regular "Track-II" dialogues at various levels and areas of mutual concern in the last 30 years, especially the last decade.[14] There are also numerous informal dialogues and meetings between the two sides covering practically all areas of mutual concern.

At this point, most of these dialogues are still at their "water-testing" stage. The two sides still hold strong suspicions against each other. Each side is protective of its vital interests. The dialogues are opportunities for the two sides to learn about the other side's positions on the key issues. It will be a long time before the two sides can upgrade these dialogues to a higher level where the two can take each other as partners and take coordinated and cooperative action on important issues of the day. Nevertheless, as Chinese Premier Wen Jiabao puts, "dialogue is better than confrontation".[15] US Secretary of State Clinton and Treasury Secretary Geithner echo the Chinese Premier with a little strategic touch on the US-China relationship: "Simply put, few global problems can be solved by the United States or China alone. And few can be solved without the United States and China together".[16] These regular meetings will allow the two sides to "explain" their positions on controversial issues, if not to solve them. These deliberate efforts set the US-China power transition apart from the past ones.

In addition to these dialogues, China and the United States have also established "hot lines". In February 2008, the two sides signed an agreement to establish direct phone lines between the Pentagon and Chinese Defense Ministry.[17] In April 2008, Chinese Defense Minister Liang Guanglie and US Defense Secretary Robert Gates made a 30-minute phone call.[18]

Third, the US embracement of China as a responsible stakeholder opens the door for China to make changes to the existing international system from within, presumably through negotiation but not as a disgruntled revolutionary seeking destruction of this system from outside.[19]

Fourth, although China wants to change the existing international order, it does not have a sound alternative design to replace it. In recent years, China has put forward a "harmonious world" construct as a Chinese vision for a new international order. Yet as the analysis in the following pages shows, this harmonious world construct does not measure up to a workable design for a new world order. It will help to improve the existing international order and may "modify" US international conduct, but its simple mentation does not require a war with the United States or the destruction of the US-led international system.

Finally, the power transition theory points out that "a wise challenger, growing in power through internal development, would wait to threaten the existing international order until it was as powerful as the dominant nation and its allies, for surely it would seem foolish to attack while weaker than the enemy".[20] A recent excellent analysis of the power transition theory reinforces this view by showing convincingly that the upstart, believing its development would eventually turn it into the "top dog" among the great powers, would try to avoid premature confrontation, even as it approaches parity, with the hegemony.[21] It is more logical, and empirically evident, that the dominant power rather than the upstart is more likely to initiate a fight. This is clearly the case with China, whose leaders have sworn to use strategy rather than force to win the contest.

In addition, as two well-established nuclear powers and extensively-connected economic growth engines, a calculated war between the United States and China is unthinkable (even Mearsheimer has to accept this). Thus, with the United States expected to uphold its military superiority well into the mid-century, the possibility of China using force to change the world (replacing the US presence everywhere) is highly unlikely. Deadly contest for change is not an option for China. The risk of war between the United States and China will be more likely a miscalculated or unwanted fight over China's unsettled problems in the Western Pacific (more discussion of this aspect in the following pages).

A Change of Guard?

The peaceful change of hegemonic leadership from the United Kingdom (UK) to the United States in the 20th century presents the power transition theory as a special case. Organski offers the following explanations:

- The US economic growth did not alarm Great Britain;
- The United States did not seek world leadership;
- The United States shared fundamental values and culture with Great Britain;
- The United States succeeded rather than overthrowing the British order;
- Great Britain was losing control of the international order, it was grateful that the United States picked up where Great Britain let go;
- Great Britain eventually became the "loyal lieutenant" to the United States.[22]

Most of these circumstantial conditions are not available in the US-China relations. Besides, there are several reasons China cannot take over the helm of the current international order. First, while China actively integrates itself into the economic, science and technology, education, and many other parts of the international system, it nevertheless refuses to connect with the prevailing democratic systems of the world. Although in the future China will become inevitably more democratic (more discussion of China's change in the following section), it will still be a "reluctant convert". China does not have the "heart and soul" to take over the leadership from the United States. China will not replace the United States to become a champion of democracy and human rights.

Second, the United States will have strong resilience to stay on top. Even when China reaches its full potential and becomes a much more powerful nation, the United States will still be too big to be No. 2 to China. A UK-like change in the US-China relationship is very unlikely. The UK is much smaller than the United States. Its hegemonic reach was historically conditioned. As Organski notes, ordinarily, the UK would have no chance to rule the world, but as the first nation to become industrialized, the UK was able to become a global hegemony while much of the world was still in the underdeveloped agrarian stage. When the United States became the hegemonic power, the UK had no choice but to take a subordinate role. This is not the case between the United States and China.

Reluctant Accommodations?

This is a very peculiar aspect of the US-China power transition. Other matters aside, the United States and China both believe that some key changes in the other will make the transition, and the world for that matter, a peaceful one. For the United States, the most desirable change in China is for its government to become a democratic institution. For China, it is a curtailment of US hegemonic conduct in international politics and the democratization of international relations. It is quite ironic that the "champion of democracy (i.e., the United States)" is accused of practicing "dictatorship" in international affairs whereas an authoritarian China promotes democracy in the world.[24] This irony, however, is surely the missing link between the United States and China, the peaceful evolution of which can make the US-China power transition a different one in history.

The US push for democratic change in China has a long history. In the early 1950s, John Foster Dulles, Secretary of State of the Dwight Eisenhower administration, initiated a policy of "peaceful evolution" to induce democratic change in the Soviet Union, China, and other communist nations.[25] Dulles saw that communism as a political system was repressive and could not last without forceful government sanctions. He anticipated that by the third or fourth generation, the communist leaders would lose their ideological zeal and gradually turn to the democratic way of government. Dulles suggested that the US Government facilitate this change through political, economic, and cultural penetration into the communist states. A peaceful evolution, rather than the use of force, would eventually transform those communist nations.

Dulles's anticipation came true with the collapse of the Soviet camp in 1990-91 (although Mikhail Gorbachev was already the 5th generation leader of Soviet communism, counting from Vladimir Lenin [1917-24], Joseph Stalin [1924-53], Nikita Khrushchev [1953-64], to Leonid Brezhnev [1964-82], but excluding the two transitional figures, Yuri Andropov and Konstantin Chernenko, who only held the Soviet communist leadership for about 2 years), but encountered strong resistance from Chinese leaders from Mao Zedong to Deng Xiaoping and the present ones (China is currently under the 4th generation of communist leadership; the Chinese Communist Party [CCP] is making dogmatic efforts to resist peaceful evolution in China).[26] The United States nevertheless has never given up the hope and effort to promote democratic change in China. President Nixon's opening of China and subsequent US engagement policies with China have all been part of these efforts.[27]

In the post-Cold War era, the United States has become even more convinced that an international order based on democracy, free commerce, and the rule of law is the only destiny for the world.[28] Promotion of this international order has been the central tenet of US national strategy accordingly.[29] The United States is willing to shed national treasure and blood to promote democracy abroad, as in the case of Iraq. China unfortunately stands as the single largest roadblock in this US mission (the Muslim world collectively is another). Thus on every occasion of international importance, the United States challenges China to take on political reform and reminds China that without completing the long-dodged political modernization, China will not be able to reach its full potential, nor will it be able to act as a responsible stakeholder to promote common good in international affairs.[30]

China, however, holds a different view. Chinese leaders argue that democracy is not the panacea for international problems.[31] They insist that developing nations, China in particular, have authoritarian governments for good reasons—Huntington's classic argument for authoritarian stability in developing societies still stands as a valid one.[32] US heavy-handed pressure for forceful and hasty political change only creates political instability in developing nations; in the post-Cold War world, it is the US hegemonic approach that is responsible for most of the international conflicts and questionable armed interventions. The United States, as the Chinese argue, has been an "irresponsible stakeholder" in world affairs.[33]

Opposing hegemony has been an enduring theme in Chinese foreign policy since the early days of the People's Republic of China (PRC) (the United States has been the primary target of this policy; China also opposed Soviet hegemony over the communist world during the latter part of the Cold War). In recent years, China has taken a step forward to propose change to the US-led hegemonic order. China's alternative is a "harmonious world construct,"[34] an idea based on a combination of Confucius' teaching, China's long-held Five Principles of Peaceful Coexistence,[35] and other Chinese views. On September 15, 2005, Chinese President Hu Jintao took the opportunity of the 60th anniversary of the United Nations (UN) to present this call to the world leaders gathering at the UN headquarters in New York. In his speech, Hu also rolled out a roadmap for the construction of this harmonious world:

- uphold multilateralism and strengthen the UN, the collective security mechanism, and the authority of the UN Security Council to realize common security;
- uphold mutually beneficial cooperation to achieve common prosperity, reduce the uneven economic development

between the rich and the poor countries, and establish a new international economic order that is fair for all, but not just for the rich Western nations (with expected reforms in international commercial, financial, trading, and natural resources-development systems);

- uphold the spirit of inclusiveness to build a harmonious world in which different political and cultural entities can co-exist; and,
- promote UN reform actively and prudently.[36]

Chinese leaders celebrate the promulgation of this harmonious world construct as a shining milestone in China's foreign policy and in world affairs. Indeed, they claim that as a "great and proud nation" ascending to the center stage of international affairs, China must have its vision for the world. This harmonious world construct presents for the first time China's comprehensive views on international relations and the Chinese way on handling international conflict. It is China's "icebreaking gift" to the world.

Moreover, Chinese leaders take the harmonious world call as a successful breakthrough in China's effort to take the initiative in world politics, to define terms in international conduct, and to take over the "power and rights to speak in international affairs". For so long, all of these have been the privileges of the United States and the West. China is determined to reverse the situation in which China is only on the defense and subject to US/West censuring.[37] This is a very important step for China in the power transition process.

Finally, the harmonious world construct gives a new lease on life to Confucianism and communism. It is a milestone in China's effort to revive the hope for a utopian world and make this dreamed world implementable.[38]

Amid this shower of praise, Chinese leaders and analysts take the harmonious world construct as an article of faith and make every effort to appreciate its "strategic profoundness" and "political correctness" and suggest ways to promote and implement this grand design. Indeed, in the last several years, numerous Chinese government propaganda and "scholarly analyses" have been disseminated to introduce, praise, and support the harmonious world construct. They believe that the time has come for China to project its views, values, and agendas to the world.[39]

However, the harmonious world construct is by no means as promising as the Chinese have claimed. Chinese leaders would be better served to take a hard look at this policy call before getting carried away by that unqualified praise and making another round of zealous promotion.

First, Chinese leaders should see that their harmonious world construct is about improvement of the existing (US/West-led) international order, but not a design to replace it. President Hu's UN speech cited earlier attests to this point. There is no reason for China to over-blow the significance of this construct.

Second, Chinese leaders should also take a hard look at the "classical foundation" of the harmonious world construct, namely, the Confucius teaching and his prescriptions for a harmonious society. There have been numerous writings in China to celebrate the redressing of Confucianism in China and the CCP's embracement of Confucius teaching as the cultural underpinning of China's harmonious society and harmonious world construct.[40] However, few have dared to discuss some of the widely known problems with Confucianism and their negative implications for the harmonious world construct.[41]

It is beyond the scope of this analysis to provide an extended discussion of Confucius' "dream of a 'communism-equivalent' harmonious world", his "love" for the hierarchical socio-economic and political relationship: ruler and servant, father and son, his preference for the rule of benevolence and rituals to the rule of law, his admiration for the high class and rulers and prejudice against the commoners, his view on the unalterable class stratifications, his way to make the people follow an order but not to understand it, and his "contribution" to China's authoritarian tradition. Suffice it to say that the entire stock of Confucius's political thought is about authoritarian order and rulership. We also know for a fact that China's whole history has been under dynastic and authoritarian rule, especially in the almost 2,000 years when Confucianism was the official political and ethical dogma, not to mention the totalitarian dictatorship under Mao Zedong. (Although Mao and his successors claim to have broken from China's dynastic past and dismissed Confucianism, the CCP has nevertheless retained most of the Chinese authoritarian tradition in its rule of China). Authoritarian rule by design does not allow political differences. It goes without saying that "harmony with cultural diversities and political differences" NT) has never existed in China. On the contrary, throughout history, Chinese have only known about "political conformity with disharmony". Thus when those unqualified claims of harmony as the mainstay of the Chinese tradition and the underpinning of the harmonious world construct come to dominate the promotion of this questionable call, they are, in essence, observing the authoritarian rule of political conformity and flattering the Chinese leaders with a "new dress" that they do not have.

Chinese leaders' call for cultural diversity and political difference puts themselves in an awkward situation: they like to cite Karl Marx's teaching that a nation's foreign policy is an extension of its internal political, economic, social, and cultural constructs; yet since there is no harmonious society in China, how can they promote a harmonious world abroad as a Chinese foreign policy? The harmonious world call, under this circumstance, appears to be just another cover for the Chinese leaders to protect their authoritarian rule in China, but not a genuine design for a new world order.

In addition, the harmonious world construct, a natural extension of China's long-held Five Principles of Peaceful Coexistence, requires the practice of Confucius' "self-cultivation" as a starting point for those who want to put all-under-heaven in good order. As Confucius's "backward logic" goes, if you want to bring peace and order to the world, you should start with putting peace and order in your country, your family, and most basically and fundamentally, you should first "purify" yourself, and make yourself peaceful and in good order. Since men are not angels nor transformable, it is difficult to put this highly altruistic harmonious world construct in operation, or put another way, to expect statesmen in the world to follow Confucius' teaching to practice this ideal statesmanship. This is also a reason why China's Five Principles of Peaceful Coexistence and all those "unselfish and mutually beneficial expectations" have largely been just goodwill calls but not operable or enforceable mechanisms in international relations (Chinese claims to the contrary notwithstanding).[42]

This critique may be hard for the Chinese leaders to swallow. But they have no need to be upset with lacking a sound and workable agenda for the world at this point. Their priority, after all, is still at home but not abroad. Indeed, as Deng Xiaoping puts it, making good on China's modernization is the CCP's overarching mission. Bringing 1.4 billion Chinese, close to a quarter of the world's population, to a higher level of human endeavor is a great contribution to the world.

China's modernization is a monumental mission. It has made impressive progress in the last 30 years. However, its eventual success is still not a foregone conclusion. Among the big challenges in the years to come, China must face squarely its long-shirked political modernization. For thousands of years, China has not had a political system that can promote harmony with diversity and difference and ensure lasting peace and stability in China. The CCP relied on the old rules to maintain stability in China in the last 30 years. It would be increasingly difficult to do so over the next 30 years.

It is fair to note that the CCP has made some political changes in the last 30 years.[43] However, most of those changes have been reluctant (the CCP's anti-West orientation dictates that political change be taken only to the extent that economic reform can continue) and cosmetic (administrative restructuring but not fundamental political change).[44] Now China's overall development has reached the point that more substantive political reform is in order. There are already noted signs of Chinese people longing to have a more democratic way to choose their representatives to the People's Congress, and eventually their local and national leaders, a true rule of law in China (not dictated by Party lines and with no exception for the CCP members), a more effective (i.e., independent) check on the government officials' rampant corruption, and so on.

The CCP leaders understand that China eventually needs a democratic government. They have no alternative but to make changes. However, the CCP has two requirements for political reform: it must preserve the CCP's rule of China, and there should be no political chaos. In fairness, these are not unreasonable demands. The CCP, after all, is committed to China's modernization and has a sound plan to approach it. Moreover, China's reform and development cannot take place in a chaotic situation. However, the CCP should turn to democratic ways to keep itself in power. It should also use democratic means to maintain political stability in China. Singapore is a good example for China, but eventually, Japan is a better model. In many ways, the CCP has a good chance to become a long-ruling party like Japan's Liberal Democratic Party (LDP).[45]

It should be noted that in recent years the CCP has taken positive steps to address the need for political reform. In 2004, the CCP for the first time passed a resolution to address the Party's ruling issue. The CCP acknowledges that it is not easy to seize power, but it is more difficult to manage a country. It also acknowledged that the CCP's ruling party status was not born, but should be earned; it is not forever. The CCP allows discussion of its legitimacy problem and accepts that it must work to keep it.[46] In 2006, the CCP put forward a resolution to construct a harmonious society in China. In 2007, Hu Jintao made a sweeping call for democratic reform at the 17th National Party Convention report. In 2009, the CCP adopted a resolution to promote "intra-Party democracy". Along the way, the CCP has accepted that freedom, equality, justice, and harmony are universal values.[47] The CCP has also accepted the concepts such as human rights, rule of law, constitutional democracy, people-based approach, political civilization, transparent government, service government, responsible government, etc.[48]

The 30th anniversary of China's economic reform test case, the Shenzhen Special Economic Zone (SEZ), was in 2010. Chinese Premier Wen Jiabao and President Hu Jintao were there to drum up the celebrations. The two also took the occasion to call for an "ideological emancipation" and charged the SEZ to take the lead in political reform in China's next round of change. Wen Jiabao put the nation on notice that without political reform, China would not be able to deepen economic reform and development; but could lose what it had already achieved through the economic reform and even short-circuit its modernization mission.[49]

All of these indicate that peaceful evolution is well underway in China. In the next 20 to 30 years, the CCP's challenge is to carry out the political reform in an orderly way.[50] There are good reasons to believe that this peaceful evolution will sail through in China. The CCP's commitments mentioned above are crucial, without which democratic change in China will be impossible. In addition, the CCP's more than 20 years of "experiment" with elections at the rural villages have prepared China's "least qualified" people for democracy. These are 80 percent of China's population. No matter how inadequate this practice is, it is a step in the right direction. Finally, China's economic development has prepared its city residents for democracy. This political reform, as the CCP rightly notes, will be gradual, but will change China in fundamental ways. China's *White Paper on Building of Political Democracy* in China has made it clear.

China's political reform will produce a "socialist democracy with Chinese characteristics". The qualifier "Chinese characteristics" suggests that China's political system will not be like any other. Many Chinese analysts take it wrong that the United States dictates the form of democracy. Nothing can be further from the truth. The United States stands for the democratic principles. It does not matter if other democracies are parliamentary or presidential. Germany and Japan are perfect examples. After their defeat in World War II, both nations were under US occupation. The United States could dictate how they rebuilt their countries, but the United States instead left them to make the one that fit their national needs. The recent example of Iraq is another. Again, the United States did not require Iraq to be rebuilt like the United States.

China's democratic change will not remove its conflicts of interests with the United States, but it will make those conflicts less contentious. While under the influence of ideological difference, every conflict automatically becomes a test of will. It is a life and death situation. With the removal of ideological difference, China may not become a "dear friend," but it will not be a condemned enemy. Russia is an example.

Flashpoints in the US-China Relations

Although China and the United States understand that the two are engaged in a power transition process; the two nations need to take careful measures to manage this contentious relationship; as US Secretary of State Hillary Clinton put it loudly in her 6th visit to Asia since taking office, "it is not in anyone's interest for the United States and China to see each other as adversaries, [so] we are working together to chart a positive, cooperative, and comprehensive relationship for this new century;"[51] logically there is no reason for China to initiate a fight over this change, and China's peaceful evolution will eventually help make the US-China relations more manageable. The two nations nonetheless have contentions over what can be called China's "nation-building" issues.

In addition to the continuation of economic development and political change discussed earlier, China's nation-building efforts include unification with Taiwan, settlement of the territorial disputes in the East and South China Seas, its maritime ambitions, and the issues of Tibet and Xinjiang. The United States is involved directly or indirectly in all of these issues. While China is determined to complete its nation-building process on its way to become a great power, the United States is there to "watch China do the right thing".

Unfortunately, because China and the United States do not see eye to eye on these key issues, many of China's acts will be perceived as wrong-doings and most of the US involvement will be taken as ill-willed interference in China's internal affairs. These clashes can turn into flashpoints, a mishandling of which can set them on fire and get the United States and China to overstep on each other's interests and overreact to each other's actions, forcing the two nations to a premature or unwanted confrontation.

Taiwan: Why China Does Not Let It Go?

This is probably the most frequently-asked and most baffling question for Americans about the Taiwan issue. From the

American perspective, China is big enough territory-wise and surely does not need the addition of Taiwan to become a great power. Moreover, Taiwan has had its *de facto* independence from China for well over half a century; there seems no compelling reason why it must be part of China. Since Taiwan has a well-developed economy and enjoys a higher level of per capita income than that in China, how much better will unification be for Taiwan? Taiwan is already a democracy. Why would the Taiwan people want to live under a repressive authoritarian rule from the other side of the Taiwan Strait? For these reasons and more, few Americans can understand why China is so obsessed with the unification of Taiwan. However, to many mainland Chinese, these questions and reasoning are insulting. The issue is not how Taiwan benefits from the unification, but what China wants from this undertaking. Chinese have no hesitation to tell Americans that they are ignorant of China's history, China's need for national unity, the complicated nature of the cross-Taiwan Strait relations, and US involvement in this almost intractable issue.

The Chinese take the Taiwan issue as part of China's contemporary history of humiliation from foreign powers. From the First Opium War of 1840 to the founding of the PRC in 1949, foreign powers launched numerous attacks and intrusions on China. China was forced to sign a world record of 745 unequal treaties with 22 foreign powers[52] and lost Hong Kong to the UK, Macau to Portugal, a large piece of territory in northern China to Russia, and Taiwan to Japan.

China has seen changes in its territory many times in history. It has been a pattern that following each dynastic fall China suffered territorial loss or internal fragmentation. But this ancient nation has a remarkable capacity to retain its unity, the persistent quest of which has resulted in making China the longest-surviving and most coherent civilization in the world and molding the Chinese "great unity mentality". Indeed, every new ruler of China takes the mission of restoring the greatness of the Middle Kingdom and recovering its "stolen" territories as a mandate from heaven. It is no exception for the contemporary Chinese leaders. The CCP has had this mission in its party platform since its founding in 1921.

Since taking control of mainland China in 1949, the CCP has made the unification of China one of its three sacred historical missions (the other two are modernization of China and safeguarding world peace). With the return of Hong Kong and Macau to PRC sovereign rule in 1997 and 1999 respectively, the unification of Taiwan with mainland China has become what many Chinese call the last chapter of this historical mission, without which, China cannot bring this history to a graceful close.

But Taiwan is more than a piece of territory in history. In 2001, China signed a "Treaty of Good-Neighborliness and Friendly Cooperation" with Russia. A key part of the treaty is about settling the border disputes between the two nations. China and Russia stated in the treaty "with satisfaction that each has no territorial claim on the other" and agreed to hold talks to finalize a few remaining border demarcations.[55] This treaty, as one noted Chinese observer pointed out, had in essence signed off China's claim to about 1.5 million square kilometers (roughly 579 thousand square miles) of territory Russia took from the Qing Dynasty in the 19th century under one of those socalled unequal treaties imposed on China by foreign powers. The size of this lost land is about 40 times that of Taiwan.[56]

Why did China give up such a large claim for no tangible return from Russia yet refuse to let a tiny Taiwan go away? In many ways, China's compromise in the Sino-Russo treaty is to buy peace from Russia for China's economic development and in case China has to use force against Taiwan and consequently confront the United States, because of the US commitment to Taiwan's defense, Russia will not make trouble for China along the borders but instead, will possibly lend support to China. Also, China's long-lost northern territory is a scarcely-populated area with snow cover for much of the time in the year. There is really not much the Chinese feel dear about.

However, Taiwan is an entirely different story. The island has a government that was once an arch enemy of the CCP. Before its defeat in 1949, this government sought the destruction of the CCP and had an on-and-off civil war with the CCP for over 20 years. After it took shelter in Taiwan, this government continued the unfinished civil war with the CCP by waging overt and covert campaigns to reclaim the mainland and fought against the CCP for the legitimate representation of China in the international community until the CCP prevailed in replacing this government in the UN Security Council in 1971. After the United States switched its diplomatic recognition of China from Taipei to Beijing in 1979, mainland China received recognition from many other nations.

By the 1990s, the Taiwan government gradually abandoned the civil-war confrontation with the CCP. But Taiwan soon posed two new challenges to Beijing. One was its democratic transition. Taiwan has become a showcase that democracy can take root on a "Confucius land" and challenged the CCP to do the same. The other was the emergence of the Taiwan independence movement. As a "by-product" of democratic change, Taiwan's pro-independence force had come to the surface. Many of the pro-Taiwan independence advocates were previously-suppressed political dissidents. While sacrificing their life for decades to fight for Taiwan's democracy, these "freedom fighters" also wanted to turn Taiwan into an independent country. Riding the waves of change, they founded the Democratic Progress Party (DPP) and subsequently won Taiwan's 2000 and 2004 presidential elections. Under the leadership of openly pro-Taiwan independence President Chen Shui-bian, the DPP had taken many provocative acts to challenge Beijing for a showdown on the issue of independence and unification.[57] The Taiwan issue subsequently became one about national secession mixed with a fight with China over political ideology and way of life; both get on the sensitive nerves of the Chinese leadership and challenge the CCP's mission and its legitimacy. For these political reasons, the Chinese leaders in Beijing see the fight for Taiwan as its vital interest and will not let Taiwan go.

In addition to the political issues, Taiwan is also a vital strategic stronghold. One hundred years ago, China gave away Taiwan as a cheap bargaining piece of war reparation to Japan following its humiliating defeat in the First Sino-Japanese War of contemporary times.[58] According to China's principal negotiator at Shimonoseki, Japan, the Plenipotentiary of His Majesty the Emperor of China,

Li Hung-Chang, the Qing government gave away the offshore island of Taiwan so that Japan would not press for more territorial concessions on China's mainland. Li, in particular, held that Taiwan was ungovernable and strategically unimportant to the Qing, for this empire still had much unconquered land to its west (Li was referring to the vast territory covering today's inner and outer Mongolia, several of China's western provinces, and all the way to the Tibetan and Uygur areas).[59]

That was then. Yet Taiwan's strategic significance took a dramatic turn at the end of World War II. General Douglas MacArthur was the first to characterize Taiwan as being a "protective shield" and a "critical salient" to the US interests in the Western Pacific. The protective shield came as a result of US victory in World War II in the Pacific.

Our strategic frontier then shifted to embrace the entire Pacific Ocean, which has become a vast moat to protect us as long as we hold it. We control it to the shores of Asia by a chain of islands, extending in an arc from the Aleutians to the Marianas, held by us and our free allies. From this island chain we can dominate with air power every Asiatic port from Vladivostok to Singapore, and prevent any hostile movement into the Pacific.

Yet the critical salient in the island chain came from the uncertain future of Taiwan. Keeping in mind the US problem with communist China (the "Who lost China" debate was being waged in Washington) and its effort to liberate Taiwan, MacArthur warned that:

The geographic location of Formosa [Taiwan] is such that, in the hands of a power unfriendly to the US, it constitutes an enemy salient in the very center of this defensive perimeter.... Utilization of Formosa by a military power hostile to the US may either counter-balance or overshadow the strategic importance of the central and southern flank of the US frontline positions. Formosa in the hands of such a hostile power could be compared to an unsinkable aircraft carrier and submarine tender, ideally located to accomplish offensive strategy, and at the same time checkmate defensive or counter-offensive operations by friendly forces based on Okinawa and the Philippines.[60]

In any case, Taiwan has been in "US hands" since MacArthur's time. The strategic nightmare has actually been on China's side. Indeed, China sees this "US-controlled unsinkable aircraft carrier" as a constant threat pointing to its "belly button" (if one takes a creative look at the bulging shape of China's eastern seaboard—does it not look like China's big belly?) Taiwan is only 90 miles from China, but it is a Pacific Ocean away from the United States. If Taiwan is vital to US national security, Chinese say that they feel it more so to China's national security consideration. Today, China wants to bring Taiwan under its control at all costs. In addition to the reasons discussed in the previous sections, Taiwan's geo-strategic significance plays a big role in China's calculation.

In addition to the historical, political, and geo-strategic significance, Taiwan is also a vibrant economy. It has 23 million people, many of whom are the world's topnotch scientists, engineers, and business gurus. Many of them also have family ties on the mainland. To the CCP leaders, Taiwan and mainland China have a wide range of intertwined political, socio-economic, cultural, and historical interests. No matter who is in charge of China, the unification of Taiwan with mainland China is an unavoidable mission. If China were to become a democratic nation, unification would presumably take place in a more amicable way. Taiwan may even want to join the union willingly.

In addition to the reasons discussed above, the Taiwan issue is intrinsically a problem between the United States and China. The United States has been involved in the Taiwan issue since the very beginning. As the Taiwan issue evolves, the United States and China have always found themselves in a test of will, strength, and wits over the handling of this thorny problem. Moreover, the significance of the Taiwan issue gets more intense in the context of the power transition. Letting Taiwan go is tantamount to conceding defeat. Chinese leaders will never entertain this option.

The United States' first involvement in the Taiwan issue took place in 1943 when President Franklin D. Roosevelt met with British Prime Minister Winston Churchill and Chinese Generalissimo Chiang Kaishek in Cairo, Egypt, to address the war against Japan. The three heads of state issued the Cairo Declaration that at the war's end, Japan "be stripped of all the islands in the Pacific which she has seized or occupied since the beginning of the first World War in 1914, and that all the territories Japan has stolen from the Chinese, such as Manchuria, Formosa, and the Pescadores, shall be restored to the Republic of China".[61] The three allies reaffirmed these terms in the Potsdam Proclamation in 1945.[62] Upon its defeat in the war, Japan complied with the demands and relinquished Taiwan (along with its other relinquishments).

The US second take on the Taiwan issue 5 years later was an uneasy one. At that time, US war-time ally and long time friend, Chiang Kai-shek, and his Nationalist government had lost the Chinese Civil War and retreated to Taiwan. The Communist leaders were contemplating an invasion of the island to finish this deadly quarrel. The Harry Truman administration was convinced that Chiang and his party were corrupt and had lost the mandate to rule China. Based on assessments and recommendations from the State and Defense departments and the Joint Chiefs of Staff, although the United States would not like to see the Chinese Nationalists and Taiwan fall into Communist hands, it nevertheless would take a hands-off approach on this issue (General MacArthur's observation notwithstanding).[63] On January 5, 1950, President Truman issued a statement reiterating US support for the Cairo Declaration and made it clear that the United States had no desire to get involved in China's internal conflict.[64]

Many took President Truman's statement as meaning the United States would not prevent the Communists from invading Taiwan. However, before the mainland Chinese got ready to launch the attack, the Korean War broke out. President Truman believed that the attacks on Korea and China's mounting pressure on Taiwan were all part of the drives of Communism. Thus, while preparing for a response to the Korean situation, Truman also ordered the Seventh Fleet to neutralize the Taiwan Strait. The President made the following statement on June 27, 1950, 2 days after the outbreak of the Korean War:

"The attack upon Korea makes it plain beyond all doubt that communism has passed beyond the use of subversion to conquer independent nations and will now use armed invasion and war. It has defied the orders of the Security Council of the United

Nations issued to preserve international peace and security. In these circumstances the occupation of Formosa by communist forces would be a direct threat to the security of the Pacific area and to United States forces performing their lawful and necessary functions in that area".

"Accordingly, I have ordered the Seventh Fleet to prevent any attack on Formosa. As a corollary of this action I am calling on the Chinese Government on Formosa to cease all air and sea operations against the mainland. The Seventh Fleet will see that this is done. The determination of the future status of Formosa must await the restoration of security in the Pacific, a peace settlement with Japan, or consideration by the United Nations".[65]

This US military act practically closed the window of opportunity for the mainland Chinese on Taiwan; as President Dwight Eisenhower later put it, "any invasion of Formosa would have to run over the Seventh Fleet,"[66] an operation that was completely beyond China's capability at the time. Of note is that Truman's statement for the first time raised the issue that *the future status of* Taiwan was undetermined.[67] A month later in a special report to the Congress, President Truman, also for the first time, set the US expectation that the *Taiwan issue be* settled through peaceful means.[68] This requirement was codified in future US policies on the Taiwan issue. It has also become a point of contention between the United States and China, which insists that it has the sovereign right to use force to bring about unification with Taiwan if necessary.

With the Taiwan Strait "off limits," China and the United States fought a bloody war in Korea instead.

Following the tenuous armistice in 1953, the United States turned around to sign a Mutual Defense Treaty with the Republic of China (ROC) government on Taiwan, turning the Seventh Fleet's temporary patrolling into a long-term US commitment to the defense of Taiwan.[69] This pact effectively put Taiwan out of reach by the mainland Chinese for the next 20 years.

The next time the United States dealt with the Taiwan issue was in 1972 when President Richard Nixon made his historic visit to China. Nixon was there to change US-China relations and solicit China's cooperation in ending the Vietnam War and counterbalancing the Soviet threat. The Chinese leaders took the opportunity to address the Taiwan issue. It was a tough business.[70] The two sides expressed their positions in the Shanghai Communiqué, which turned out to be a masterpiece of diplomatic communication in modern international relations known as the "agreement to disagree," as the following:

- The Chinese side reaffirmed its position: the Taiwan question is the crucial question obstructing the normalization of relations between China and the United States; the Government of the PRC is the sole legal government of China; Taiwan is a province of China which has long been returned to the motherland; the liberation of Taiwan is China's internal affair in which no other country has the right to interfere; and all US forces and military installations must be withdrawn from Taiwan. The Chinese Government firmly opposes any activities which aim at the creation of "one China, one Taiwan," "one China, two governments," "two Chinas," an "independent Taiwan" or advocate that "the status of Taiwan remains to be determined".
- The US side declared: The United States acknowledges that all Chinese on either side of the Taiwan Strait maintain there is but one China and that Taiwan is a part of China. The United States Government does not challenge that position. It reaffirms its interest in a *peaceful settlement* of the Taiwan question by the Chinese themselves.[71]

China's positions are straightforward. However, the US terms are carefully worded. The United States "acknowledges" but does not endorse the Chinese claims. While the mainland Chinese intend the PRC to be the "unified China," the United States holds the "one China" as an undefined future entity. For the Chinese leaders, there is only one destiny for Taiwan: unification with the mainland; it is a matter of "when" and "how". But the United States uses the neutral term of "settlement," suggesting that the final resolution of the Taiwan issue can be unification or separation, as long as it is settled in a peaceful way. This is a "polite" check on the Chinese intent to "liberate" Taiwan, with the use of force if necessary.

In spite of the disagreements, the two sides moved on. Seven years later, President Jimmy Carter took a giant step to normalize relations with the Beijing government. At the same time, he also terminated US official relations with Taiwan and let the defense treaty expire a year later. Congress was furious with Carter's moves (the President took the actions when Congress was in the Christmas recess)[72] and quickly took counter-measures to pass the Taiwan Relations Act (TRA) of 1979 to define US positions and commitments to the China-Taiwan affairs as follows:

- to declare that peace and stability in the area are in the political, security, and economic interests of the United States, and are matters of international concern;
- to make clear that the United States decision to establish diplomatic relations with the PRC rests upon the expectation that the future of Taiwan will be determined by peaceful means;
- to consider any effort to determine the future of Taiwan by other than peaceful means, including by boycotts or embargoes, a threat to the peace and security of the Western Pacific area and of grave concern to the United States;
- to provide Taiwan with arms of a defensive character; and,
- to maintain the capacity of the United States to resist any resort to force or other forms of coercion that would jeopardize the security, or the social or economic system, of the people on Taiwan.[73]

Mainland Chinese hate the TRA, for it reiterates the US view that Taiwan's status is undetermined; defines what the Beijing government deems rightful measures, especially the use of force, as "grave concern" to the United States; continues the provision of arms to Taiwan; and promises US military intervention if China were to use force to coerce Taiwan. Chinese denounce the TRA, arguing that it is a US law and should have no international standing. However, this law reflects the will and position of the superpower. Chinese leaders understand that it will be at their own peril if they ignore it.

Chinese leaders nevertheless regretted their compromise on the arms sales item. Shortly after the normalization of relations with the United States in 1979, China sought to put an end to it. In 1982, China got the Ronald Reagan administration to issue the third joint US-China communiqué to address the arms sales issue. Yet it was a non-committal promise from the United States:

> The United States Government states that it does not seek to carry out a long-term policy of arms sales to Taiwan, that its arms sales to Taiwan will not exceed, either in qualitative or in quantitative terms, the level of those supplied in recent years since the establishment of diplomatic relations between the United States and China, and that it intends to reduce gradually its sales of arms to Taiwan, leading over a period of time to a final resolution. In so stating, the United States acknowledges China's consistent position regarding the thorough settlement of this issue.[74]

While negotiating with the Chinese, the Reagan administration privately provided six assurances to Taiwan that the United States 1) had not agreed to set a date for ending arms sales; 2) had not agreed to hold prior consultations with the PRC regarding arms sales to Taiwan; 3) would not play a mediation role between the PRC and ROC; 4) would not revise the TRA; 5) had not altered its position regarding sovereignty over Taiwan; and 6) would not exert pressure on Taiwan to enter into negotiation with the PRC.[75]

For better or for worse, the Shanghai Communiqué of 1972, the Joint Communiqué to establish US-China diplomatic relations of 1979, the Joint Communiqué on Arms Sales to Taiwan of 1982, and the Taiwan Relations Act (TRA) of 1979 have become the basic documents "governing" the relations among China, Taiwan, and the United States. However, these documents have created no fewer problems than they were intended to solve. The annual arms sales process between Taiwan and the United States, for instance, has become a constant test of will among China, Taiwan, and the United States.[76] This process also brings ups and downs in US-China relations. In the most recent cases, President

George W. Bush's authorization of sales in October 2008 and President Barrack H. Obama's reauthorization in January 2010 have prompted the Chinese government to take strong actions such as suspending US-China military-military exchanges and high-level official visits and threatening to punish US firms that sell weapon systems to Taiwan. More seriously, during these last two rounds of confrontation, many Chinese called on the Chinese government to take stronger actions against the United States. Some wanted the Chinese government to set rules for the United States to follow. Others suggested that China take counter-measures to inflict real pain on the United States (i.e., punish US firms that produce arms for Taiwan and force them to pay for their acts). Many even asked the Chinese government to prepare for a showdown with the United States on the arms sales issue, and the Taiwan issue as a whole, in 10 years.[77]

Even the documents themselves are points of contention between China and the United States. China always holds the United States accountable to the three joint communiqués. However, those communiqués are executive agreements. They are not subject to congressional approval; hence have no legally binding effects. Every new President has to reaffirm the new administration's commitment to those communiqués or they will become obsolete. Indeed, since Congress has never endorsed the terms of those communiqués, the "One-China" principle, which is China's most-stressed item, is not a treaty-bound US commitment at all. The Taiwan Relations Act of 1979, however, is a US public law. No matter how strongly China opposes it, every US President has to follow the law to handle US relations with Taiwan, whether they like it or not.

Moreover, there is plenty of ambiguity in those documents. Taiwan's pro-independence forces look to the TRA as their source of US support because of its strong pro-Taiwan positions and push the Taiwan independence agenda to the brink from time to time with the expectation that the United States will eventually back them up.

China, however, insists that the United States would honor the One-China principle and reacts strongly to Taiwan's pro-independence moves with the expectation that the United States will not intervene.

The United States for some time relied on this "strategic ambiguity" to maintain a delicate balance between the two sides across the Taiwan Strait. However, the recurrent tension in this area has forced the United States to rush to the rescue from time to time. This so-called strategic ambiguity eventually fell out of favor during George W. Bush's terms in the White House. In 2001, in the aftermath of the US-China military airplane collision incident, President Bush categorically put it that "the United States would do whatever it takes to help Taiwan defend itself".[78] Yet in 2003, the President, while having a meeting with the Chinese Premier Wen Jiabao at the White House, responded to a question from the press that he would not want Taiwan to make trouble.[79] In other words, the United States made it clear that if Taiwan provoked China's attack by pressing the independence agenda, it should not expect the United States to come to its defense; but if China lost its patience and forced unification upon Taiwan, the United States would intervene. Strategically, President Bush had in essence removed all the ambiguities in the US commitment. Operationally, the US response will depend on how the situation goes.

In the course of its development, the Taiwan issue has become a bizarre tug of war. On one end of the rope stands China, determined, focused, and making every effort to pull Taiwan into its fold. On the other end of the rope, there are two disoriented contestants, Taiwan and the United States, each having an internal tug of war over the China-Taiwan issue.

Inside Taiwan, it is a three-way situation. The DPP tries to pull Taiwan away from China. The Kuomintang (KMT) stands for eventual unification of Taiwan with China, not on China's terms, but on democratic principles—China must become a democracy or the KMT will not lead Taiwan to join China.

The 23 million Taiwan people are torn between these two parties. Repeated public opinion polls in Taiwan show that except for a small percentage of steadfast pro-independence and pro-unification extremes, most people have to agree that the current status quo of *de facto* but not *de jure* independence is a choice of the lesser evil, because they understand that outright promotion of formal Taiwan independence will provoke a war with China, whereas a compromised unification at this time is asking for trouble. Why submit to an authoritarian regime in Beijing while they can enjoy democracy and freedom in Taiwan?

The tug of war took a dramatic turn in 2008 when the KMT regained control of the Taiwan government. The KMT's landslide victories in the legislative and presidential elections clearly indicated that the Taiwanese people were frustrated with the DPP in its handling of Taiwan's economy and, more pointedly, Chen Shui-bian's confrontational relations with mainland China and the United States during his two terms in office (2000-08). Taking these elections as a mandate for change, President-elect Ma Ying-jeou set his agenda for a change in the cross-Strait relations. It had three components: a peace agreement with the PRC, a revitalization of Taiwan's economy, and an expansion of Taiwan's international space.

Shortly after taking office, Ma responded positively to PRC President Hu Jintao's call for an end to hostility and to sign a peace agreement. Ma proposed that the two sides return to the so-called "1992 consensus," in which the two sides agreed on "one China," but left open its definition and political content, and start the process of reconciliation.[80]

At the same time, Ma also made good on his campaign promises to open direct commercial/passenger flights between Taiwan and mainland China, ease restrictions on Taiwan-China economic exchanges, allow Taiwan to take advantage of China's booming economy, and get mainland Chinese tourists to visit Taiwan, a multi-billion US dollar business and a service market for more than 40,000 jobs. This was Ma's package to revitalize Taiwan's economy. Ma understood that Taiwan as "a beacon of democracy to Asia and the world" (President Bush's congratulations) must regain its economic cutting edge, lost under the DPP and Chen Shui-bian's reign. An aggressive expansion of Taiwan's economic exchange with China was the way to go.

The idea of a peace agreement between China and Taiwan first came from Kenneth Lieberthal, a noted China observer and one-time Senior Director for Asia in the Bill Clinton administration's National Security Council. Lieberthal proposes that the two sides sign a 20-to-30-year "agreed framework" so that China will not use force to threaten Taiwan and the latter will not seek formal independence and let time wash away the differences between the two sides.[81] Ma Ying-jeou and Hu Jintao have exchanged goodwill across the Taiwan Strait for such an agreed framework.

However, the tug of war will continue. Ma Ying-jeou has made it clear that in addition to the above-mentioned "China no use of force" and "Taiwan no move to formal independence," there will be "no hasty unification". Indeed, it took Taiwan well over half a century to become a thriving democracy. It will take much more time for China to reach this stage where a peaceful unification on democratic principles can take place. But these "no's" rest on a strong US backing. As China becomes more powerful and capable, US ability to dictate the conditions on the Taiwan issue will decline. In addition, rapid and extensive economic integration is taking place between the two sides across the Taiwan Strait. In June 2010, the Ma Ying-jeou administration signed the Economic Cooperation Framework Agreement (ECFA) with mainland China.[82] Economic integration will get deeper and broader between the two sides. Even if the DPP were to regain control of the government in Taiwan, it would find it difficult to undo the economic changes. To avoid a "willy-nilly" unification with the mainland or a desperate fight for independence and drawing China and the United States into an unwanted fight, Taiwan would be better off negotiating an agreement to guarantee its rights and benefits while it still has the bargaining advantages now.

Western Pacific: Troubled Waters?

In addition to the Taiwan issue, the United States and China have some very unsettling business in the Western Pacific involving direct confrontations as well as indirect conflicts involving China's maritime neighbors. Both will impact the preservation or alteration of the international order in this region, with the United States standing for the former and China, driven by its growing ional power, pushing for the latter.

For well over 60 years, the United States has maintained an order of hegemonic stability in the Western Pacific. This situation is changing. A recent writing by Aaron Friedberg, a Princeton University professor and former adviser to Vice President Dick Cheney on national security affairs, provides a rather telling characterization of this changing situation. It is worth quoting it here at length:

By the early 1990s, with the vestiges of Soviet air and naval power rotting at their bases in the Russian Far East, the Pacific had become, for all intents and purposes, an American lake. US forces were invulnerable and able to operate with impunity wherever and whenever they chose. Using forward-deployed ships, aircraft and troops operating from local bases and facilities in Japan, South Korea, Thailand, and Singapore, as well as those that could be dispatched from Hawaii and the West Coast, the United States could defend its friends, threaten its enemies and move its forces freely throughout the Western Pacific. American air and naval units conducted routine deployments and reconnaissance missions just outside (and at times, no doubt, within) China's airspace and territorial waters with little fear of harassment or interdiction, while US satellites passed overhead, unseen and unmolested.

Even beyond East Asia, the US Navy was in complete command of the world's oceans. If ordered to do so, the Navy could interdict commercial shipping and stop or sink vessels bound for China, regardless of whether they were traveling across the Pacific or east across the Indian Ocean.... In sum, at every level of potential conflict, from limited engagements at sea to transcontinental nuclear war, the Americans held the upper hand.

Fast-forward to the present. America's ability to project power into the Western Pacific, once unchallenged, is now threatened by the maturation of what Pentagon planners refer to as China's "anti-access/area-denial" strategy.... In a future crisis, Washington might have little choice but to pull them [US forces] far back from China's coasts, well beyond the effective range of their aircraft....

This combination of [PLA] rapidly advancing offensive and defensive capabilities is beginning to raise doubts in the region about America's ability to defend its allies and project its power. What is worse, over the next several years there will be an increasing danger that, in an extreme crisis, China's leaders might believe that they have a chance of starting a war by effectively knocking the United States out of the Western Pacific....[83]

Friedberg's final remarks may be too alarming. But China's ambitions give the United States little room for comfort. China wants to develop its maritime power (wmCg), which covers, most importantly but is not limited to, the security of China's extended ocean fronts and territorial waters, sovereign control of Taiwan and its surrounding territory, "recovery" of the "stolen" islands in the South and East China Seas, [84] effective management of its claimed Exclusive Economic Zone (EEZ), security of the sea lines of communication (SLOC), and a powerful blue-water navy that can project China's power and protect China's expanding interests.

The Chinese believe that this maritime power is indispensible for China to become a full-fledged global power.[85] Currently, China has secured its extended ocean fronts—no foreign power is to repeat a humiliating invasion of China from the sea again. China has also developed an increasingly credible deterrence against Taiwan and possible US military intervention in an event of China-Taiwan confrontation over unification or separation—with the access-denial capability Friedberg has mentioned in the quote.[86] On the distant SLOCs, China enjoys a free ride arguably provided by the United States. But eventually, China will prefer to rely on its own forces to protect its interests. At the moment, the most troubling issues for China in the Western Pacific are the conflicts with the United States over the EEZ, the territorial disputes in the South and East China Seas, and the lack of a credible blue-water navy to sustain China's interests. All of these add complications to the contentious US-China power transition.

US-China Conflict over the EEZ. This is a direct confrontation between China and the United States. It centers on the US military activities in the Chinese-claimed EEZ. The issue stems from the two sides' diametrically-opposing views on the legal and practical nature of the US military activities in this area. The opposing views and acts have gotten the two nations to confront each other in hostile ways in the Western Pacific.

The most notable confrontation so far is the collision of a US EP-3 surveillance plane with a People's Liberation Army (PLA) fighter jet about 70 miles off China's southern coast over the South China Sea on April Fool's Day 2001 (it was unfortunately not a joke).[87] Since then, China and the United States have continued to clash in the South and East China Seas. China has reportedly "harassed" the entire US ocean surveillance fleet at various occasions such as the *USNS Bowditch* (September 2002), *Bruce C. Heezen* (2003), *Victorious* (2003, 2004), *Effective* (2004), *John McDonnell* (2005), *Mary Sears* (2005), *Loyal* (2005), and *Impeccable* (2009).[88] The latest incident in the South China Sea involving the USNS *Impeccable* generated a new round of outcry between the two nations. Dennis Blair, former Commander of the US Pacific Command, called it the most serious confrontation since the EP-3 incident.[89] In addition to the clashes over the surveillance ships, China has also taken issue with the US aircraft carrier group making military exercises in the Yellow Sea and its occasional transit of the Taiwan Strait.[90]

China argues that the UN Convention on the Law of the Sea (UNCLOS) has established the 200 nautical miles (nm) EEZ between the territorial waters and the high seas as a special area different from either and governed by its own rules (see Appendix I, Article 55 and Article 86). China also holds that freedom of navigation and over-flight in the EEZ have certain restrictions, namely, the activities must be peaceful and non-threatening to the coastal nations. China charges that US military surveillance ships and reconnaissance flights in the Chinese-claimed EEZ have hostile intent against China and therefore do not fall in the scope of peaceful and innocent passage. China has repeatedly asked the United States to reduce this activity and eventually put a stop to it.[91]

The United States categorically rejects China's claims, arguing that China misinterprets the UNCLOS at best, but more pointedly stretches the interpretation intentionally to stage this confrontation with the United States at worst. The United States holds that the UNCLOS sanctions on foreign military activities are only for the 12-nm territorial waters, but not the EEZ (see the underlined phrase in the UNCLOS in Appendix I, Article 19). The United States also argues that China's reservation to the UNCLOS on foreign military activities in the EEZ does not enjoy broad support from the other signatory parties. Indeed, of the 161 nations ratifying the treaty, only 14 reserve the right to require approval for foreign military activities in their claimed EEZs. China's position therefore is an exception rather than the rule.[92] Robert Scher, Deputy Assistant Secretary of Defense for Asian and Pacific Security Affairs, puts it straightforwardly:

"Further, we reject any nation's attempt to place limits on the exercise of high seas freedoms within an EEZ. It has been the position of the United States since 1982 when the Convention was established, that the navigational rights and freedoms applicable within the EEZ are qualitatively and quantitatively the same as those rights and freedoms applicable on the high seas..".

"Our military activity in this region is routine and in accordance with customary international law as reflected in the 1982 Law of the Sea Convention".[93]

The US side also points to its experience with the Soviet Union during the Cold War. The two superpowers had an agreement to avoid incidents on the high seas (the 1972 US-Soviet Union Incidents-at-Sea Agreement [INCSEA]). When Soviet military vessels came to US shores, the United States shadowed and watched them closely, but did not demand their departure as the Chinese do now. Chinese argument that the United States would not tolerate Chinese military surveillance ships near US shores does not stand. China has gone too far in its demands.[94]

The US side has also hinted to China that as its interests expand globally, China may need to send its navy to far-away areas to protect those interests; it would be therefore in China's interest to keep the EEZ open for foreign military activity. China at this point does not buy this argument. In its effort to fight against piracy at the Gulf of Aden, China explicitly asked for permission from the Somalia government to let the Chinese naval forces operate in Somalian troubled waters.

Aside from these arguments, the United States holds that, as Friedberg rightly puts it in the quote earlier, it has been conducting this business for well over 60 years; no one is to tell the US military to stop this practice. Admiral Timothy Keating, while visiting Beijing as commander of the US Pacific forces, put it on record that the United States does not need permission from China to sail its aircraft carrier group through the Taiwan Strait.[95]

These opposing views and confrontations are difficult to reconcile, given: 1) the two nations have had troubled relations throughout the years and do not trust each other; and, 2) the two are engaged in the ongoing power transition, and the fight over the EEZ is a test case on the national strength of the two power transition contestants. The stakes are high on both sides.

There is unfortunately no easy fix to this problem either. The UN Convention on the Law of the Sea is not likely to come up with a solution to these disputes any time soon. In the meantime, China and the United States have to take their arguments in their own hands to confront each other.

The US-China contention in this area came to a head in 2010. In March, North Korea allegedly sank a South Korean military vessel in the two Koreas' disputed waters in the Yellow Sea. In an effort to deter North Korea, the United States and South Korea decided to conduct a joint military exercise in the Yellow Sea. The United States would send an aircraft carrier strike group to boost up the war drills. However, China vehemently opposed this projected show of force. China was not happy with the way the United States and South Korea handled the case. Chinese analysts pointed out that the United States and South Korea made a mistake in not inviting China and Russia to the investigation (the ones in this investigation were the United States, Britain, Australia, Sweden, and South Korea). China thus refused to endorse the "biased results".[96] China held that the US-South Korea joint military exercise would have little or no effect on North Korea but instead would raise new tension in the region. More pointedly, China simply did not want the US warships to come to the Yellow Sea.

The Yellow Sea is about 300 miles wide, and lies between China and the two Koreas. US warships could easily sail in the

Chinese-claimed EEZ.[97] In addition to the contention over the EEZ, China also looks at this issue through its historical and national security lenses. Chinese PLA Major General Luo Yuan put it that the Yellow Sea was once an "amusement park" for the foreign naval powers and many of the humiliating invasions of China took place there. China did not want to see this gathering of hostile foreign warships in this area again. Moreover, Luo argued that the intended war games would be too close to China's "center of gravity," its capital, and would be too much of a threat to China's national security. Finally, Luo contended that although the war games were directed toward North Korea, given the US-China contentions over the EEZ in particular and power transition in general, the real intent of the United States sending those warships to the Yellow Sea was a check on China's position on the EEZ in particular and a show of strength against China in general.[98]

The United States and South Korea eventually conducted the show of force in July 2010 in the Sea of Japan, not the Yellow Sea. Although the Pentagon rejected allegations that the United States caved in to China's pressure and insisted that the aircraft carrier battle group would go to the Yellow Sea in future joint military exercises, most likely in the second phase of the planned war games, many took this as a US compromise.[99]

But the United States soon had an opportunity to "get even" with China. In November 2010, tension in this region flared up again. The two Koreas exchanged artillery shelling at their disputed area. Some of North Korea's artillery shells landed on the South Korea-controlled Yeonpyeong Island, killing South Korean soldiers as well as civilians. President Obama and South Korean President Lee Myung-bak immediately ordered the two nations' combat forces to carry out the second phase of the planned war games. This time, the aircraft carrier USS *George Washington* and its battle group steamed into the Yellow Sea. In the midst of an international condemnation of North Korea and support for the United States on this crisis, China had to tune down its rhetoric, although the Chinese Foreign Ministry spokesman did voice China's objection again to the US warships coming to the Yellow Sea. China nevertheless swallowed a bitter pill. But the contention between China and the United States on US military activities in the Chinese-claimed EEZ did not stop there. The two would come to fight again as the United States promised to continue these activities in the future.

With the absence of mutually (and internationally) acceptable grounds, the ultimate arbiter over the US military activities in China's claimed EEZ will be the two nations' national power, especially their military power. China at this point, and for some time to come, does not have the capability to carry out its demands. It can only make repeated protests or harass US operations in the Chinese-claimed EEZ. However, China is making steady efforts to improve its fighting capabilities. China's Marine Administration now has many well-equipped patrol ships and airplanes to conduct "law enforcement" acts in its claimed EEZ on a regular basis. China's navy will come for reinforcement if they encounter hostile acts from opponents. It will only be a matter of time when China will take a more forceful stand on this issue. According to the Pentagon's and other credible institutions' assessments, it will take China probably another 10 to 15 years to reach that level.[100] In the realm of international relations, this is a very short time span. Indeed, China has already made the call that the United States should prepare itself to accept this change and accommodate China's demands.

US-China competition or confrontation in the Western Pacific is a difficult issue. Unlike the two nations' encounters in other regions of the world, where there is a good chance that UN sanctions are in order or conflict is on less important interests, the two could find it easier and beneficial to cooperate. With the Chinese PLA Navy's (PLAN) escort mission in the Gulf of Aden and its cooperation with US and international forces as an example, the two nations' fight in the Western Pacific is direct, with vital interests at stake. It is difficult for the small Asian nations to intervene and the issues are hard to settle peacefully. It is an emerging reality that will be difficult for the two nations to come to terms in the context of the ongoing power transition.

South China Sea Disputes. The South China Sea encompasses a portion of the South Pacific spanning from the southern tip of

Taiwan to the Strait of Malacca. The area includes numerous small islands, rocks, and reefs, scattered roughly around the four island groups. This area is known as the Pratas in the northeast, the Macclesfield Bank in the middle, the Paracel Islands in the west, and the Spratly Islands in the south. Many of the "features," however, are submerged under water, visible only during low tides. There is, therefore, no precise count of the features in the South China Sea.

China has a long history of fisherman using these waters as well as official claims to the islands. They were arguably the first to assign them names, used them as navigational references, and attempted to designate them as Chinese territories by putting them in the jurisdiction of southern Chinese coastal provinces and marking them as such on maps.[101] For centuries, the Chinese took it for granted that their historical reach established their ownership over those islands and the waters around them. They never felt the need to maintain effective control or management of those faraway and uninhabitable islands. This was not a problem when the Middle Kingdom was powerful and its influence in its surrounding areas was strong. Yet when China was in dynastic decline, which has been a "cyclical illness" of China throughout its history, its imperial reach also retracted. It so happened that China's latest dynastic decline coincided with the forceful arrival of the European colonial powers. This time, in addition to suffering from internal turmoil, China also "lost" practically all of its offshore "territories" (in quotation marks because they are in dispute) to foreign powers: Taiwan and its surrounding islands were ceded to Japan; the South China Sea islands all "acquired" European names (the British were arguably the first Europeans to set foot on the South China Sea islands; indeed, the Spratly and Pratas islands were both renamed after British sailors);[102] the French took possession of the Paracel and Spratly islands in the 1930s to expand the reach of its colonial protectorate, Annam (the predecessor and central region of present day Vietnam); and during World War II, Japan took control over all of the South China Sea islands in its drive to create the Greater East Asia Co-Prosperity Sphere.

At the end of World War II, Japan complied with the demands by the US-led allies, as articulated in the Cairo Declaration (1943) and reaffirmed in the Potsdam Proclamation (1945), respectively, to relinquish all the territories it "had stolen" during its imperial expansion (see Appendix II). However, by the time Japan came to sign a peace treaty with its wartime opponents and victims to legalize the termination of war and its relinquishments at the peace conference in San Francisco, there was no undisputed recipient to accept the territorial "spoils". China was divided between two governments, each claiming to represent the whole. The national leaders gathering in San Francisco for the peace conference with Japan could not decide which China, the ROC on Taiwan or the PRC on the mainland, they should designate as the legitimate recipient of Taiwan and its surrounding territory. In fact, neither Beijing nor Taipei was invited to the conference. In the end, the Peace Treaty with Japan only reiterated Japan's renunciation of its right to Taiwan and Pescadores but did not specify the recipient (see Appendix IV, Article 2[b]). With respect to the South China Sea islands, the delegates to the peace conference rejected a Soviet proposal to give them to China[103] and did not endorse a claim by Vietnam at the conference (see Appendix IV, Article 2[f]).[104]

China denounced the design of the peace treaty with Japan as well as the outcome of the San Francisco peace conference.[105] Chinese Foreign Minister Zhou En-lai issued a statement prior to the conference condemning the United States for its alleged role in "depriving China of its right to recover its lost territories" and "creating a treaty for war but not peace in the Western Pacific". At the same time, China reiterated its claim to Taiwan, its surrounding islands, and all of the South China Sea islands.[106]

In retrospect, China had several opportunities to secure its claim and control of the South China Sea islands regardless of what the United States and other nations did at the peace conference in San Francisco. In 1943 and in a world still heavily ruled by "jungle power" (in the way of the centuries-old power politics, that is, great powers did what they wanted but small nations suffered what they must, and great powers got to decide post-war international order), China could have demanded the "return" of the South China Sea islands in the Cairo Declaration. Indeed, the United States, the UK, and China were the only three "Great Allied Powers" gathering in Cairo to map out the post-war

East Asia territorial rearrangement (Vietnam, Malaysia, and the Philippines were not even independent countries yet). Moreover, in 1946, the ROC government dispatched warships to "recover" the Paracel and Spratly islands.[107] In a world that emphasized effective control rather than historical claims, [108] China could have kept its troops there to exercise effective control of those territories and establish China's unbroken and unchallengeable possession of those islands. Chinese leaders are themselves to blame for failing to do so and neglecting the South China Sea Islands for decades thereafter.[109] Their repeated protests against the United States and the other claimants and their statements about the South China Sea Islands "historically belonging to China" or as "China's intrinsic and inseparable territories" although necessary for China to uphold its claims, sounded painfully hollow.[110] Chinese leaders wasted all their time and energy engaging the Chinese in "perpetual revolution and class struggle" against each other at home, while leaving the disputed territories unattended offshore.

In the meantime, Vietnam and the Philippines continued their efforts (in acts, not only in words) to secure their claims and exercise effective control over the South China Sea islands.[111] By the early 1970s, word came that the South and East China Seas had vast deposits of fossil fuel and natural gas. The negotiation of the UN Convention on the Law of the Sea was also making progress—the world would soon divide up the "ocean commons" and allow the ocean littoral nations to claim the 200 nm EEZs and take possession of their naturally extended underwater continental shelves. These new developments prompted the South China Sea littoral nations to "scramble for effective occupation" of the islands in the South China Sea.[112] This scramble for territory continued well into the 1990s and left the disputes over the South China Sea islands as follows:

- The Pratas Islands: completely occupied by Taiwan but disputed by China;
- The Paracel Islands: mostly occupied by China but disputed by Vietnam;
- The Macclesfield Bank: disputed among China, Taiwan, and the Philippines;

- The Scarborough Shoal: disputed among China, Taiwan, and the Philippines;
- The Spratly Islands: disputed among China, Vietnam, Taiwan, the Philippines, Malaysia, and Brunei; of the more than 30,000 features, about 50 are considered to be islands; they are occupied by the following disputants:

  — China: 6;

  — Vietnam: 29;

  — Malaysia: 5;

  — Philippines: 9;

  — Taiwan: 1;

  — Brunei, none, but has EEZ claims.[113]

In the face of these disputed claims, China continues to hold that it is the owner of all the islands, reefs, and other features in the South China Sea and accuses all others of "stealing and occupying China's territories". Vietnam holds the second largest claim. In addition to disputing China over the Paracel islands, Vietnam claims ownership of all of the Spratly islands. Its claim puts Vietnam in dispute with China, Taiwan, and its Southeast Asian neighbors, Malaysia, Brunei, and the Philippines.

China was upset with the other claimants' rush to take possession of the South China Sea islands. It used force against Vietnam in 1974 to "regain" control of the key parts of the Paracel island group, and again in 1988 to fight for the islands in the Spratly area. There have also been armed conflicts between China and the Philippines over their disputed features.

In the midst of the fight for territory in the South China Sea, however, China launched its economic reform (in 1978). Its modernization mission dictated that China undertook measures to create an amicable internal and external environment. The most important of China's external requirements was to promote a constructive relationship with the United States (US investments, markets, and cooperation in practically all areas were instrumental for China to get started with its economic reform and development; Robert Zoellick was right to claim credit for the United States in his "responsible stakeholder" speech discussed earlier).

China's second external priority was to mend fences with its neighbors. A major part of China's problems with its neighbors was territorial disputes. Knowing that territorial disputes were difficult to settle but refusing to let this stand in the way of its modernization mission, China proposed to its neighbors in the early 1980s a policy of "shelving the disputes and moving on to promote joint development of natural resources at the disputed areas".[114]

China's efforts brought it an extended period of relative peace and stability in its surrounding areas. China was able to normalize relations with all its neighbors, especially the Southeast Asian nations, and focus on its economic development. However, 30 years afterwards, China realized that it had paid a heavy price for this policy—China left its disputed territories largely unattended for another 30 years. (The first 30 years were from 1949 to 1978 when the Chinese were condemned to repeated political movements, and the second 30 years from 1978 to 2008 when China turned its attention to economic development). China's territorial disputants, however, got three decades to reinforce their effective control of the disputed territories. Indeed, Vietnam and Malaysia have turned their possessions into popular ocean vacation resorts, fishing outposts, ocean natural resources exploration stations, or military garrisons. Permanent structures such as airplane runways, seaports, offices, and housing are well in place.[115] It would be very difficult, if not impossible, for China to negotiate the "return" of those islands.

The policy of shelving dispute-promoting joint development is now under heavy criticism in China. Many Chinese feel that China is foolish to pursue such a one-sided policy.[116] They argue that China is the only one to follow this policy. The other claimants welcome China's "self restraint," but none feels obligated to reciprocate in kind (much like China's "altruist" calls discussed earlier, such as the Five Principles of Peaceful Coexistence and the Harmonious World concept that expects other nations to practice altruism and exercise self constraint in international affairs even though few, if any, would do it wholeheartedly).

Indeed, all of the other claimants know that China's policy is based on the premise that the sovereignty of those islands belongs to China. China, for its part, has always maintained this bottom line in its dealing with the other claimants.[117] Deng Xiaoping, the architect of this policy, made it clear right at the beginning that "sovereignty is not negotiable".[118] The other claimants are not stupid. They see China's policy of shelving disputes as a matter of convenience. They believe that China will try to gradually coerce the disputants to agree with China's position; once China becomes stronger and the time is right, China will certainly become more assertive and will settle the disputes in its favor, with the use of force if necessary. The disputants therefore believe that their best bet is to take advantage of China's "benign neglect," "grab" as many islands as they can, and take their time to reinforce their effective control of the disputed territories.

Many Chinese also complain that China's call for joint development of natural resources in the disputed areas has only met with disappointment. So far, there are numerous drill rigs in the South China Sea, producing sizeable tonnages of crude oil and natural gas annually; but it is like "a feast for all but China". In the end, "China shelves disputes, only to make it possible for all others to work for their developments".[119]

Finally, Chinese analysts note that the other South China Sea claimants have been taking collaborative efforts to deal with China. By establishing the Association of Southeast Asian Nations (ASEAN) Declaration on the South China Sea and the Code of Conduct, the other disputants hold China to multilateral bargaining. At the same time, all of the disputants increase their defense spending and purchase advanced weapon systems to strengthen their naval and air forces.[120] The message is clear: they are preparing to protect their possessions. Many Chinese therefore ask the Chinese government to abandon this policy and take more assertive measures to settle the disputes in China's favor and before it is too late for action.

The Chinese government is caught between the need to continue its modernization mission, which is projected to take another 30 years to turn China into a true great power (review China's plan discussed earlier), and the need to fight for its claimed territories, which cannot wait, but can cause unpredictable interruption to the modernization mission. It appears that the Chinese government is trying to juggle the two simultaneously.[121] While continuing to advocate the shelving dispute by promoting a joint development policy, [122] China also takes concrete measures to exert effective control over the disputed territories. For instance, China's State Oceanic Administration (SOA) has started administrative, monitoring, and law enforcement patrols in the South and East China Seas, especially around the Spratly Islands and the disputed areas between China and Japan (discussed later), with well-equipped special-function vessels. According to China's SOA, in 2010 it has dispatched patrol ships 160 times and surveillance planes in 523 flights, covering ocean waters from China's northern sea shore, where the Yalu River meets the sea, to the Okinawa Trough on the edge of the Chinese-claimed underwater continental shelf (more on this in the next section) and the James Shoal at the southern tip of the South China Sea.[123]

In China's 12th Five-Year Plan released in March 2011, China for the first time included a special chapter on its maritime interests and development. In addition to specifying the guidelines for maritime development, China also plans to build 16 surveillance aircraft and 350 patrol vessels. In the meantime, the Chinese Foreign Ministry created a new Department of Boundary and Maritime Affairs. The PLAN also constructed a new naval base on Hainan Island focusing on the South China Sea and has been making efforts to expand its naval power eventually to a blue-water navy.

In addition to the above, China is also making efforts to prevent the involvement of the United States in these disputes. Throughout the years, China has been very suspicious and sensitive to the US position on the South China Sea disputes.[124] The Chinese blamed the United States for making the sovereignty of the South China Sea open for dispute at the San Francisco peace conference in 1951. They were also upset with the United States freely using the South China Sea to wage the Vietnam War (transporting forces and launching air and naval attacks on Vietnam), ignoring China's claim and protests, and making Southeast Asia and the South China Sea one of the three "anti-communism breakwaters" in the Western Pacific during the early years of the Cold War (through the Southeast Asia Treaty Organization [SEATO]; the other two are the US-Japan and Korea alliances and the US-ROC [Taiwan] defense pact).[125]

The Chinese were "grateful," however, when the United States took a "hands off" stand on the South China Sea disputes following its rapprochement with China in 1972. For instance, the United States turned a "blind eye" to China's military operation against Vietnam in 1974 (China-Vietnam naval clash over the Paracels), 1979 (China-Vietnam Border War), and 1988 (China-Vietnam naval clash over the Spratlys).

But they got upset again when the United States took issue with China's military clash with the Philippines in 1994, warned of China's "creeping encroachment" of the South China Sea territory, and hinted that the US-Filipino defense treaty would cover the Philippines' claimed South China Sea territories.[126] Chinese leaders have taken watchful note of the US adjustments in its position toward the South China Sea disputes since the end of the Cold War. Although the United States has openly maintained a neutral position,[127] China nevertheless holds that the United States sides with the Southeast Asian claimants privately.

More recently, the Chinese see growing US domestic pressure on the US Government to take stronger stands against China on the South China Sea disputes. US anti-China critiques strongly urged the Obama administration to be more assertive in Southeast Asian affairs. They also charge that China's claim on the South China Sea islands is overbearing. They are concerned that China's military modernization is upsetting the strategic balance in Southeast Asia and threatening US navigation freedom (such as the harassment of US surveillance ships and flights). They press the US Government to modify its strategy toward China in Southeast Asia and the South China Sea, and urged the US Government to support Vietnam, the Philippines, and Malaysia on their claims.[128] "The United States should take sides," as some in the United States have demanded.[129]

Chinese note that the Obama administration appears to take those domestic pressures seriously. In less than 2 years since taking office, Secretary of State Hillary Rodham Clinton has visited this region six times. She has repeatedly told the Asia community that the United States is back (from George W. Bush's "neglect") and is here to stay.[130] Secretary of Defense Robert Gates echoes Clinton's call by emphasizing the United States is a "residence power" in Asia and reaffirms US commitments to this region.[131] President Obama has also visited Asia twice and characterized himself as the "first Pacific President".[132] Through these high-sound-bite outreaches, the Obama administration has put forward a strategy toward Asia: strengthen and reinvigorate old alliances, make new friends, and support multilateral institutions in this region.[133]

Chinese watch the Obama team's moves with much suspicion. They dismiss the above as pretext for the United States to reposition itself in the Western Pacific. They argue that the United States has never left the Asia-Pacific, even though it has been busy fighting wars elsewhere; and this stormy repositioning is only an attempt to counter-balance China's expanding power.[134] Thus instead of welcoming the "return" of the United States to Asia, China was preparing for new tension in the two nations' relations.[135] Unfortunately, it did not take them long to see a downturn this way. Indeed, an eventful 2010 unfolded in a series of confrontations between the United States and China that touched upon almost all the sensitive issues between the two nations.

The year 2010 started with President Obama's authorization of $6.4 billion worth of arms sales to Taiwan (on January 29) and a meeting with the Dalai Lama at the White House (on February 17). Both, according to the Chinese, were acts stepping on China's core interests and against repeated Chinese protests. They set off a firestorm in Beijing. The Chinese government summoned the US Ambassador and the Defense Attaché to receive China's protest, and informed them that high-level military exchanges with the United States were to be suspended and those US corporations that make arms for Taiwan would be sanctioned.

In the following month (March), US Deputy Secretary of State James Steinberg and Senior Director for Asian Affairs at the National Security Council Jeffrey Bader visited Beijing with an attempt to "bring US-China relations back on track". Their meeting with the Chinese officials, however, was an unsuccessful one. Chinese officials took the occasion to lecture their American guests on China's core interests. But since the two sides did not see eye to eye on these issues, neither did they agree on the way to handle the issues, their difference remained as wide as ever.

It was later revealed that during this meeting, Chinese officials for the first time included the South China Sea territorial dispute in the list of Chinese core interests.[136] This Chinese move, even if it were meant to be a water-testing one, was very disturbing to the United States, for China has long held that it will use all instruments of national power, especially the use of force, to deal with issues involving its core interests. Raising the stakes on the South China Sea dispute is very dangerous; in addition, since China has such a broad claim on the South China Sea, not just land features, but also waters, and given China's position on foreign military activities in its claimed zones, putting the South China Sea as one of China's core interests has far-reaching consequences. Thus, 2 months later in May, when Chinese officials brought this issue directly to Clinton while she was in Beijing for the Second US-China Strategic and Economic Dialogue, Secretary Clinton rejected it flatly: "We don't agree with that".[137]

In the meantime, tension in Northeast Asia flared up around the alleged North Korea sinking of a South Korea warship and its aftermath. China refused to endorse any US-led measure to condemn North Korea and opposed vehemently a planned US-South Korea joint military exercise in the Yellow Sea. Specifically, China opposed the United States sending the *George Washington* aircraft carrier strike group to the troubled waters. Chinese argued that the true intent of this planned US show of force was not to deter North Korea, for that "outlawed" nation has never been deterred anyway, but to tell the Chinese that they should not try to push the US forces out of the EEZ.

The push and shove between the two nations came to a head in July in Hanoi, Vietnam, at the ASEAN Regional Forum. Secretary Clinton came prepared to give China an official response on the South China Sea issues. She declared the following:

- The United States has a national interest in the freedom of navigation, open access to Asia's maritime commons, and respect for international law in the South China Sea.

- The United States supports a collaborative diplomatic process by all claimants for resolving the various territorial disputes without coercion. We oppose the use or threat of force by any claimant.
- While the United States does not take sides on the competing territorial disputes over land features in the South China Sea, we believe claimants should pursue their territorial claims and accompanying rights to maritime space in accordance with the UN Convention on the Law of the Sea. Consistent with customary international law, legitimate claims to maritime space in the South China Sea should be derived solely from legitimate claims to land features.[138]

The Chinese charged that, taken out of context, the above sounded righteous; but delivered at the ASEAN Regional Forum, every foreign minister in the audience (there were 27 of them at the forum)[139] knew what Clinton was after, and every point made in her speech was an attack on China.

Clinton's first point is a forceful statement. If it stands, this statement can become a doctrine in US foreign policy on a par with other US foreign policy doctrines, most notably the Monroe Doctrine that put the European powers on notice and defined US interests in the Western Hemisphere, and the Carter Doctrine that warned the Soviets not to tamper with the Persian Gulf and made the security of the region a vital interest of the United States.[140] This "Hillary Clinton Doctrine" is put forward against another great power, China, and defines the US position on the key issues at stake.

Clinton's second point goes against China's long-held position of settling disputes with the other claimants in bilateral ways. The United States is concerned that China may have too great an advantage over the other disputants one-on-one. In addition, by opposing the use or threat of force in settling the South China Sea disputes, Clinton was in essence telling the Chinese that they should not make the South China Sea disputes a core interest of China.

Clinton's third point goes against another Chinese long-held position of settling the disputes "in accordance with the special historical, political, economical, geographical, and other related circumstances". To the Chinese, UNCLOS is a necessary reference, but they do not want to subjugate the disputes to the ruling of the UNCLOS, for it will be disadvantageous to China's claims, which are largely historical but not records of effective control.

Clinton's final point takes issue with an ambiguous Chinese claim on the South China Sea. It is the area delimitated by the 9 dashed border lines. China has had these dashed lines around the South China Sea on its maps since 1947, when the first map was published by Chiang Kai-shek's Nationalist government shortly before its fall and retreat to Taiwan. However, neither the Nationalist government nor the PRC government has ever clarified whether those dashed lines are temporary markers of China's territorial boundary that cover both the water as well as the land features in the South China Sea and would be eventually formalized as permanent Chinese border lines. By taking an official stand on this issue, Clinton is dismissing those Chinese markers. The United States is now a disputant in the South China Sea disputes.

The Chinese were furious. They had asked Clinton not to bring this issue to the ASEAN Regional Forum prior to the meeting. They were angry that the US Secretary of State not only ignored their pleadings, but also took such a forceful stand at the forum. Chinese Foreign Minister Yang Jiechi immediately responded with "a very strong and emotional statement essentially suggesting that this was a pre-planned mobilization on this issue.... He was distinctly not happy".[141] China rejected the US attempt to "internationalize and complicate" the South China Sea disputes and vowed not to cave in to the US pressure. In an unmistakable show of its resolve, China had the PLA carry out a large-scale live-fire military exercise in the South China Sea, reportedly involving all of China's naval fleets (the Northern, Eastern, and South China Sea fleets), right after this confrontational exchange.[142] The PLA naval exercise was also an apparent counter-measure against the up-coming first-ever US-Vietnam military exercises in the South China Sea.

The US-Vietnam military exercises were to commemorate the 15th anniversary of the US-Vietnam rapprochement. But put in the context of this recent tension between China and the United States, China clearly interpreted it as part of the Obama strategy to make new friends and a US effort to form a US-Vietnam "united front" against China. The timely arrival of the *George Washington* carrier strike group (immediately following its joint exercises with South Korea in Northeast Asia) gave the Chinese solid evidence to support their views.

The Chinese see that the United States is abandoning its half-hearted neutral stand and moving toward an active involvement approach.[143] To the Chinese, this is like a nightmare come true—the last thing they want to have is a confrontation with the United States over the South China Sea disputes. Unfortunately, they see it becoming a reality. By any account, these open and subtle exchanges constitute a defining moment in the US-China power transition. South China Sea disputes have also become a complicated part of this contentious process between China and the United States. The Chinese believe that this development is inevitable and beyond China's control.

East China Sea Disputes. China has tough challenges in the East China Sea. It has territorial disputes with a great power, Japan. Moreover, China also has to deal with the United States as a result of the US treaty obligation to defend Japan if China and Japan were to use force against each other to settle the disputes.

China and Japan have two closely related disputes in the East China Sea. One is about the delimitation of the two nations' maritime boundary; the other, the sovereign right over a group of islands known as the Diaoyu Dao in Chinese and Senkaku gunto in Japanese in the disputed area of the two nations' overlapping ocean claims. It is very difficult, if not impossible, to see the settlement of one without the other.

China and Japan are maritime neighbors on the two sides of the East China Sea, with China's eastern seaboard from Fujian Province to Shanghai on the west and Japan's Ryukyu island chain on the east. The distance between the two sides is about 360 nm at its widest stretch in the north and about 200 nm at the narrowest points in the south. For centuries, there was no maritime boundary between China and Japan. However, with the birth of UNCLOS, the two nations, which are parties to the treaty, found the need and requirement to establish proper dividing lines in their shared waters and the seabed underneath.

These "revolutionary" provisions, however, were bound to create overlapping claims and bring neighboring littoral nations to confront each other. During the long and exhaustive negotiations for the Law of the Sea, nations were divided on how to handle inevitable conflicts resulting from overlapping claims. Some advocated a one-fits-all "median line" to settle overlapping claims. Others insisted on an "equitable principle" for claimants to negotiate solutions to their disputes. The two sides could not reach an agreement at the conclusion of the UNCLOS in 1982. They compromised by recommending claimants follow the rules of the International Court of Justice to settle their disputes; and whatever method they use, they should have a formal agreement on the delimitations (see Appendix I, Article 83 [1]).

The UNCLOS came into effect in November 1994. Two years later, Japan promulgated its *Law on the Exclusive Economic Zone and the Continental Shelf*, which claimed a 200-nm EEZ all around Japan and asserted the use of median lines to delimitate overlapping claims with its ocean neighbors on the opposite sides. China adopted its *Law on the EEZ and Continental Shelf* in 1998 and claimed 200 nm EEZs along China's coast lines and its offshore islands as well.[144] China and Japan's claims in the East China Sea unsurprisingly overlapped. China was upset that Japan had taken the initiative to assert a median line as the delimitation in the two nations' expected overlapping claims. China's main objection was that it saw a natural prolongation of China's underwater continental shelf from its eastern seaboard stretching all the way to the Okinawa Trough; and therefore China was entitled to extend its jurisdiction over the continental shelf as such and use the western edge of the Okinawa Trough as a natural delimitation line between the two nations' claims. From China's claim, there was no ground for Japan's asserted median line. Moreover, China took Japan's assertion as a unilateral act, deemed it invalid without an agreement between the two nations and therefore dismissed it altogether. Although China and Japan subsequently held negotiations, their differences were oceans apart and no agreement was reached.

This dispute has evidently affected the two nations in their efforts to explore natural resources in the disputed area (China's drilling for natural gas and fossil oil near the alleged median line and Japan's protest is a case in point) and the overall China-Japan relations from time to time (when tension flairs up in the disputed area).[145] Complicating the dispute on the maritime delimitation was the two nations' fight over the sovereign ownership of the Diaoyu/Senkaku Islands in the disputed area. Those islands consist of five tiny uninhabited islands and three barren rocks that are barely visible on the ocean surface. They lie at the edge of the East China Sea continental shelf and the southern tip of the Okinawa Trough. The islands by themselves have little material value. However, they bear high-stakes political and economic consequences for China and Japan.

Indeed, the current fight over these islands came initially out of the two nations' reaction to the speculation that the East China Sea had large fossil deposits[146] and the expectation that the possession of those islands lends strength to a claim to a sizeable portion of the undersea natural resources (according to one study, the area is about 20,000 square nm[147]). In fact, Japan's median line delimitation was based on its assertion that those islands belonged to Japan; and the islands were entitled to have EEZ and continental shelf as well. If China were to "recover" the Diaoyu/Senkaku Islands and had its way on the extended continental shelf, China would have that valuable asset instead. This is a fight neither side can afford to give up.

But the political reasons for the two nations' fight over those islands are equally significant. China and Japan are battling over those islands for their unsettled past, as well as for their unfolding future—both want to be great maritime powers; and the fight over their maritime boundary and the possession of those islands thus is a test case on their ambitions. Moreover, it is not only a fight for China, but also a fight with the United States over its alleged role in creating this dispute between China and Japan, its commitment to support Japan if China and Japan were to use force against each other over those islands, and a test of strength between China and the United States in their power transition process. The stakes are high. The dispute is intractable. The following is a list of the opposing arguments.[148]

- China holds that Chinese were the first to discover those islands and used them as a navigation reference for centuries; Chinese fishermen came to the area around the islands regularly; and dynastic China's envoys made stops at those islands on their way to China's vassel state, the Ryukyu island kingdom, until Japan conquered the latter in 1879. China claims that those islands are "intrinsically integral and inseparable territories of China since antiquity" and "China's sovereign ownership of those islands [is] indisputable".
- Japan does not dispute China's historical claims, but argues that China has never exercised effective control of those islands, and the "physical connection" of those islands to China is questionable and not intrinsic. Japan, for the record, took over and had official control of those islands from 1895 to 1945 and since 1972.
- China claims that the Diaoyu/Senkaku Islands are part of China's extended continental shelf and Taiwan's surrounding islands; Japan "stole" Taiwan and its surrounding islands, including the Diaoyu/Senkaku Islands, from China through the Treaty of Shimonoseki of 1895 all of those islands therefore were covered in the Cairo Declaration and the Potsdam Proclamation and should be returned to China.
- Japan argues that it acquired the Diaoyu/Senkaku Islands through a Cabinet Decision prior to the Treaty of Shimonoseki as a *terra nullius*, land that is not claimed by any person or state; they were not mentioned in the Cairo Declaration and Potsdam Proclamation; and therefore are not required to be returned to China.
- China condemns the United States for its inclusion of those islands in the trusteeship in 1951[151] and the handover

of those islands to Japan in 1972. China charges that the US policy was an ill-willed act toward China and a brute ill-treatment of China's territorial integrity.

- The United States makes no apology for China's accusations. But the United States has always held that it takes no position in the territorial dispute and insists that the trusteeship and handover have no bearing on the sovereignty of those islands. Moreover, the United States has also made it clear that the dispute should be resolved peacefully and, if Japan were to be attacked as a result of this dispute, the United States would honor its mutual defense treaty obligation to come to Japan's defense. This position cannot be more unequivocal and forceful from the recent remarks by Secretary of State Clinton:

Well, first let me say clearly again the Senkakus fall within the scope of Article 5 of the 1960 US-Japan Treaty of Mutual Cooperation and Security. This is part of the larger commitment that the United States has made to Japan's security. We consider the Japanese-US alliance one of the most important alliance partnerships we have anywhere in the world and we are committed to our obligations to protect the Japanese people.[152]

- China holds that the Okinawa Trough marks the end of "China's underwater continental shelf," and the depth of the Okinawa Trough meets the UNCLOS requirement to be taken as a break in its extension.[153]
- Japan argues that the Okinawa Trough is only an accidental dent, and the Ryukyu island chain is the true edge of the East China Sea continental shelf. Japan and China therefore share this continental shelf, and the two nations should delimitate their maritime boundary at the median line (with Japan continuing its possession of the Diaoyu/Senkaku Islands).
- China holds that it has followed a policy of "shelving disputes while promoting joint development" with good faith, and accuses Japan of taking advantage of China's self-constraint and altering the status of the disputes.[154]

- Japanese officials, most recently Minister of Foreign Affairs Seiji Maehara, call the Chinese policy a "one-sided stand" and insist that "there is no territorial dispute" between Japan and China.[155]

The list can go on and on, but these "he said, she said" contentions will never settle the dispute; they are only making it increasingly irreconcilable. Indeed, China feels that in the past 100 years it has lost wars and territories to Japan; to this date, it has not "recovered the lost territories," namely Taiwan and the islands in the South and East China Seas, and not even received a formal apology from Japan. There is ample evidence in China that this dispute with Japan, and the United States as well, is already a heavy-loaded nationalistic and emotional issue; and there is no room for China to back down in this dispute.

Moreover, the Chinese profess to have learned their lessons on the disputed island territories the hard way and vow to take corrective measures to assert China's interests. In the words of Sun Shuxian, the Executive Deputy Commander of China's National Marine Surveillance Fleet, in international law, there are two customary practices for ruling on maritime disputes: one is to see if you have effective control and management of the disputed territory; and the other is the preference of effective control over historical claims. For instance, we have been arguing that these islands have been ours since antiquity; these words are hollow; what really counts is your actual control and effective management. China's marine surveillance and law enforcement patrol must make its presence in the disputed area and establish records of effective control".[156]

Sun's remarks are China's battle cry. China's actions are already underway. The Chinese SOA made the debut of its control and administration mission on the Diaoyu/Senkaku Islands in December 2008. The Chinese celebrated this first successful operation. Two Chinese marine surveillance and law enforcement vessels caught the Japanese defense force off guard. They broke into the Japanese-guarded 12 nm zone around the Diaoyu/Senkaku Islands and stayed there for about 8 hours.[157] A Chinese Foreign Ministry spokesman dismissed Japan's protest, saying that "China does not see its normal surveillance and law enforcement activities in its maritime territory 'provocative;' and China will decide when to send these vessels to the Diaoyu/Senkaku Islands again on its own terms".[158] Since then, China's marine surveillance ships have made many more "visits" to the Diaoyu/Senkaku Islands. The SOA has stated that it would turn these "visits" into regular official duties for the Marine Surveillance Fleet.[159]

The Chinese have noted that at this point that its marine surveillance and law enforcement fleet is still much smaller than that of Japan. The Chinese government has specified in its recently released 12th Five-Year Plan that it would turn this force into a formidable one in the coming years. Funds have been earmarked to build 30 to 50 big size and highly capable vessels. The first one, "*Yuzheng* 310", a 2,580-tonnage vessel with a platform for two Z-9A helicopters and advanced satellite communication systems, made its maiden voyage on November 16, 2010. Its destination was the Diaoyu/Senkaku Islands.[160]

China's efforts are changing the situation around the Diaoyu/Senkaku Islands. Clashes between China and Japan over the Diaoyu/Senkaku Islands and reports about China's determination to develop its marine surveillance and law enforcement forces and to assert and protect China's maritime interests hit Chinese media headlines at an alarming rate. Although most of the reports are only about China's efforts to gain control of the Diaoyu/Senkaku Islands, one cannot but wonder if those efforts do not imply the eventual eviction of Japan's forces out of the disputed area. Since there is no reason to expect that Japan will sit idle while China is making its advances, a showdown between China and Japan, with the danger of armed conflict, is only a matter of time; and this time is coming fast. And the United States, as promised by Secretary of State Clinton, will have to rush to the rescue.

What about Tibet and Xinjiang?

These are China's explosive issues. Unlike the small and uninhabitable islands in the South and East China Seas, Tibet and Xinjiang make up about one-third of China's landmass and have a population of about 3 million in Tibet and 22 million in Xinjiang.[161] These two regions are also different from Taiwan in a significant way in that while the people in Taiwan are Han

Chinese, the ones in Tibet and Xinjiang, excluding the Han Chinese residents, are not. The ethnic groups of Kazakh, Kirghiz, Russian, Tajik, Uyghur, and Uzbek, to name the major ones, in Xinjiang are of mixed Caucasian descent. Their problems with the Chinese are intertwined with many issues such as territorial disputes, religious intolerance, cultural clashes, human and political injustice, economic inequality, and so forth. In many ways, their fight with the Chinese is no less complicated than the problems in Afghanistan, the Balkans, or the Middle East.

Tibet and Xinjiang have been under China's effective control for well over 60 years; yet they are still as unsettled as ever. The relations between the people of these two regions and the Han Chinese are anything but harmonious. Prejudice in racial, cultural, social, political, and economic terms between the majority Han Chinese and the Tibetans and the various minorities in Xinjiang still run deep. These two regions also rank among the lowest in economic development, education standards, and in most vital indicators in China. As a consequence of these problems, clashes between these "different races" and the Han Chinese take place from time to time. The drive for separation or independence is also a recurrent theme. Every time there is social-political clash in these two regions, it naturally comes to riots and intensifies the animosity between people in these two regions and the Han majority. The riots of 2008 and 2009 in Tibet and Xinjiang, respectively, are cases in point. These conflicts are also connected to the separation/independence movements waged by the "brethren" of Tibetans and Xinjiang ethnic groups abroad. On top of these, there is the involvement of foreign nations, most notably the United States. All of these factors make these problems complicated and explosive.

For a long time, the Chinese government took heavy-handed measures to deal with these problems. In 2000, however, the CCP added a new piece. It launched a "Great Western Development Project" for Tibet and Xinjiang and the several underdeveloped provinces around these two regions.

The main components of this project included development of infrastructure[162] (transport, hydropower plants, energy, and telecommunications), enticement of foreign investment, [163] increased efforts on ecological protection (such as reforestation[164]), promotion of education, [165] and encouragement of talent flow into the western provinces.

The idea behind this project is consistent with the CCP's economic development drive in the past 30 years. That is, economic development is the answer to most of the social-political problems. Chinese leaders believe that with an improved standard of living, people will have less need for social-political unrest; for the people in Tibet and Xinjiang, economic development will turn their attention away from the fight for separation or independence and reduce their incentive to join their poor brethren outside Chinese borders. As Zhang Chunxian, the CCP chief of Xinjiang, recently put it, economic development is the "master key" to Xinjiang's problems.[166] The central CCP leadership has also made new efforts to drum up support for the development of the Western regions in the same light.[167] With the Great Western Development Project laying the initial groundwork in the last 10 years and the new blessing from the central CCP leadership, Zhang vowed to accelerate this development program and narrow the gap between the western region and the more developed eastern parts of China in the next 20 to 30 years.

Development takes time. Between now and then, Chinese leaders must find ways to get the people in these two regions engaged in the development efforts. At the same time, the Chinese government has to deal with the external forces that are persistently pressing for the separation/independence of the two regions from China. The Chinese leaders are particularly concerned with the US factor in these two explosive problems. They hold that the United States has many reasons to play these two issues as leverage against China; it has the capacity to influence the course of the separation/independence movements; it has been actively involved in the affairs of these two regions; and will continue to be so in the future.

Tibet and China can be divided into three broad periods. The first goes from mythical or legendary times to the beginning of the 7th century when Tibet emerged as a unified kingdom in the Himalaya Mountain region. The second period goes from the 630s

AD when Tibet under its founding ruler, Songtsen Gampo, and Tang China fought their first of many wars, through the Mongol-ruled Yuan Dynasty (1271-1368), the Chinese restored Ming Dynasty (1368-1644), the Manchu-ruled Qing Dynasty (1644-1911), the Chinese ROC (1911-49), to 1950, when Tibet became a formal part of the PRC, to the present.

There is much controversy involved in the presentation of this long history. Chinese and Tibetans-in-exile hold opposing views. Whereas China routinely produces its interpretation of this history to legitimize its rule of Tibet, the Tibetans-in-exile make every effort to dispute China's claims and provide their own versions of this history to justify their struggle for Tibet independence. Between these two opposing forces stand some Western scholars who try to offer balanced analyses. Nevertheless, all should bear in mind that there is no agreement on this controversial matter.

China's position is repeatedly stated in a number of government White Papers on Tibet and Tibet-related issues. Its key claims are as follows:[168]

- Tibet has been an inseparable part of China since antiquity.
- In 641, the founder of unified Tibet, Songtsen Gampo, negotiated a marriage with Chinese Prince Wen Cheng and a niece of the Chinese Tang Emperor. Tibet and China subsequently became relatives. (Note: by virtue of this marriage, Songtsen Gampo and the Chinese emperor Tang Taizong had an "uncle-niece relationship". In accordance with Confucius' teaching, it implied a hierarchical junior-senior relationship between the two nations).

In 1271, the Mongols established the Yuan Dynasty and unified a war-torn China. Tibet was also part of the Mongol conquest and subsequently became an administrative region directly under the administration of the central government of Yuan.

- Every Chinese government since then—the Ming, Qing, and ROC—has followed the Yuan practice of exercising sovereign and administrative control over Tibet.

- In 1727, the Qing assigned the first high commissioner to be stationed in Tibet.
- During the Qing Dynasty, the central government held the power to confirm the reincarnation of all the deceased high Buddhas of Tibet, including the Dalai Lama and Bainqen Erdeni. The central government also sent high commissioners to supervise the installation ceremony of the new Dalai Lama and Bainqen Erdeni over the centuries.
- The ROC government continued the relationship with Tibet established by the previous dynasties. Upon the death of the 13th Dalai Lama in 1933, the ROC government followed the tradition to supervise the search for the reincarnate successor. In 1939, the ROC government approved the selection of Lhamo Toinzhub (the Dalai Lama's original name), and in 1940 President Chiang Kai-shek issued an official decree conferring the title of the 14th Dalai Lama on Lhamo Toinzhub. The ROC high commissioner and other Chinese officials also supervised the installation ceremony.
- The PRC liberated Tibet in 1950 as it did many other Chinese provinces. The PRC government also followed its predecessors in handling the change and affirmation of the Dalai Lama and Bainqen Erdeni.

The Tibetans-in-exile dispute every Chinese account of the Tibet-China relationship. Their positions can be found mostly at *Tibet.net*, the official website of the Central Tibetan Administration (CTA, English version), *xizang-zhiye.org* CTA's Chinese version), *dalailama.com* (the Dalai Lama's site), and other Tibetan publications. Their key positions are as follows:

- Tibetans and Chinese each have their own accounts of the origins of their civilizations. The two peoples have no connection in their ancestry. The few presumable Tibetans that ancient Chinese knew about were the Qiangs. However, the Chinese always characterized the Qiangs as aliens or nomadic barbarians. Chinese anthropologists and historians also admit that there is no conclusive evidence to show if the Qiangs are the mainstay of the Tibetans.[169]

Ancient Chinese never made it to the Tibetan plateau. As such, Tibet was never an inseparable part of China in antiquity.

- The marriage of Songtsen Gampo and Chinese Prince Wen Cheng brought a period of relative peace between Tibet and Tang China. Yet it did not make the union or subordination of Tibet to China. Songtsen Gampo unfortunately died young in 650. Her successors soon resumed warfare with the Chinese. In the next nearly 200 years, Tibet and China continued their fights and failed attempts to make peace. It was in 823 when the two sides reached a firm agreement for peace and signed a landmark peace treaty to settle their animosity and disputes.
- The Tang-Tubo Peace Treaty of 823 AD is not a treaty of union between Tibet and China, contrary to the Chinese claim; but a treaty to end war, settle borders, and make peace between the two nations. The following are from the inscriptions on the only surviving stone monument erected in 823 (according to historical records, the two sides made three stone monuments; this surviving one is at the front of the Jokhang Monastery in Tibet; the second one was erected at the Tibet-China border; and the third one was at China's capital Changan, today's Xian the latter two vanished long ago): (an unofficial translation:... Today, Tubo [Tibet] and Han [Tang China] each has secured its border at this demarcation, to its east is the Great Tang's territory; and to the west, the territory of the Great Tubo; each pledges not to be enemy of the other, not to wage war against each other. In case of border closing and intrusion, each side should properly question the intruders, and then release them with clothes and food provided. Today both nations are equals; this treaty is for a great harmony between the two).[170]

Of note is that China has never mentioned the above in any of its White Papers about Tibet.

- The Tibetans-in-exile accept that since the Mongol-ruled Yuan, Tibet had been subject to interference from China.

However, Tibet was able to retain its independence and maintain its own government.[171] Moreover, more than half of the time during the 678 years between the founding of the Yuan Dynasty in 1271 and the fall of the ROC in 1949, Tibet was dealing with the Mongols and the Manchus; the Chinese were a conquered people, they did not have much to do with the relations between the Mongol and Manchu-ruled "China" and Tibet.

The above-presented assertions, Chinese included, did not really matter when China made Tibet a formal part of the PRC in 1950. Indeed, in those days when powerful nations did what they wanted and small nations suffered what they must, few condemned China for its incorporation of Tibet. However, these arguments would not have been necessary had China turned Tibet into a happy member of the Chinese union. In fact, for at least the first 30 years of the PRC, China's administration of Tibet was a great failure.[172]

The most devastating blow to the Chinese rule of Tibet was no doubt the defection of the Dalai Lama and his followers to India in 1959. Today, the Dalai Lama is the longest-exiled prominent political and religious figure in the world. He also has a large number of followers. Presently, there are about 145,000 Tibetans living outside of Tibet, about 101,000 of which in Dharamshala, where the Tibetan Government-in-exile resides, 16, 000 in Nepal, 2,000 in Bhutan, and 26,000 in various other parts of the world.[173] There are also various Tibetan-in-exile organizations in the United States and Europe pursuing the cause of Tibet independence.

Although in the last two decades China has taken measures to improve the standard of living in Tibet, Chinese leaders nonetheless have many limitations in dealing with the Dalai Lama and the Tibetans-in-exile. The Tibet question remains an unsettling block in China's nation-building business[174]. It is also a thorny problem between the United States and China because of the US involvement in this issue, which has become even more complicated as a contentious component of the ongoing US-China power transition.

A comprehensive analysis of this issue goes beyond the scope of this analysis. The following highlights the milestones and the latest conflicting stands on all sides about this complicated issue.

- In October 1950, the newly-founded PRC ordered the PLA to move into Tibet, putting it under China's effective control ever since.[175]
- In March 1959, the Dalai Lama defected from Tibet. He and his followers established a Tibetan Government-in-exile in Dharamshala, India, and pursued "a policy of seeking independence for Tibet".[176]
- In the early 1970s, the Dalai Lama saw that outright independence for Tibet was difficult. He thus started discussions with his followers about finding a middle-way approach to settle the Tibet issue with China.[177]
- In the late 1970s, Chinese leaders abandoned Mao's "perpetual revolution" and turned to China's economic reform. As part of their effort to create an amicable environment for development, Chinese leaders reached out to the Dalai Lama for possible reconciliation. Deng Xiaoping reportedly learned that the Dalai Lama's elder brother, Gyalo Thondup, was living in Hong Kong. He thus extended an invitation for Thondup to visit Beijing. Thondup at that time was a member of the Tibetan Government-in-exile. With consent from the Dalai Lama, Thondup went to Beijing as the Dalai Lama's personal representative and met with Deng Xiaoping in 1979. That was the first official contact in 20 years between the Chinese government and the Dalai Lama since his defection. Thondup reportedly got the Chinese government to open up Tibet for family reunions and a promise from Deng that "except for Tibet independence, everything else is open to negotiation".[178]
- In 1987, the Dalai Lama put forward a Five-Point Peace Plan for Tibet. The points are: 1) transformation of the whole of Tibet into a zone of peace; 2) abandonment of China's population transfer policy, which threatens the very existence of the Tibetans as a people; 3) respect for the Tibetan people's fundamental human rights and democratic freedoms; 4) restoration and protection of Tibet's natural environment and the abandonment of

China's use of Tibet for the production of nuclear weapons and dumping of nuclear waste; and 5) commencement of earnest negotiations on the future status of Tibet and of relations between the Tibetan and Chinese people.[179]

- In 1988, the Dalai Lama delivered the Strasbourg Proposal to specify his thoughts on the implementation of the Five-Point Peace Plan[180].
- The Five-Point Peace Plan and Strasburg Proposal make up the core of the Dalai Lama's middle-way approach. Its starting position is that the Dalai Lama does not seek Tibet's separation/independence from China. In return, the Dalai Lama asks for the establishment of a greater Tibet with a high degree of autonomy and the freedom to self rule. Finally, the Dalai Lama preaches peaceful means to reach agreement with the Chinese government through dialogue and negotiation.
- In 2002, the Chinese government and the Dalai Lama's representatives held their first round of talks in Beijing. By January 2010, the two sides have met nine times[181].
- Through the talks, Chinese leaders "arrogantly reject the Dalai Lama's Middle-Way Approach".[182] China's position is imperiously stated by Zhu Weiqun, the Executive Deputy Director of the CCP's Central United Front Work Department and key figure in charge of the talks with the Dalai Lama's representatives.
- Chinese leaders deny the existence of a "Tibet Question," claiming that Tibet has always been China's territory and there is no room for its separation. They therefore insist that the Dalai Lama accept this position and "correct his mistake in pursuing Tibet independence and continuing to advocate the position that Tibet was an independent country prior to the Chinese occupation as stated in his Five-Point Peace Plan and other documents".[183]
- Chinese leaders denounce the Tibetan Government-in-exile, asserting that no other nation in the world recognizes its legitimacy. China therefore refuses to hold talks with this organization.

- Chinese leaders accept, however, that there is a "Dalai Lama Question"; it is about his return to China or the continuation of "his self-imposed exile" abroad. Chinese dialogue with the Dalai Lama therefore is always about the terms for his return and with his personal or private representatives, but not representatives of the Tibetan Government-in-exile.
- Chinese leaders reject the Dalai Lama's plan for the future of Tibet. First, they charge that the Dalai Lama is asking for too much territory beyond the current confines of the Tibet Autonomous Region to build his "Greater Tibet Peace Zone". Second, they repudiate the Dalai Lama's request for the Chinese to stop population transfer into Tibet and eventually return the "Chinese settlers" back to China. Third, they categorically dismiss the Dalai Lama's call for the PLA to withdraw from the Tibet region. Fourth, they snub the Dalai Lama's idea of making Tibet a "buffer zone" between China and India. Finally, they reject the Dalai Lama's design of a greater Tibet as a highly autonomous and self-governing entity in China.[184]
- The United States is supportive of the Dalai Lama's initiatives. It holds the following positions on the Tibet issue:
- The United States "recognizes the Tibet Autonomous Region (TAR) and Tibetan autonomous prefectures and counties in other provinces as part of the PRC;"
- It urges "China to respect the unique religious, linguistic, and cultural heritage of its Tibetan people;"
- The United States maintains "contact with representatives of a wide variety of political and non-political groups including Tibetans in the United States, China, and around the world;"
- US Government officials have met and will continue to meet with the Dalai Lama in his capacity as an important religious leader and Nobel laureate; and
- The United States encourages Chinese leaders to hold talks with the Dalai Lama to resolve the Tibet issue peacefully.

In addition to the above, the US Tibetan Policy Act of 2002 also authorized the establishment of a statutory position of Special Coordinator for Tibetan Issues in the State Department (the individual who heads this office is also an Assistant or Undersecretary of State); required a number of annual reporting requirements on Sino-Tibetan negotiations both by the State Department and by the congressionally established Congressional-Executive Commission on China (CECC); mandated the provision of Tibetan language training to interested foreign service officers in the US Government; required US Government officials to raise issues of religious freedom and political prisoners; and urged the State Department to seek establishment of a US Consulate in Lhasa.[185]

- The Chinese point to the above as the United States having a two-faced policy on the Tibet issue. On the one hand, the President claims that the United States does not challenge China's sovereignty over Tibet. On the other, Congress makes every effort to undermine the President's statement. The Chinese understand that this is a typical play of the US divided government. They nevertheless see that the President's statement has no legally-binding power; US Congress has never endorsed it; it is, after all, congressional acts and resolutions that exert more influence in the US policy toward Tibet.
- The Chinese hold that the United States has always wanted Tibet to become an independent country. In recent years, Chinese analysts scanned through many declassified US foreign policy documents (the US Government publication of the Foreign Relations of the United States, for instance) and came up with documented evidence to support their views. They found that the United States was actively involved in helping Tibet to establish independent nationhood in the late 1940s and early 1950s. They also found that the United States continued to encourage Tibetans to pursue the course of independence throughout the 1950s, provided Tibetans with weapons and trained Tibetan fighters, and eventually helped the Dalai Lama to flee from China in 1959.[186]

- The Chinese analyses are further supported by American writers revealing US involvement in the Tibetan affairs.[187]
- In addition, Chinese analysts have also documented US congressional efforts to support the Tibet independence movement.[188]
- The Chinese hold that since the end of the Cold War, and especially since China showed signs of its rising, US policy on Tibet has become part of the US efforts to slow down or even derail China's development. The Chinese argue that the United States does not really care about human rights and economic wellbeing in Tibet; US policy on Tibet has to serve overall US interest regarding China; US concerns about political, religious, and ethnic rights in Tibet are only smokescreens for the United States to leverage influence over changes in China.[189]

In all fairness, one can see that the Dalai Lama is reconciliatory. Indeed, in a note presented to the Chinese government by the Dalai Lama's dialogue representatives in their latest round of talks in February 2010, the Dalai Lama has gone so far as to reaffirm unequivocally that he does not seek separation or independence of Tibet from China; he respects the Chinese constitution; he does not challenge the leadership of the CCP, the PRC central government, and its socialist system.[190]

Chinese officials, however, are unreasonable. They have shown their "historical limitations" in their pre-emptory dealings with the Dalai Lama. Chinese officials see that the Dalai Lama's proposed highly-autonomous Tibet is nothing more than a state in a federalist system like that of the United States. They accuse the Dalai Lama of attempting to undermine the Chinese political system. The Chinese leaders are unfortunately still stuck in the mindset of China's outdated tradition of "central dictatorship". They dogmatically refuse to accept that as China's economic and political changes continue, the CCP and Chinese government will have to become more democratic and decentralized eventually; and a key change will be that China's provinces and cities will have governors and mayors chosen by the people from below but not appointed by the central government from above. When that change takes place, China's provinces and cities will become more autonomous, although they may not be as independent as US states and cities. The Dalai Lama's proposal is right on target. But the tragedy is that he is ahead of the Chinese leaders in embracing democracy, and his proposal for a highly-autonomous Tibet comes at a wrong time and at a wrong place. In China, unfortunately, it is still a crime just to advocate these ideas.

The Chinese officials are also unreasonable in the way that they do not even seem to care that the Dalai Lama could pass away eventually and his leaving could create a whole host of new issues that would further complicate the Tibet problem and loosen up the Tibetans-in-exile to pursue their course with resort to violent means. Zhu Weiqun said that China would not be afraid to meet force with force if the Tibetans were to turn violent. As Zhu put it, "we have fought before; you should remember your defeats in the past; and there is no chance for you in the future".[191] This future, according to Wang Lixiong, a noted Chinese dissident writer and self-made Tibetan observer, for the Tibetans as well as the Chinese, is doomed.[192]

Xinjiang, China, and the United States. In many ways, Xinjiang is more complicated and explosive than Tibet. Unlike the homogenous Tibet, Xinjiang has many different ethnic groups longing for different futures. While the Tibetans have the Dalai Lama as a religious leader preaching for non-violent ways to pursue their goals, the ethnic groups in Xinjiang are fragmented and have no commonly-accepted leaders. Worse, many in Xinjiang are influenced by their radical and extremist Muslim brethren in the troubled areas of Central Asia and the Middle East, and look to their experience for answers to the Xinjiang problem.

What is the Xinjiang problem? It is about the fate of a piece of land in the very center of Asia known in Chinese as the "Western and New Territory" or in Uyghur separatist terms, "East Turkistan".[193] The issue is whether it should stay as an "intrinsic and inseparable part of China," or become an independent homeland for the Uyghur people, or to be partitioned along ethnic lines to accommodate the interests of the East Turkic ethnic groups and the Han Chinese.

The Xinjiang problem has a long history. The Chinese claim of this land, for instance, goes back to dynastic China's Western Han era of 200 BC. Over the ages, there have been changes of possession among the Chinese, Mongols, and the Turkic ethnic groups. This land has also witnessed great power interference from time to time, most notably by Russia and Great Britain. After a long fight against the Turkic ethnic groups and Russia since the 1750s, China's last dynasty, the Qing, secured control of the entire region and named it the Xinjiang Province of China in 1884. However, the Qing Dynasty fell in 1911. Xinjiang once again fell prey to internal turmoil and external interference. There were repeated attempts to create East Turkistan as well. In 1949, the CCP-led PLA "liberated" Xinjiang, and it has been under the tight control of the PRC ever since.[194]

However, the CCP did not put the Xinjiang problem to rest for good. The East Turkistan separation movement did not go away, either. The reasons are twofold. First and foremost, China failed to develop a sound political and economic system that could accommodate the complicated relations in Xinjiang. Contrary to the CCP's propaganda, Xinjiang has never become a melting pot for the Han Chinese and various Turkic ethnic groups in any measure. Second, the external environment surrounding Xinjiang provides "fertile grounds" for the separatist movement to grow. Indeed, Xinjiang's unsettling and conflict-laden neighbors, namely Afghanistan, Pakistan, and the Turkic republics of the Soviet Union, gave Xinjiang more than enough reasons to be unsettled as well.

A turning point came at the end of the Cold War. The collapse of the Soviet Union gave independence to a number of former Soviet republics in central Asia bordering Xinjiang. They are Kazakhstan, Kyrgyzstan, Tajikistan, Uzbekistan, and Turkmenistan. These are the countries defined primarily by the kind of people who bear the name of these new nations (the suffix "stan" simply means the land).

The Uyghurs, who are the second largest subdivision of the so-called East Turkic people (the Kazakhs are the largest; Kazakhstan is also the largest of all the new "East Turkic stans") and arguably the most active of all, are stuck in Xinjiang, China. They are the majority ethnic group in Xinjiang. The official title of this Chinese province bears the name of the Uyghurs as the "Xinjiang Uyghur Autonomous Region". Nevertheless, they are the only ones of the East Turkic people without an independent homeland.[195]

The sense of deprivation is understandable. China's unsettled relations with the Uyghurs were not making things any easier for the latter. Against this backdrop, Uyghur separatist movements naturally resurfaced. The East Turkistan Islamic Movement (ETIM) and East Turkistan Liberation Organization (ETLO) came in the early 1990s. Both organizations used violent means to pursue their causes. They also made contact with Osama bin Laden and his al Qaeda network and the Taliban of Afghanistan.

The terrorist attacks on the United States on September 11, 2001, brought the superpower to fight against al Qaeda and the Taliban right across the border of Xinjiang. Some of the Uyghur fighters were captured, exposing the ETIM and ETLO connections to these terrorist groups. The United States, China, the Shanghai Cooperation Organization (SCO), and the UN subsequently put these two organizations on their terrorist organization lists.[196] Although these international pressures did not put an end to the Uyghur separation organizations, they did force them to reduce their activities.

By the mid-2000s, the pro-Uyghur independence activists gathered in Munich, Germany. They formed the World Uyghur Congress (WUC). It is an international organization of exiled Uyghur groups said to represent the collective interests of the Uyghur people both inside and outside of Xinjiang. It was founded in mid-April 2004 in Munich, Germany, as a collection of various exiled Uyghur groups including the Uyghur American Association (UAA) and East Turkestan National Congress (ETNC). Rebiya Kadeer is the current president, elected in 2006. There is no known link between the WUC and the ETIM. The WUC aim is to promote the right of the Uyghur people to use peaceful, non-violent, and democratic means to determine the political future of East Turkestan. The organization is funded in part by the National Endowment for Democracy (NED), which gives the WUC $215, 000 annually for "human rights research and advocacy projects". The NED is a US non-profit organization founded in 1983 to promote democracy by providing cash grants funded primarily through an annual allocation from the US Congress. President Kadeer met former US President George W. Bush in June 2007.

The Uyghur American Association (UAA) is a Washington DC-based advocacy organization. It was established in 1998 by a group of Uyghur scholars to raise American public awareness of the Uyghur people in East Turkestan and other parts of the world. The UAA receives $249, 000 annually from the NED for the human rights research and advocacy projects.[197]

The WUC got a boost in 2005 with the release of Rebiya Kadeer and her arrival in the United States. Kadeer is a very dynamic and charismatic leader. She soon took over the leadership of WUC. Under her leadership, the WUC distanced itself from the militant groups. It will take a long-term approach to pursue their goals. They are relocating their action center to Washington and they will lobby the US Government to put pressure on China.

The Chinese are very concerned with the "US factor" in the Xinjiang problem. They note that since the end of the Cold War, the United States has become the principal foreign power to interfere with the Xinjiang problem. They all hold that, much like the Tibet issue, the United States uses the Xinjiang problem to put pressure on China. Chinese analysts also see that the US strategic design against China in this area has not been affected by the War on Terrorism. They believe that the United States has an interest in keeping China's troubled areas unsettled and unstable so that the United States will have more strategic flexibility against China.

The Chinese are especially concerned with the US Congress and some powerful non-governmental organizations (NGOs) in their support for the Uyghur separatist organizations. They have noted that Congress uses resolutions, although non-binding, to put pressure on China. Congress also uses resolutions to force the President's hand. Chinese analysts note that although other great powers such as Great Britain, Germany, Russia, Japan, Turkey, and the Soviet Union supported Uyghur movements in the past, since the end of the Cold War, the United States has become the principal foreign power to support the Uyghurs. Chinese analysts have documented Uyghur activists' meetings with President Bill Clinton and Vice President Al Gore and US Government and NGO support to the WUC. They provide funds and moral support and put pressure on the Chinese government.[198]

US-China Power Transition: At Odds, But Not At War

In the years ahead, the conflicts discussed in the previous sections and the ongoing power transition will continue to push China and the United States over the brink to confront each other from time to time or to pull the two together for cooperation when the two nations' common interests dictate.

China's Options

By many accounts, China does not want to have war, hopefully not for the next 30 years. This is so, not because the Chinese are inherently peace-loving as Chinese analysts have long claimed,[201] but because China's modernization mission demands a war-free environment. There is a theoretical reason for this option as well. Indeed, in a power transition process, if the upstart sees that its comprehensive national power will surpass that of the extant hegemonic power by virtue of its expected development, it will be foolish for the rising power to initiate a premature fight with the latter.[202]

The Chinese apparently have taken both their practical need and the logical prescription by the power transition theory into account. Indeed, there have been repeated calls in China for the Chinese leaders to continue their tao-guang yang-hui strategy for the next 30 years and more.[203] Chinese government is well advised to go along. However, the Chinese also understand that conflict with the United States is inevitable, and their response is unavoidable. To deal with this difficult relationship, they have a formula called "at odds, but not at war". This strategy is more proactive than the tao-guang yang-hui, which is primarily about avoiding confrontation. Thus in addition to developing its capabilities through the modernization mission, China will engage with the United States, confront the United States if necessary, but stop short of going to war. It is a strategy loaded with Sun Tzu's teaching, the most familiar of which is about subjugating the enemy without fighting.

US Options

The "law of physics" informs us that the United States and China should not go to war against each other. However, as discussed in this analysis, the two nations have plenty of reasons to do otherwise. Perhaps the most fundamental conflict is over the way of government between the two nations. For well over 60 years, the United States has been at odds with China over its government and its conduct in domestic as well as international affairs. The conflict is in essence part of the Cold War the United States fought with the Soviet Union. The Soviet communists are long gone. Yet the Chinese Communist Party has preserved its authoritarian rule and relied on that rule to bring about China's rise in the last 30 years. The economic success has given the CCP's rule a new lease on life. The Chinese leaders are determined to continue their authoritarian government in China for the next 30 years or longer.

The United States, however, insists that China's authoritarian regime, no matter how useful it is for China's development, is a transitional fix. The United States will not only continue to take issue with China over its repressive government, but will also engage with China in attempts to manage its rise, shape the way China develops, and guard against China in case it turns bad. With respect to China's unsettled external problems, the United States will continue to be at odds with China's authoritarian government over the nature of its claimed interests and the way this government handles disputes. In short, the ideological divide between China and the United States ensures that the two governments do not take each other with trust and do not see eye to eye on each other's vital interests.[204] Underpinning the US sense of ideological superiority over China is the superpower's influential and globally-positioned material power. This power allows the United States to apply a heavy-handed approach to international affairs. The US dealings with China are no exception.

The rise of China is now putting the US capability in question. Chinese PLA Senior Colonel Liu Mingfu argues that ideological conflict is only a smokescreen, and the real problem of the United States with China is its hard power development. Liu asserts that even if China were to become a democracy tomorrow, the United States would still have problems with China, because the United States, in President Obama's words, does not accept second place (if this sounds familiar, it is because Liu is talking like the American "offensive realist" John Mearsheimer).[205]

In recent decades, there have been unabated assertions about the decline of US power. Some also believe that the decade-long war on terrorism has cost the United States tremendously, and the recent financial crisis has dealt the United States another heavy blow. However, many hold that the United States will be able to rebound and continue to maintain its leading power for a long time to come.[206] By many accounts, these optimistic views have it right. Most Chinese analysts also agree with this assessment,[207] although they also understand that the United States will be able to continue to find fault with China and use its heavy-handed approach toward China in the years to come.

Do's and Don'ts on the Core Interests

The Chinese have no illusions about US staying power. They are no strangers to US heavy-handed approaches, either. Their most important concern is that the United States can be unappreciative of China's core interests, challenge China at will, and force China off balance from its strategy of at-odds-but-not-at-war from time to time. The hot-tempered confrontations between China and the United States in 2010 are timely reminders of this contentious nature of the two nations' relations:

- In January 2010, President Obama notified Congress of his authorization to sell more than $6 billion worth of weapon systems to Taiwan.
- In February 2010, President Obama met with the Dalai Lama at the White House.
- These two acts were considered to be the United States stepping on China's core interests and set off a firestorm in

China. China subsequently suspended high-level military and security exchanges with the United States.

- In March 2010, a South Korean warship was sunk in the disputed waters between the two Koreas. China refused to join the United States in condemning North Korea. Months later, China also refused to endorse the US-led investigation results.
- In March 2010, the US State Department released its annual report on world human rights conduct, sharply criticizing China's human rights record. In response, China's State Council issued a report denouncing US gun policies, widespread homelessness, and racial discrimination.
- In June 2010, China opposed the US plan to send its aircraft carrier strike group to the Yellow Sea to conduct a military exercise. As an ostensible show of resolve, the PLA conducted a live ammunition exercise in the troubled area.
- In July 2010, the Chinese government raised the intensity of its opposition to US warships or warplanes entering the Yellow Sea to conduct military exercises. At the same time, the PLA held another military exercise "Warfare 2010" in the Yellow Sea. The United States and South Korea eventually held their joint military exercise in the Sea of Japan.
- In July 2010, in Hanoi, Vietnam, US Secretary of State Clinton and Chinese Foreign Minister Yang Jiechi carried out by far the most hot-tempered spat between the United States and China on the South China Sea issues.
- In August 2010, US aircraft carrier USS *George Washington* made its first visit to Vietnam. It was there to celebrate the 15th anniversary of US-Vietnam relations. US destroyer USS *John S. McCain* participated in the first US-Vietnam joint naval exercise. The Chinese took these US moves as attempts to turn Vietnam into a counterbalance against China. In an unmistakable response, the

three PLA navy fleets held joint exercises in the South China Sea.

- In September 2010, the China-Japan trawler incident broke out around the Diaoyu/Senkaku Islands in the East China Sea.
- In October 2010, US Secretary of State Clinton stated that the US-Japan defense treaty covers the disputed islands. The United States would come to Japan's defense were China to use force to settle the dispute.
- In November 2010, the two Koreas exchanged artillery fire on and around the South Korea-controlled Yeonpyeong Island in the Yellow Sea. The USS *George Washington* aircraft carrier strike group and South Korean forces held joint military exercises off the North Korea shores in the Yellow Sea shortly afterwards.
- In December 2010, President Obama phoned Chinese President Hu Jintao to warn that China's muted response to the Korean Peninsula tension was emboldening North Korean provocations and asked China to stop practicing "willful blindness" to the rogue regime's transgressions.
- In January 2011, US Secretary of Defense Gates made an icebreaking visit to Beijing. The PLA, however, made a clumsy test flight of its long-speculated stealth fighter jet J-20. It was an act unmistakably intended to send a defiant message to the United States.

While the above events were taking place, "Chinese foreign policy hawks" made their timely debut. These are some high-powered and well-connected individuals with military and foreign policy backgrounds. They follow the examples of their American hawkish counterparts to make provocative calls.

Specifically, they pressed the Chinese government to take stronger action against the United States. They wanted the Chinese government to set rules for the United States to follow, get the United States to pay for its bad behavior, and to feel the pain of punishment. Some even asked the Chinese government to prepare a showdown with the United States on the arms sales to Taiwan issue in the foreseeable future, at the most, in 10 years.[208]

Adding fuel to fire, the Chinese government released a high-profile speech by China's State Councilor and its current foreign policy helmsman, Dai Bingguo, in which he spelled out for the first time China's core interests in three broad areas:

- The fundamentals of the Chinese political system and political stability, namely the Communist Party leadership, socialist system, and the socialist development with Chinese characteristics;
- China's sovereignty security, territorial integrity, and national unity; and,
- Basic requirements for China's sustainable economic development.[209]

Compared with the enduring core interests of the United States, which are national security, economic prosperity, and the preservation of liberty, [210] China's core interests are short-term-based. The first item is in essence about the CCP's regime survival. The second item lacks clarity. Does it include the disputed territories? Put in a different way, Dai's statement is like a note to the United States: do not mess with China's government, its territorial disputes, and China's resources supply. One can clearly hear a defiant tone in Dai's statement. The conflicts of interest and the downturns in the US-China relations are disturbing. Henry Kissinger, perhaps the only surviving architect of the US-China relations we know of today, was undoubtedly concerned. "Avoiding a US-China Cold War" was his disquieting call.[211] These concerns eventually required highest-level attention and forced the two governments to turn Chinese President Hu Jintao's long-delayed goodwill visit to the United States into a "presidential conflict management workshop" in January 2011. However, this presidential meeting clearly had not made much progress. Although the two presidents listed 20-plus important areas where the United States and China could cooperate, they nevertheless could not reach agreement on the two nations' core national interests. The opposing stands are clearly evident in the joint statement following the meeting. The two differing statements below cannot be any more disagreeable. They remind us of the terms in the Shanghai Communiqué of 1972 in which the United States and China awkwardly agreed to disagree.

The United States stressed that the promotion of human rights and democracy is an important part of its foreign policy. China stressed that there should be no interference in any country's internal affairs.[212]

China has long held that the United States uses promotion of democracy as a pretext to advance its interests. In this Obama-Hu "workshop," China apparently took the US insistence on its policy to promote human rights and democracy in China as another US disregard of China's core interest (an attack on Dai Bingguo's first point about China's political system) and therefore fought back. Kissinger was quick to point out that "if the United States bases its approach on China on democratic change, deadlock is inevitable".[213] His remarks hit the nail right on its head.

China, however, still managed to score a few points in this "presidential bargaining". The following statement has long been China's standard line for protecting its authoritarian government and economic development under authoritarian rule. It is now part of China's core interests.

The United States and China underscored that each country and its people have the right to choose their own path, and all countries should respect each other's choice of a development model.

Americans can be confused: when did the Chinese people have the right to choose their own path? Nevertheless, the United States went along with China on this statement.

The Chinese development model mentioned above happens to have much appeal to the developing nations. It also poses a challenge to the US-advocated approach (much of this challenge has been discussed in the literature about the "Washington Consensus" and the "Beijing Consensus").[214] One has to wonder how much arm-twisting had taken place in this "presidential workshop" to put this line in the joint statement. Furthermore, China also got the United States to make the following statement: "The two sides reaffirmed mutual respect for national sovereignty and territorial integrity".

This line is absolutely China's concern, because the United States has long passed the days when it had to worry about national sovereignty and territorial integrity. But given that the United States and China do not see eye to eye on China's territorial disputes, the above line, while allowing China to remind the United States of China's loosely-defined core interests, are only empty words.

The conflict on the core interests continued to trouble China and the United States. The two nations had to address this issue again in the 3rd US-China Strategic & Economic Dialogue in May 2011. This time, Chinese State Councilor Dai Bingguo had something positive to report:

The United States reaffirmed (again) the following positions: the United States 1) welcomes a strong and successful China to play a bigger role in international affairs; 2) respects China's core interests; 3) has no intention to contain China; and 4) no intention to stir up trouble inside China. In return, China reaffirmed its adherence to the peaceful development approach and its promise not to challenge the United States.[215]

In less than 10 years after their first goodwill exchange (China's peaceful development initiative and the US responsible stakeholder call discussed earlier), China and the United States came to reassure each other again on the essential issues in the two nations' relations and the power transition process.

As the power transition unfolds, there will be new conflicts. China and the United States need to reassure each other time and again. In the meantime, the two sides need to have a better understanding of what they should or should not do regarding each other's core interests so as to avoid unnecessary conflicts.

On the East and Southeast Asia Regional Order. US core interests are preservation of US-led regional security, economic prosperity, and pursuance of democracy (for US domestic affairs, it is the "Blessings of Liberty" as stated in the US Constitution). The rise of China has caused the United States to wonder: Will China follow the example of US President James Monroe (the 5th President from 1817 to 1825) and assert a sphere of influence in East and Southeast Asia? Will the rise of China come at the expense of US core interests in this region?

These questions are understandable, but the concerns are not necessary for at least three main reasons. First, the Chinese know that it is not practical. Dai Bingguo ridiculed the idea of a Chinese version of Monroe Doctrine in his remarks mentioned earlier. Indeed, in the next 30 years, China still needs to carefully handle relations with its Asian neighbors so that China can continue its modernization mission, rather than trying to become a "boss" in this region.

Second, the nations in Asia will not accept a Chinese Monroe Doctrine either. Unlike the weak nations in Central and South America of President Monroe's time, many of China's Asian neighbors are formidable powers. Japan, in particular, is not quite ready to yield its leading position in Asia to China yet. Of note is that almost all of the East and Southeast Asian nations want the United States to stay engaged in this region. It is a widely-shared view that the nations in Asia-Pacific want the United States to maintain security and order in this region and serve as a counter-measure against China.[216]

Finally, the US alliance and coalition network in the Western Pacific is solid. It is stable and powerful enough to maintain the US-led regional order in the years to come. China is understandably uncomfortable with this US-led "encirclement;" but it has no reason to be paranoid. The US effort is part of its "hedging" strategy to guard against a China that might turn aggressive, but not a strategy to contain or attack China.

China can use its economic power to attract the Asian nations. But China should bear in mind that it does not have an alternative regional order to offer. The ASEAN-China Free Trade Area may be China's platform to make its impact. But this impact, if there is any, will be decades away. More importantly, as noted Chinese analysts admit, "except for Pakistan, China has no reliable ally in Asia. China is strategically the most isolated rising power in contemporary world history". The key problem, as Chinese analysts rightly point out, is China's refusal to connect with the prevailing international political institutions. This problem clearly sets China apart from the other Asian nations that have made or are making their transition to democracy.[217] Indeed, China has money nowadays, but it does not have political appeal. Its harmonious world concept may sound good, but it is not implementable (review the discussion of China's harmonious world construct earlier in this analysis). When it comes to human aspirations, people still turn to the United States. The recent upheavals in the Middle East are perhaps the best testimony.

For the above reasons, the United States does not need to be nervous about China's "potentials" to change the regional order in the Western Pacific Rim. China should guard against the temptation to make unqualified and certainly premature changes in the Asia-Pacific region.

On the Taiwan Issue. It is fair to say that the United States and China would have been at odds with each other whether they had the Taiwan issue or not. It is also fair to say that US-China conflict over many other issues normally does not contain the threat of war. However, because of the Taiwan issue, the United States and China have to prepare to see each other in arms. One can also make an argument that if the US-China power transition were to end in war, it would be most likely triggered by a fight over the fate of Taiwan.

There is no question that the Taiwan issue is complicated. However, there is also room for mutual understanding, a little of which can take the United States and China a long way toward preventing unwanted fights. The recent US decisions to sell arms to Taiwan and China's hot-tempered reactions are cases in point.

In all fairness, China overreacted. First, those two US decisions to sell weapons to Taiwan (President Bush in October 2008 and President Obama in January 2010) were in essence rehashing of the same package of weapon systems offered to Taiwan in 2001. Taiwan's legislature did not appropriate funds to purchase those weapon systems in the last years. Yet Taiwan's executive office kept asking for the sale time and again. The United States was simply answering the calls.

Second, the United States did not sell those weapon systems to support Taiwan independence. Rather, the weapons were intended to help enhance Taiwan's defense. In fact, for the last 30 years, the United States has followed closely the provision in the

TRA to provide Taiwan with weapons of a defensive nature. Although Chinese can dispute that the 150 F-16 fighter jets President George HW Bush sold to Taiwan can be offensive weapons as well, they have to admit that Taiwan has never been able to use them as such.

Third, China did not seem to understand the complicated nature of the US arms sales to Taiwan and clumsily interpreted them only as the US intent to use them as leverage against China. Although US arms sales to Taiwan do have such intent at times, this business is also a reflection of the US gun culture, helping the weak side to self-defense, economic support for the defense industry, and many others. It is also a business, as Secretary of Defense Gates put it, which has been going on for over 30 years; and the executive office is not in a position to terminate it.

Fourth, Gate's remarks brought out a point that the Chinese still do not seem to understand about how the US Government functions. The provision of weapons to Taiwan is codified in the TRA. It is a legal requirement for the President. As long as Taiwan requests arms, the President will follow the law to entertain its needs. Moreover, the President is also required by the US Arms Export Control Act to notify the Congress of the decision to sell arms to Taiwan (or to any other nation). No matter how low key the President elects to make the notification, the authorization becomes a public record in the Federal Registry and the media are there to bring it to the public's attention. China should take these factors into account before preparing its unconditioned and outrageous reaction to the next US move on this issue.

Finally, if China wants to get the United States to stop selling arms to Taiwan, it can do one of the following two things: to get Taiwan to give up its need for arms or to get the US Congress to repeal the arms provision in the TRA, or to abolish the TRA altogether. Chinese should see that the 1982 US-China Joint Communiqué, which suggested that the United States would reduce the arms sales and eventually put an end to them (see the full quote in the previous section about Taiwan), is an empty-worded US presidential statement with China. It is not endorsed by the Congress, hence has no legally-binding power. The executive office does not have the power to put an end to the arms sales business. For all the years since then, China has tried to hold the President accountable to the 1982 agreement. Unfortunately, as the saying goes, China has been barking up the wrong tree. In practical terms, China should find it easier to persuade Taiwan to give up its needs than to get the US Congress to amend or abolish the TRA.

China may dismiss all of the above and prepare to take stronger actions if the United States were to authorize another sale of arms to Taiwan. However, China should learn the lessons from their last two unproductive reactions. The suspension of military exchanges hurt both sides and had to be resumed eventually. A more measured approach should be considered.

On the South China Sea Disputes. The hot-tempered exchange between Secretary of State Clinton and Chinese Foreign Minister Yang Jiechi is a good example of the United States and China overreacting to each other's moves. A high degree of distrust between the two sides regarding each other's intentions and approaches toward the South China Sea problems certainly made the situation worse.

Aside from the above, the Chinese strongly hold that if Secretary Clinton did not disregard China's private request for her not to bring the difference between China and the United States over the South China Sea issues to the floor of the ASEAN Regional Forum and make China lose face in front of so many foreign ministers of the Asia Pacific region, China would not have had to react so strongly.[218] It appears that being a little culturally sensitive and considerate when dealing with China can be more productive.

On the China-Japan Dispute in the East China Sea. China has set itself on a path of no return on the dispute over the Diaoyu/ Senkaku Islands. It is a matter of when and how China settles the issue with Japan.[219]

Japan is equally firm on this dispute. After all, Japan has had effective control of those islands for almost 40 years now. (If China and Japan were to submit this dispute to the international court, Japan would have an advantage simply because of its effective control of the disputed territory). In October 2010, Secretary of State Clinton made clear that the US-Japan mutual defense treaty is applicable to those islands. If China were to use force to settle the issue, the United States would come to Japan's defense. China is certainly not happy with this US intervention. Yet it has to take this into account. For the United States, since it has insisted that this dispute be settled in a peaceful way, the United States should stand firm on this position and prevent a war between China and Japan so that the United States does not have to fight either.

On the Tibet and Xinjiang Issues. China's concern with the US factor in the problems of these two regions is understandable. However, China should pay more attention to its own policies and conduct in these two regions, for unlike the disputed territories in the Western Pacific, namely Taiwan and the islands in the East and South China Seas, China has effective control over Tibet and Xinjiang. If China does it right, it can keep the Tibetans and Uyghurs happy in the Chinese union. There is little the United States would do to undermine China's efforts. After all, the United States has time and again stated that it does not challenge China's sovereignty over these two regions. Its concern is mostly about human rights violations.

It is good that China has the Developing the Western Region program going. It is fair to expect economic development to improve the overall situation in Tibet and Xinjiang. However, as the noted Chinese dissident observer of Tibet and Xinjiang affairs Wang Lixiong points out, economic development is no substitute for the efforts to win the hearts and souls of the people in those two regions. Political reform is eventually in order.[220] In this respect, China should welcome US assistance rather than rejecting it.

The United States needs to take two things into account. One is to hold a fine line between concern for human rights violations and support for separatists movements. The other is to take an unassuming approach to work with the Chinese government on the human rights issues. The Australian experience with the Chinese government can be useful.[221]

On China's Military Power. Of all the expanding elements of China's comprehensive national power, none is more of concern to the United States than China's military power. Will China's military power catch up with that of the United States? What should China and the United States do in a peer competition, if not collision, of these two mighty military machines?

The answer to the first question is straightforward. China has the capacity for its military to become a peer competitor to the US military. All China needs are motivation, smart policies, resources, and time to bring about its military's potentials. The United States inadvertently provided China with the motivations in the 1990s. One was a wakeup call to the Chinese with the US-led revolution in military affairs (RMA), which gave rise to an innovative fighting power that was put on a full play during the Gulf War I of 1991 against Saddam Hussein's invasion of Kuwait and the Kosovo air campaign of 1999. Chinese leaders were shocked to see how much the US military power had advanced. They had long regretted that China missed several RMA's in the past (e.g., the transitions from "cold-weapon warfare" with the use of mainly knives to "hot-weapon warfare" with the application of fire power and guns and to "mechanized warfare" with the employment of tanks, battleships, and airplanes), and determined that China must take measures to catch up with this RMA in the information age.[222]

The other catalyst for change was the Taiwan Strait crisis of 1995-96, during which the United States made a strong show of force in the Western Pacific, perhaps the largest since World War II. Chinese leaders suddenly found themselves confronting the Taiwan independence movement (prior to that time, the Taiwan issue was mostly an unfinished war between the CCP and KMT and Taiwan independence was not in question), but its ability to deter Taiwan's push for independence and likely US military intervention abhorrently inadequate. To protect its claimed core interests, China must upgrade its military power immediately.

Finally, the US-China power transition also surfaced in time to remind the Chinese leaders that they needed a strong military to support and protect China's rise to power. Although Chinese leaders spoke out loud their proposition for China's peaceful rise, they had every reason to observe the old saying that, if you want peace, prepare for war.

These challenging situations required China's policy adjustment. Back in the early days of China's economic reform, Deng Xiaoping put China's military modernization on the back burner. He was on record as instructing China's military leaders that military modernization had to wait until China quadrupled the size of its economy, hopefully by the end of the 20th century.[223] However, the new circumstances dictated that China set its military modernization in motion ahead of schedule. "To build a prosperous nation with a strong military" was China's answer to the challenges.[224]

With an adjustment in its national strategy, China followed a two-pronged approach to improve its military power. On the one hand, China purchased advanced battleships and fighter jets from Russia as quick fixes for dealing with the Taiwan issue. On the other hand, China made an all-out effort to embrace the RMA and transform its military machine.

To China's fortune, its growing economy provided timely resources for these huge undertakings. Indeed, as Ross and Monroe put it, China's powerful economy was fueling a credible military force. (See the quotes from Ross and Monroe in the earlier section). From the mid-1990s to the present, China has topped the world in spending the most amount to purchase advanced conventional weapon systems abroad (mostly from Russia, see the Stockholm International Peace Research Institute Yearbooks of Armaments, Disarmament, and International Security for the records). At the same time, China also evidently increased its military spending to cover the other expenses of its military transformation. However, this extraordinary increase in defense spending did not seem to bother the Chinese leaders—they, after all, had plenty in their treasury. Indeed, as China's economy expected to have decades to grow before reaching its full capacity, China can bear this burden; and China's military modernization will have bountiful funding for its development. In this sense, China is more like the United States when it was on its way to becoming a great military power than the Soviet Union on its way to bankruptcy.

The result of China's efforts is clearly identifiable. The Pentagon has documented the developments in the growth of Chinese military power through its annual report to the Congress since 2000. The following has been a consistent assessment and concern over the years:

> The People's Liberation Army (PLA) is pursuing comprehensive transformation from a mass army designed for protracted wars of attrition on its territory to one capable of fighting and winning short-duration, high-intensity conflicts along its periphery against high-tech adversaries—an approach that China refers to as preparing for "local wars under conditions of informatization". The pace and scope of China's military transformation have increased in recent years, fueled by acquisition of advanced foreign weapons, continued high rates of investment in its domestic defense and science and technology industries, and far-reaching organizational and doctrinal reforms of the armed forces. China's ability to sustain military power at a distance remains limited, but its armed forces continue to develop and field disruptive military technologies, including those for anti-access/area-denial, as well as for nuclear, space, and cyber warfare, that are changing regional military balances and that have implications beyond the Asia-Pacific region.[225]

As of 2011, China is second to the United States in many areas of military power such as defense spending; aerial-based weapons, ballistic, and cruise missile programs; naval combatant, submarine, and amphibious warfare ships; and land-based capabilities. In 2007, China became the third nation (in addition to the United States and Soviet Union/Russia) to test its anti-satellite capability. Earlier in 2011, China also test-flew its advanced stealthy fighter jet, the J-20 (an ostensible matchup to the US F-22), and then in mid-2011 speculation spread that China would soon test-sail its first aircraft carrier (the Soviet-built *Varyag*).[226]

In addition to these quantitative changes, China has also brought about qualitative transformation through the implementation of the RMA to its military organization, command and staff, doctrine, education, logistics, medical support, defense industries, and many other areas. In recent years, the Chinese military has also put its new capabilities and improved war machines to test in frequent military exercises inside China as well as with foreign militaries abroad. A more capable military force is unquestionably emerging in China.[227] Riding the tides of its transformation and development, China's military is now eager to carry out its new mission in the new century, which in good part will be in contact and conflict with the United States.[228]

This leads us to find answers to the question of how the Chinese and US militaries get along in this ongoing power transition between the two nations. As discussed earlier, neither side wants a war with the other. Yet the United States and China have plenty of conflict that can drive the two into unwanted confrontations. It is imperative that the two sides find ways to minimize the dangers. The United States and China presumably can take many different measures to avoid unintended confrontations, but the most basic one is arguably to establish an effective, reliable, and stable contact between the two militaries. It is quite a problem that more than 30 years after establishing normal relations, the two nations still have not found the way to do the same for the most sensitive component of their national power, the military.

The reasons, incongruously, are simple. The two sides have incompatible views about the problems in their military relations and in the words of Chinese Senior Colonel Zhao Xiaozuo, "culturally unmatched approaches" to promote their goals.[229]

On the US side, the United States took the rise of China as a disruptive process and believed that Chinese military power would be a key instrument for these disruptions. The United States thus conceived a wide range of objectives to minimize the dangers of the Chinese military. Secretary of Defense William Perry put the US interests succinctly in a speech back in the mid-1990s. His words still ring true today.

> Engagement opens lines of communication with the People's Liberation Army—the PLA. A major player in Chinese politics, the PLA wields significant influence on such issues as Taiwan, the South China Sea, and proliferation. And if we are to achieve progress on these issues, we must engage PLA leaders directly.... [B]y engaging the PLA directly, we can help promote more openness in the Chinese national security apparatus, including its military institutions. Promoting openness or transparency about Chinese strategic intentions, procurement, budgeting, and operating

procedures will not only help promote confidence among China's neighbors, it will also lessen the chance of misunderstandings or incidents when our forces operate in the areas where Chinese military forces are also deployed.[230]

The United States has pursued these goals in the last two decades. Yet its efforts so far have met with frustration. In the meantime, US-China military-to-military relations have gone through six "roller-coaster" ups and downs:

- US suspension of military-to-military contacts following the Tiananmen Square tragedy in 1989, including sanctions on arms sales and other items to China that still remain effective to this day.[231]
- China's suspension of military-to-military contacts in protest against the United States allowing Taiwan's President Lee Teng-hui to make a private visit to his Alma Mater, Cornell University, in 1995 and the US intervention in the Taiwan Strait crisis of 1996.
- China's suspension of military-to-military contacts following the US accidental bombing of the Chinese Embassy in Belgrade, Yugoslavia, in 1999.
- US suspension of military-to-military contacts following the EP-3 incident over the South China Sea in 2001.
- China's suspension of military-to-military contacts following President Bush's authorization of arms sales to Taiwan in 2008.
- China's suspension of military-to-military contacts following President Obama's decision to sell arms to Taiwan and meeting with the Dalai Lama at the White House in 2010.

Frustrated with these ups and downs, many in the United States question the value of military-to-military contacts with China. They cannot tolerate the Chinese military's role in China's domestic affairs (e.g., the Tiananmen crackdown); the PLA's provocations (e.g., the EP-3 incident); and the Chinese government using the suspension of military-to-military relations as leverage against the United States (e.g., the last two rounds of suspension). Some also complain that the military-to-military contacts benefit China more than the United States, for the United States is generously open but China is tightly concealed. Opponents to US-China military-to-military contacts suggest that the United States should limit these exchanges to high-level strategic dialogues, and keep the PLA out of touch with the US military at the operational level. The United States would be better off keeping its military superiority over China and focus on measures that will ensure the safety of US military in the Western Pacific, even if meant to stand firm on China's military challenges.[232]

The Chinese, however, have an entirely different take on US-China military relations. They hold the following views:[233]

- The most fundamental problem in the US-China military-to-military relationship is the lack of trust between the two nations. Without this trust, this relationship is not sustainable.
- China blames the United States for its continued perception of China as an enemy. With its antagonistic view, the United States takes every development in China as a threat. Particularly, the United States never respects China's rightful need to modernize its military power.
- The Chinese maintain that they have a consistent and pragmatic view of its relationship with the United States: it is neither a friend nor an enemy. China accepts that it will never become an allied friend to the United States, but it can try to avoid becoming a deadly enemy. China holds its relationship with the United States as the most important one among its key foreign relations and will do everything possible to preserve this relationship. The Chinese argue that the United States has an ambivalent attitude toward China; and US policy toward China has vacillated between engagement and containment, with ample evidence of the United States leaning toward the latter.[234]
- The Chinese hold that the United States does not appreciate China's position on its core interests and keeps stepping on these interests. During Chairman of the Joint Chiefs of Staff Admiral Mike Mullen's recent visit to

Beijing, Chinese leaders repeatedly reminded him that China's sovereign interests are untouchable, whereas all other issues can be discussed through military-to-military exchanges.[235]

- China also holds that the United States has a hidden agenda in its military-to-military exchanges with China. It is the US mission to shape the direction of the PLA's development so that it can integrate China's armed forces into the US-led international security order. China adamantly opposes the US attempt to "liberalize" China's armed forces and does not want the United States to turn the PLA into a junior partner of the US military.[236]
- The Chinese argue that the United States demand for China's national security transparency is unfair. As a weaker state to the United States, they argue, China is entitled to have some secrecy.

In early 2011, after almost a year of suspension of high-level military-to-military exchanges and an eventful year of intense conflict, the two sides guardedly resumed military-to-military contacts. However, with what the Chinese PLA Major General Luo Yuan characterizes as the "main obstacles" remaining unchanged, i.e., the distrust mentioned above, the institutionalized arms sales to Taiwan, continued US military activities in Chinese claimed EEZs, and the restrictions set by the US Congress on US-China military-to-military exchanges, [237] it is only a matter of time before another breakdown brings these guarded exchanges to a halt. Indeed, 3 days after Admiral Mullen left China, President Obama received the Dalai Lama again at the White House (on July 16, 2011). China unsurprisingly launched a strong protest. Although China did not suspend the hardly-resumed military-to-military exchanges this time as a response, one can be sure that China took note of this new "US blatant interference in China's core interest" (in the Chinese Foreign Ministry Spokesman's terms). China would most likely add this "record" to the pending presidential decision on a multibillion-dollar deal to upgrade Taiwan's F-16 fighter planes as reasons for the next stormy setback in the two nations' military-to-military relations.[238]

As it stands, the ups and downs will continue to be the defining character of the US-China military-to-military relations. The lack of mutual trust sets limits on the contacts between the two militaries. The conflicts between the two nations over the issues discussed in this analysis are like time bombs waiting to trigger breakdowns of these tenuous relations from time to time. However, the two nations' extensive common interests in many other areas dictate that the two nations cooperate. As some Chinese analysts point out, as long as the overall relations between the two nations hold, the United States and China can only be at odds but not at war over the conflicts. US-China military-to-military relations will suffer the ups and downs, but they will eventually continue.

In the short term, this may be the agony the two militaries have to put up with. However, in the long run, this kind of relationship is not conducive to the two nations' need to manage the power transition process. It is therefore in the interest of the United States and China to develop an effective, reliable, and sustainable relationship for the two nations' militaries.

Presently, the two militaries have a few high-level contacts such as exchange of visits by senior civilian and military officials, defense telephone link (DTL) between the Pentagon and the Chinese Defense Ministry, military representatives in the US-China Strategic and Economic Dialogue, the Defense Policy Coordination Talks (DPCT), US-China Defense Consultative Talks (DCT), the Military Maritime Consultative Agreement (MMCA), and others. At the mid-level contacts, there are occasional naval ports of call and exchange of short-term visits by the officers of the two militaries.

These contacts, however, are rather superficial. Decades of experience in these "business-like" contacts between the two militaries have informed us that the two sides hardly develop any true understanding or long-term relationships; and there is little progress in promoting trust between the two sides through these contacts. At times of conflict between the two nations, these superficial contacts cannot be employed to help ease tensions—the defense hotline never got through and there were no communication between the two militaries other than speculations or angry exchanges of blows at each other's defense headquarters press conferences.

Is there any other option except for the two militaries to go beyond the extant superficial contacts? There is indeed one that has never been tried. This approach is to exchange resident students (military officers) in the two nations' military schools at all levels.

The United States has decades of experience with international officers/students in US military schools. There are plenty of positive aspects to this program. US officers develop long-term relations with their international counterparts that can go a long way to help strengthen US military relations with those foreign nations. They benefit from the international students' perspectives in their day-to-day contacts. The international fellows in turn receive valuable professional military education in the United States that is mostly not available in their own countries. Moreover, the international students also learn about democratic values and principles. Many of them bring their learning home and use it to improve their countries' political and military conduct. All in all, having the international students in the US military schools has been a valuable investment. It also pays valuable dividends at crucial times. As a former US Army War College Commandant Major General (retired) Robert Scales remarks, the professional conduct exercised by the Egyptian military during Egypt's recent political change was a great example of foreign militaries learning from their US counterparts in handling civil-military relations. Many of the senior Egyptian military officers in charge have been to US military schools.[239]

Chinese military schools have international officers as well. According to China's *National Defense White Papers*, China receives foreign military students/officers from more than 130 countries in the world. The PLA also sends hundreds of its bright officers to military schools in other countries, some of which are North Atlantic Treaty Organization (NATO) members and US close allies such as the UK, Japan, and South Korea. It is time Chinese military schools accept resident students from the US military.

US-China power transition is a long process. The conflicts between the two nations over their core interests are not easy to settle. These conflicts will continue to affect the two nations' military relations. However, the two militaries must not wait until the political climate is perfect to develop their relations. Developing a long-term and collegial relationship between the two militaries will be beneficial to both countries. Exchanging residence students/officers at each other's military schools is the way to go.

Final Thoughts

The United States and China have been at odds ever since the founding of the PRC in 1949. The outstanding conflicts discussed in this analysis have also existed for a long time. However, the rise of China and the power transition have seriously complicated these conflicts. China, for instance, holds that it must settle those disputed core interests, most notably Taiwan, before it can become a true great power. US interference therefore is perceived by China as attempts to obstruct China's rise.

To the United States, China's rise and its external impact are very worrisome. Among many other factors, the fact that this rising China is in the hands of an authoritarian government, whose leaders do not share with their American counterparts on the fundamental values underpinning the US-led international order, is very troublesome to the United States. The United States has many reasons to be concerned with China's rise coming at the expense of the US core interests.

It is fortunate that the United States and China both understand that there is a power transition going on between the two nations that complicates their capricious relations. Both understand the inherent danger of this power transition and agree to take careful measures to manage this process.

The bottom line is that neither the United States nor China wants war, yet there are conditions under which the two sides can be pushed over the edge to fight even if they do not want to. The Taiwan issue, as the Chinese rightly put it, is the most difficult one in US-China relations. The Chinese insist that China cannot become a true great power without completing its mission of national unity; and the most outstanding piece is Taiwan. The Chinese certainly hold that US involvement in the Taiwan issue in general, and the arms sales in particular, are the main obstacles in

China's mission. In many ways, one can argue that the settlement of the Taiwan issue is also the time when the United States and China can come to terms with the power transition business. If the US-China power transition "catches fire," the trigger will most likely be the Taiwan issue.

As the power transition unfolds, there will be new problems. Of note is that by the second half of the next 30 years, there will be new dynamic in the two nations' relations, driven primarily by the changing power balance between the two. The United States should take Organski's observation below seriously.

> It might be expected that a wise challenger, growing in power through internal development, would wait to threaten the existing international order until it was as powerful as the dominant nation and its allies, for surely it would seem foolish to attack while weaker than the enemy. If this expectation were correct, the risk of war would be greatest when the two opposing camps were almost exactly equal in power, and if war broke out before this point, it would take the form of a preventive war launched by the dominant nation to destroy a competitor before it became strong enough to upset the existing international order.[240]

For China, the following remarks by another noted observer of great power politics, Barry Buzan, are of particular importance.

> There are three main elements that define the tensions in play. First, that China has depended on the US-led international order to provide the stability that it needs for its development. Second, that China wants to avoid being drawn into conflict with the United States as earlier non-democratic rising powers have been. And third, that China resents, and up to a point opposes, US hegemony and the unipolar power structure. The danger is that as China rises it will become less dependent on the United States, and more opposed to its leadership, and that the United States will feel more threatened by its increasing power and revisionism.[241]

Endnotes

1. Chinese can trace China's torturous rise all the way to the mid-19th century and argue that China under Mao had made good progress

in this mission. However, as this analysis recounts, those past efforts could not measure up to genuine development and were, at best, false starts. It was not until the economic reform when China set itself on a path to undisputed economic development and made the rise of China an "earth-shaking" event that the power transition process began.

2. It is important to note that one should not look at power transition as a discrete event. At present, China's comprehensive national power has not measured up to the bench mark of 80 percent of US power as defined by Organski and Kugler (AFK Organski and Jacek Kugler, *The War Ledger*, Chicago, IL: The University of Chicago Press, 1980, p. 44); there is no solid evidence that China will displace the United States in the foreseeable future; however, these conditions do not reject the possibility that China and the United States are engaged in a power transition process. The fact that the United States will uphold its superiority does not reject the possibility of power transition, either. The power transition theory does not rule out the possibility that the dominant power can defeat the upstart and retain the international order.

3. Fareed Zakaria, *The Post-American World*, New York: WW Norton, 2009.

4. Martin Jacques, *When China rules the World: the End of the Western World and the Birth of a New Global Order*, New York: Penguin Press, 2009.

5. Steve Chan, *China, the US, and the Power-Transition Theory*, New York: Routledge, 2008, presents perhaps the most insightful critiques. See especially Chapter 2 on power scores and the identity of central contenders.

6. See Liu Mingfu (*The China Dream*), Beijing, China: China Friendship Publishing Company, 2010.

7. See the literature on international rivalries.

8. See the Hu Jintao's Report to the Chinese Community Party's (CCP's) 17th Party Convention, China's 11th Five-Year Plan (2006-10), and China's Modernization Reports from 2001 to the present.

9. In August 2010, China's gross domestic product (GDP) surpassed that of Japan to become the second largest economy in the world, trailing only the United States. However, China's per capita income level is still way below that of Japan (No. 23) and the United States (No. 6) by 2009 measures. China's goal is to close the gap of its comprehensive national power to that of the United States and other advanced nations. Per capita income is a better measurement for that purpose. China's current standing in per capita income is from the International Monetary Fund (IMF), World Bank, and Central Intelligence Agency (CIA) estimates. The IMF estimate of China's per capita income ranking in 2009 was No. 98 out of 192 nations in the world (World Economic Outlook Database, April 2010). The World Bank ranking for China was No. 87 (World Bank: World GDP 2009 divided by its World Population 2009 to obtain the per capita income figures). The CIA estimate of China's per capita income level was No. 102 (*The World Factbook 2010*). The average of the three estimates puts China at No. 96 out of 192 nations in 2009.
10. A Chinese design to measure a nation's national power. It takes into account hard and soft power (military, economic, demographic, and cultural factors). According to Reports on International Politics and Security published in January 2006 by the Chinese Social Sciences Center, a government-sponsored think-tank, the list of top 10 countries with the highest comprehensive national power (CNP) score was as follows:
11. ("Keywords in US-China Relations"), ºNlQn (*www.people.com.cn*), May 10, 2010, available from *world.people.com.cn/GB/57507/11556559.html*.
12. See detailed reports at the Chinese internet, *www.people.com.cn*, and the US Treasury Department site, available from *www.ustreas.gov/initiatives/us-china*.
13. (People Net), ("Interview with Foreign Minister Yang Jiechi on the Second Round of China-US Strategic and Economic Dialogue"), May 25, 2010, available from *world.people.com.cn/GB/11691562.html*.
14. Chinese Embassy to the United States, ("Commemorating the 30th Anniversary of the Normalization of US-China Relations"), (*Chinese Embassy to the US News Report*), No. 10, December 31, 2008, available from *www.china-embassy.org/chn/zt/7685938/t529960.htm*.

15. People Net ("Meeting with US Secretary of State Hillary Clinton and Treasury Secretary Timothy Geithner"), May 25, 2010, available from *world.people.com.cn/*.

16. Hillary Clinton and Timothy Geithner, "A New Strategic and Economic Dialogue with China," *The Wall Street Journal*, July 27, 2009.

17. Liu Jun ("Crisis Management Pushes for US-China Military Hotline"), (*Beijing Evening News*), March 4, 2008.

18. *CCTV* (Chinese Central TV), ("Taiwan Strait Crisis Prompted China and the US to Establish Military Hotline, First Phone Call Lasted 30 Minutes"), April 16, 2008.

19. See Yang Jiemian, "China's Diplomacy and Theoretical Breakthrough during the 30 Years of Reform and Opening to the Outside World," (International Studies), Issue 6, 2008; Mao Zedong ("From Opposing Hegemony as an Outsider to Fixing Hegemony as an Insider"), (Theory Studies Monthly), Issue 5, 2007; and Yan Jianying ("On China's Counter-measures against US Hegemony in the Early 21st Century"), (Journal of Changchun Teachers College), Vol. 25, No. 1, January 2006, for a discussion of China's evolving approaches against hegemony.

20. AFK Organski, *World Politics*, 2nd Ed., New York: Alfred A. Knopf, 1969, p. 371.

21. Steve Chan, *China, the US, and the Power-Transition Theory*, New York: Loutledge, 2008, chapters 4 and 5.

22. Organski, pp. 361-363. Chinese analysts also note that there are many commonalities between the United States and the United Kingdom (UK). However, they are not available between the United States and China.

23. Fareed Zakaria's calls notwithstanding. See Fareed Zakaria, "Are America's Best Days behind Us?" *Time*, March 14, 2011; and *The Post-American World*, New York: WW Norton, 2009.

24. The George W. Bush administration is widely criticized for its "go-it-alone" and heavy-handed approaches in international affairs. The invasion of Iraq, without a mandate from the United Nations (UN), was criticized by friends and foes all over the world. US positions on climate change, environmental control, and many other key issues are also questionable.

25. Dulles' remarks about this policy can be found in the following documents: Speech before the California State Chamber of Commerce, December 4, 1958; Speech before the US House of Representatives Foreign Affairs Committee, January 28, 1959; and Address to the Award Dinner of the New York State Bar Association, January 31, 1959.

26. See Qiang Zhai, "Mao Zedong and Dulles' 'Peaceful Evolution' Strategy: Revelations from Bo Yibo's Memoirs," *China Heritage Quarterly*, No. 18, June 2009, for Mao's fights against "peaceful evolution"; Deng Xiaoping's *Selected Works*, Vol. III, for Deng's efforts against peaceful evolution in China; and Jiang Zemin and Hu Jintao's continuation of this struggle in their efforts.

27. See Richard M. Nixon, *Beyond Peace*, New York: Random House, 1994. Also, remarks by Secretary of State Warren Christopher at his confirmation hearing, "Our policy will seek to facilitate a peaceful evolution of China from communism to democracy....," US Senate Foreign Relations Committee, January 13, 1993. In addition, there is a large literature on US engagement policy toward China.

28. See Henry Kissinger, *Diplomacy*, New York: Simon & Schuster, 1994, for an excellent account of the evolution of the US beliefs in the world order and its mission to promote it. Review also Francis Fukuyama's "The End of History?" *National Interest*, Summer 1989.

29. See the literature on "democratic peace" from the early 1990s on for its influence on the US sense of mission and its determination to promote democracy in the world. See also the US *National Security Strategies* from the George HW Bush administration to the latest *National Security Strategy* of 2010.

30. President George W. Bush's *National Security Strategies* of 2002 and 2006 have perhaps the strongest words on China's incomplete transition to modernity and its role as a stakeholder.

31. American analysts also agree that democratic peace theory may not be as solid as the proponents have established. Recent studies continue to challenge the theory.

32. Samuel P Huntington, *Political Order in Changing Societies*, New Haven, CT: Yale University Press, 1968. Chinese government and

policy analysts have always used Huntington's theory to justify China's authoritarian rule. Readers may want to review Joseph T. Siegle, Michael M. Weinstein, and Morton H. Halperins' challenge to Huntington's work in their study on "Why Democracies Excel," *Foreign Affairs*, September/October 2004.

33. Li Zhongzhou, "An Irresponsible Stakeholder," *China Daily*, June 26, 2007.

34. I use the term "construct" for the lack of a better word. Chinese unqualifyingly call the harmonious world construct a "theory". This is a typical Chinese misuse of the term "theory" in China. The harmonious world is more of a Chinese government foreign policy call. Xu Shaomin is one of the very few Chinese critiques of the harmonious world construct. He rightly points out that this harmonious world construct is not a "theory" as many other Chinese analysts have claimed; it is a questionable design for world peace; it is at best a Chinese government policy call. See Xu Shaomin ("Harmonious World Construct: A Policy Call or a Strategy?"), available from *www.chinaelections.org*.

35. The Five Principles of Peaceful Co-Existence are: 1) mutual respect for sovereignty and territorial integrity; 2) mutual non-aggression; 3) non-interference in each other's internal affairs; 4) equality and mutual benefit; and 5) peaceful co-existence. Chinese Premier Zhou Enlai first specified the five principles in their entirety in a meeting with the visiting Indian government delegation in Beijing on December 31, 1953. By the way, the Indians also claim ownership of these five principles.

36. Hu Jintao, "Build Towards a Harmonious World of Lasting Peace and Common Prosperity," Speech at the UN Summit, New York, September 15, 2005, available from *www.china-un.org/eng/zt/shnh60/t212915.htm*. Two years later, at the CCP's 17th Party Convention, Hu provided a further elaboration of this construct. See Hu Jintao, "Report to the 17th CCP Party Convention, Section XI," October 25, 2007.

37. See Chen Xiangyang (H–T3–), ("Effectively Challenge the West's 'Speech Hegemonism'"), March 29, 2010. Jiang Yong ("China Has Things to Say, the World Is Listening"), (*Decision Studies*), March 2010.

38. Yang Jiemian, ("Idea of 'Harmonious World' in China's International Strategic Development"), (*International Studies*), No. 5, 2009; Li Dan (Ng9N), ("Harmonious Society and Harmonious World: China's New Construct for Internal and External Order"), (*Journal of Changsha University of Science & Technology* [*Social Science*]), Vol. 23, No. 2, January 2008; Cheng Yunchuan, ("The Contemporary Value of Advocating the Harmonious World Construct"), (*Fujian Forum*), No. 2, 2010; Ban Xiuping. ("160 Years after the Communist Manifesto: to Build a 'Harmonious World'"), (*Journal of Bohai University*), No. 1, 2009; Zhang Dianjun ("From 'World Revolution' to 'Harmonious World' Construct"), (*Gansu Theory Research*), Vol. 199, No. 3, May 2010.

39. It is not an unfair statement that most, if not all, of the Chinese "scholarly analyses" of the harmonious world idea since the promulgation of it by the Chinese senior leaders have been part of the Chinese government propaganda, for these "analyses" have only been limited to the introduction of the background and reasons for the Chinese government to make such a call, the content of this call (mostly a repetition of what Hu Jintao has stated), its connection to the Confucius teaching and Chinese tradition (only the good aspects), unconditional support to the call, and unqualified praise for the international significance of the call. There is no rigorous "scholarly" or theoretical scrutiny of this call. See Ren Jingjing ("The General Principle of China's Peaceful Development Strategy—A Review of the Studies on the 'Harmonious World' Construct"), (*Scholarly Review*), Vol. 39, No. 3, 2008; and Fan Baihua and Ren Jingjing, ("Studies on the 'Harmonious World' Construct: Past and Future"), (*Journal of the Party School of the Central Committee of the CCP*), Vol. 12, No. 4, August 2008 for a rather rare and fair assessment of the Chinese "researches".

40. Confucianism was badly dismissed during the Chinese "Cultural Revolution". See the CCP resolution to build a harmonious society in China, passed at the 6th Plenanium of the 16th CCP Central Party Committee, October 11, 2006.

41. There is, however, a large literature on the problems with Confucianism as the foundation for government. One can get

to see some from the following publications. Hu Ruijun, ("The Legitimacy Foundation for the Construction of a Confucian Political Order"), (*Journal of Central-South University [Social Science]*), Vol. 14, No. 3, June 2008; Zhou Yuanyuan, ("An Analysis on the Shortcoming of Confucius Rule by Virtue"), (*Party School Distance Learning Special Edition*), January 2006; Liu Fangling, ("Confucian Requirement for Order and Absolute Monarchy"), (*Academic Forum of Nandu [Journal of the Humanities and Social Sciences]*), Vol. 25, No. 4, July 2005; Zhang Zihui ("Reflection of the Rule by Etiquette in the Ancient Times and Constructing Harmony at Present"), (*Journal of Nanchang University [Humanities and Social Sciences Edition]*), No. 4, 2009; Shen Xiaoyan, ("Confucian Rule of Ritual and Modern Democratic Politics"), (*Bi-monthly Journal of Marxism and Reality*), No. 1, 2007; Wang Bo, ("Consistency and Conflict between the People-based Thought of Confucianism and the Feudal Autocracy"), (*Social Sciences of Yunnan*), No. 4, 2004.

42. Although the Chinese Constitution of 1982 guarantees freedom of speech, the Chinese government often uses the criminal law's *subversion of state power* clause to imprison those who are critical of the government. The People's Republic of China (PRC) is known for its intolerance of organized dissent towards the government. Dissident groups are routinely arrested and imprisoned, often for long periods of time and without trial. Incidents of torture, forced confessions, and forced labor are widely reported. Freedom of assembly and association is extremely limited. China has signed the International Covenant on Civil and Political Rights, but has not ratified it.

43. It is ironic that China and India are the two original "authors" of the peaceful coexistence principles, yet those principles did not prevent the two from going to war against each other in 1962. They have not helped the two to resolve their outstanding border disputes, either.

44. See Li Junru ("The CCP Central Cadre School's Vice President on China's Political Reform and its Future Trends"), (*Beijing Daily*), September 8, 2008; and Yu Keping and Yan Jian, (*Democracy is a Good Thing: An Interview with Professor Yu Keping*), Beijing,

China: Social Sciences Chubanshe, 2006, for their arguments about political changes in China.

45. Ren Jiantao (ûNQR›m), a professor at the prestigious Zhongshan University of Guangzhou, points out that most of the CCP's political changes are "crisis driven" and "piecemeal". There is no grand design for a political modernization in China. It is unfortunate.("Group Discussion: Reflection on China's 30-year Political Reform and its Future"), (*Leaders*), June 2009.

46. Japan has a parliamentary political system. The majority party gets to form the cabinet. For most of the time in the post-World War II era, Japan's Liberal Democratic Party (LDP) has been the majority party in the Japanese Diet (parliament) and ruled Japan accordingly. The difference between the Japanese LDP and the Chinese CCP is the two parties' embracement (in the case of Japan) and dismissal (on the Chinese part) of the democratic values and operating mechanisms. There is a large literature on the Japanese "one-party-rule democracy". There are also publications in Chinese about Japan being a possible model for China. This analysis contends that the CCP has a good chance to follow the footsteps of Japan to evolve into a Japanese-like political system.

47. CCP, Resolution on Enhancing the Party's Ruling Capacity, September 19, 2004.

48. At the joint press conference with President Obama in Washington, DC, in January 2011, Chinese President Hu Jintao carefully and reluctantly admitted that the Chinese government agreed with the universal values.

49. Yu Keping ("Let Democracy Bring Fortune to China"), November 10, 2008.

50. Wang Guanqun, "Chinese Premier Calls for Further Reform, Ideological Emancipation," *Xinhua News Agency*, August 21, 2010, available at *www.gov.cn/english/2010-08/21/content_1685351.htm*; Chen Hong, "President Hails Shenzhen SEZ a World 'Miracle'," *China Daily*, September 7, 2010. It is quite an irony that Liu Xiaobo, a political dissident and 2010 Nobel Peace Prize winner, was advocating the same changes but was charged with plotting to subvert the Chinese government and is serving an 11-year term

in prison for what he said and wrote. This is typically a Chinese tradition that only the rulers can set fires, but no layman is allowed to light a lantern.

51. Ye Jiang ("A Comparison between 'Global Governance' and 'Harmonious World' Constructs"), (*Journal of Shanghai Administration Institute*), Vol. 11, No. 2, March 2010.

52. Secretary of State Hillary Rodham Clinton, "America's Engagement in the Asia-Pacific," Honolulu, HI, October 28, 2010, available from *www.state.gov/secretary/rm/2010/10/150141.htm.*

53. Zhang Yaoguang (*Chinese Ocean Political Geology: Ocean Geo-Politics and the Temporal and Spatial Changes of Ocean Geology*), Beijing, China: Science Press, 2003, p. 47, has documented 40 such attacks. Many other writings casually mention 84 attacks from the sea (a typical Chinese style of writing—mentioning facts without providing sources). Du Bilan mentions the following numbers: from 1840 to 1949, foreign powers launched 479 attacks from the sea, 84 of which are large-scale ones, and mobilized 1, 860 warships with more than 470, 000 soldiers and armed personnel. See also China's State Oceanic Administration. ("Building a Strong Ocean Nation, Pushing for Chinese Rejuvenation"), March 20, 2007.

54. Gao Fang ("The Origins of the Unequal Treaties in Contemporary Chinese History"), (*Nanjing Social Sciences*), No. 2, 1999.

55. Treaty of Good-Neighborliness and Friendly Cooperation between the People's Republic of China and the Russian Federation, July 24, 2001. Those border demarcations have been completed. See Jiang Changbin ("Inside Story about Sino-Russo Border Problem Negotiation: Why Use Unequal Treaties as Basis"), (*Huanqiu Magazine*), October 19, 2005, available from *www.xinhuanet.com*.

56. See Yan Jiaqi, "'More on Sino-Russo Border Disputes' from International Law," (a Hong Kong-based journal), Issue 1, 2003; and "The Aigun Treaty" from International Law," January 6, 2003, available from *www.chinaaffairs.org*. Yan mentions in the writing that Mao and Deng refused to give the claim.

57. During Chen Shui-bian's two terms in office, he had encouraged the growth of the Taiwan identity, the "de-China" movement,

and many other socalled "incremental changes toward Taiwan independence" acts. Perhaps the most provocative one was his push for referendums to decide important issues related to cross Taiwan Strait relations.

58. See the full text of the Treaty of Shimonoseki at the Taiwan Documents Project, available from *www.taiwandocuments.org/shimonoseki01.htm.*

59. See *The Memoirs of Li Hung-Chang*, William Francis Mannix, ed., Boston, MA: Houghton Mifflin Company, 1913.

60. Douglas MacArthur, "An Unsinkable Aircraft Carrier: Highlights of MacArthur's Statement on Formosa," *Time Magazine*, September 4, 1950.

61. "Cairo Declaration," *The Department of State Bulletin*, December 4, 1943.

62. "Potsdam Proclamation Defining Terms for Japanese Surrender," *The Department of State Bulletin*, July 29, 1945.

63. See a declassified memorandum of conversation between Secretary of State Dean Acheson and Senators William F. Knowland and Alexander H. Smith on the strategic assessments of Taiwan and Chinese Civil War. *Foreign Relations of the United States*, Vol. VI, 1950, pp. 259-260.

64. For President Truman's statement, see *Public Papers of the Presidents of the United States: Harry S. Truman*, 1950, p. 492.

65. *Ibid.*

66. Dwight D. Eisenhower, *The White House Years: Mandate and Change, 1953-1956*, Garden City, NY: Doubleday & Company, Inc., 1963, p. 463.

67. Secretary of State John Foster Dulles later went on record to make clear the US change on its position. Dulles stated that "technical sovereignty over Formosa and the Pescadores has never been settled" and that "the future title is not determined by the Japanese peace treaty [with the United Nations in 1951], nor is it determined by the peace treaty which was concluded between the Republic of China and Japan [in 1952]," *Foreign Relations of the United States*, 1954.

68. *Public Papers of the Presidents of the United States: Harry S. Truman, 1950*, p. 527.

69. Statement by Secretary of State John Foster Dulles, *Foreign Relations of the United States*, Vol. VI, p. xx.

70. See Henry Kissinger's accounts of the painstaking negotiations with the Chinese on the Taiwan issues in "The Beijing-Washington Back-Channel and Henry Kissinger's Secret Trip to China, September 1970-July 1971," National Security Archive Electronic Briefing Book No. 66, William Burr, ed., available from the National Security Archive Website.

71. *Joint Communiqué of the United States of America and the People's Republic of China (the Shanghai Communiqué)*, February 28, 1972.

72. See President Carter's writings for his decision to normalize relations with China at the time.

73. The Taiwan Relations Act, US Public Law 96-8, 1979.

74. "US-China Joint Communiqué of August 17, 1982," *The Department of State Bulletin*, October 1982.

75. See Harvey Feldman, "President Reagan's Six Assurances to Taiwan and Their Meaning Today," The Heritage Foundation *WebMemo*, No. 1653, October 2, 2007.

76. See Shirley A. Kan, "Taiwan: Annual Arms Sales Process," *CRS Report for Congress*, June 5, 2001, for the 4-staged talks between Taiwan and the United States until 2001 when President George W. Bush stopped this annual process but based future arms sales talks on a need-based process. See also Shirley A. Kan, "Taiwan: Major US Arms Sales since 1990," *CRS Report for Congress*, December 2, 2009, for a detailed account for the arms sell to Taiwan.

77. Jin Yinan ("Arms Sales to Taiwan: From Pragmatism to Hegemonic Practice"), (*Study Times Monthly*), No. 2, 2010; *Xinhuanet*, ("Don't Expect the United States to Abandon Arms Sales to Taiwan"), February 8, 2010; Yang Tiehu ("News Analysis: The US Must Pay a Heavy Price for Its Arms Sales to Taiwan") February 2, 2010; Yang Tiehu ("China Should

Also Wield a Big Stick and Resolutely Oppose US Arms Sales to Taiwan"), (*Global Times*), February 1, 2010; Su Nan, ("PLA Rear Admiral Suggests Sanctions on US Firms That Sell Arms to Taiwan"), (*China News Agency*), January 7, 2010; Yang Tiehu ("Expert: China Has More Retaliation Measures That Can Inflict Pains on the United States"), (*Global Times*), February 1, 2010; Yang Tiehu ("Military Analysis: The US Should Not Be Allowed to Make Unbridled Arms Sales to Taiwan"), (*People's Daily Net*), January 13, 2010; Guo Xuetang ("Why We Should 'Set Rules' for the US to Follow"), (*Wenhui Bao*), January 18, 2010.

78. President George W. Bush interview with ABC News reporter Charles Gibson about his first 100 days in office on *Good Morning America*, April 25, 2001.

79. John King, "Blunt Bush Message for Taiwan," CNN Washington Bureau, December 9, 2003. See also Thomas J. Christensen, Deputy Assistant Secretary for East Asian and Pacific Affairs, "A Strong and Moderate Taiwan," Speech at the US-Taiwan business Council, September 11, 2007.

80. See PRC position on this issue at (Xinhuanet Background Information), ("The 1992 Consensus"), which emphasizes the "undefined nature of the one-China," available from *news.xinhuanet.com/ziliao/2003-01/23/content_704746.htm.* Butsee Ma Ying-jeou's position on this issue, which emphasizes the two sides holding on to their different interpretations: Ma Ying-jeou, ("Ma Ying-jeou Reiterated the Position of 1992 Consensus as One China with Each Side's Own Interpretations"), (*Lianhe Zaobao*), October 28, 2010.

81. Kenneth Lieberthal, "Preventing a War over Taiwan," *Foreign Affairs*, March/April 2005.

82. See the full text of the agreement at *www.chinataiwan.org/english/News/NaT/201009/t20100921_1537360.htm*. See also a survey on this agreement at *www.taiwansecurity.org/2010/GVMaApproval_ECFA-072810.pdf.*

83. Aaron L. Friedberg, "Menace: Here Be Dragons: Is China a Military Threat?" *The National Interest*, September/October 2009. Admiral Robert Willard, commander of the US forces in

the Pacific, agreed that China has achieved "initial operational capability" for a land-based anti-ship ballistic missile that could threaten US aircraft carriers in Asian waters. The Dongfeng (East Wind) 21D is intended to end an era of unrivalled US global sea and air power. Mark Stokes, a defense analyst and former official at the Pentagon, added that "this is a game-changer in the sense that it would force the US Navy to operate farther away from the Chinese coast, at least in the initial phase of a conflict". See Kathrin Hille of *Financial Times* reporting from Beijing, "Chinese Wonder Missile to Test US Supremacy," January 18, 2011.

84. When it comes to territorial disputes, Chinese have always claimed that other nations stole or occupied China's territories. See discussion in the following sections.

85. See Daniel M. Hartnett and Frederic Vellucci, Jr., "Continental or Maritime Power? A Summary of Chinese Views on Maritime Strategy since 1999," Alexandria, VA: The CNA Corporation, October 2007.

86. See Marshall Hoyler, "China's 'Antiaccess' Ballistic Missiles and US Active Defense," *Naval War College Review*, Vol. 63, Issue 4, Autumn 2010; Sheng Lijun, "China's Rising Sea Power: the PLA Navy's Submarine Challenge," *Contemporary Southeast Asia*, Vol. 28, Issue 3, December 2006; and the Annual Report on the Military Power of the PRC since 2000, Washington, DC: US Department of Defense, for discussion of China's access denial capability development.

87. See Shirley A. Kan *et al.*, "China-US Aircraft Collision Incident of April 2001: Assessments and Policy Implications," Washington, DC: Congressional Research Service (CRS) Report for Congress, October 10, 2001; and Eric Donnelly, "The United States-China EP-3 Incident Legality and Realpolitik," *Journal of Conlfict & Security Law*, Vol. 9, No. 1, 2004, pp. 25-42, for a discussion of the incident and disputes on military operations in the Exclusive Economic Zone (EEZ).

88. Xinhua News Agency, ("US Military Surveillance Ships to Collect Military Intelligence in Chinese Waters"), *Xinhuanet.com*. On these monitoring and patrolling acts, see also *China Marine*

Administration Law Enforcement Annual Report 2006, available from *www.soa.gov.cn*; Jim Garamone, "Chinese Vessels Shadow, Harass Unarmed US Surveillance Ship," March 9, 2009, available from *www.navy.mil*.

89. Admiral Blair made this remark at the Senate Armed Service Committee Hearing. Reported by the Staff Writers, Washington (AFP), March 11, 2009.

90. Liu Juntao ("[Foreign Minister] Yang Jiechi Met with [Secretary of State] Hillary Clinton and Stressed [Chinese] Opposition to Foreign Military Force to Have Military Exercise in the Yellow Sea"), (*people.com.cn*), July 23, 2010; (*People Daily*), ("Chinese Ask US Military to Stop Surveillance in China's Exclusive Economic Zoon"), August 28, 2009.

91. Huang Xueping, Chinese Defense Ministry Spokesperson, "Defense Ministry Spokesperson Press Remarks," Xinhua News Agency, March 11, 2009; Ma Chaoxu, "Chinese Foreign Ministry Spokesperson Press Remarks," Xinhua News Agency, May 6, 2009.

92. The United Nations Convention on the Law of the Sea (UNCLOS) allows member nations to hold reservations. See Under Secretary of Defense for Policy, "Maritime Claims Reference Manual," *DoD 2005, 1-M*, June 23, 2005, for a documentation of the nations signing, ratifying, or rejecting the treaty. The 14 nations that hold reservations are Bangladesh, Brazil, China, Finland, Egypt, Guyana, India, Iran, Kenya, Malaysia, Nicaragua, Pakistan, Portugal, and Uruguay. See also Raul Pedrozo, USN Captain, JAGC, "Close Encounters at Sea," *Naval War College Review*, Vol. 62, No. 3, Summer 2009.

93. "Testimony of Deputy Assistant Secretary of Defense for Asian and Pacific Security Affairs OSD Robert Scher, before the US-China Economic and Security Review Commission," February 4, 2010, available from *www.uscc.gov/hearings/2010hearings/written_testimonies/10_02_04_wrt/10_02_04_scher_statement.pdf*.

94. Author's conversation with senior US military leaders. See Eric A. McVadon, "The Reckless and the Resolute: Confrontation in

the South China Sea," *China Security*, Vol. 5, No. 2, Spring 2009, for an excellent analysis of this issue.

95. US Pacific Command, "Press Roundtable in Beijing, China, by Admiral Timothy J. Keating," Commander's Transcript from January 15, 2008, available from *www.pacom.mil/web/site_pages/commander/080115-keating-china.shtml*.

96. Shen Dingli ("Cheonan Incident Made a Stir in China's Neighboring Waters"), (*Society Observer*), No. 9, 2010; Shi Yongming ("The Cheonan Incident and International Crisis Management"), (*Peace and Development*), No. 5, 2010.

97. China and the two Koreas all claim a 200 nautical mile (nm) EEZ. Their claims overlap. A reasonable solution, according to the UNCLOS, is to draw a median line between them. However, the three parties have not yet made such a settlement.

98. Luo Yuan ("China Has Five Reasons to Oppose US-South Korean Military Exercise in the Yellow Sea"), (*Shanghai Morning News*), July 21, 2010.

99. See Geoff Morrell, Pentagon Press Secretary, "News Briefing," US Department of Defense, Office of the Assistant Secretary of Defense (Public Affairs), July 14, 2010, for the Pentagon's explanation and critiques.

100. See Pentagon's *Annual Reports to Congress on the Military Power of the People's Republic of China since 2000.*

101. Han Zhenhua (*A Study of the History and Geography of the South China Sea Islands*), Beijing, China: Social Science Literature Publishing, 1996; Liu Nanwei ('RWSZ), (*A Documentation of the Names of the South China Sea*). Beijing, China: Science Publishing, 1996. "Spratly," "Spratas," "Paracel," "Macclesfield," and so on are European assignments and colonial legacies. See also Chinese Foreign Ministry, ("The Issue of South China Sea Islands Sovereignty, [5] International Recognition of China's Sovereignty over the Spratly Islands"), available from *www.mfa.gov.cn/chn/pds/ziliao/tytj/t10651.htm*.

102. See Sun Donghu ("The Origins of South China Sea Islands' Foreign Names and Their Historical Influence"), (*Geography Studies*), No. 2, 2000.

103. The Soviet Union proposed an amendment to Article 2 (b) and (f) as follows: Japan recognizes full sovereignty of the Chinese People's Republic of China over Manchuria, the Island of Taiwan (Formosa) with all islands adjacent to it, the Penlinletao Islands (Pescadores), the Tunshatsuntao (Pratas islands), as well as over the Islands of Sishatsuntao and Chunshatsuntao (the Paracel Islands), and Nanshatsuntao islands including the Spratlys, and renounces all right, title and claim to the territories named herein.

    The delegates rejected the Soviet amendment by a vote of 46 to 3, with 1 abstention. See US State Department, *Conference for the Conclusion and Signature of the Peace Treaty with Japan, Record of Proceedings*. Washington, DC: US Department of State, Publication 4392, December 1951, p. 292.

104. The Prime Minister of the newly established Republic of Vietnam, Tran Van Huu, who attended the peace conference at San Francisco, claimed Vietnam's ownership of the South China Sea islands during his speech at the conference (every delegate had at least one opportunity to speak at the conference, the big powers of course got more than their share of the time to speak there). However, there was no action taken on that claim—it went unnoticed. See US State Department, *Conference for the Conclusion and Signature of the Peace Treaty with Japan, Record of Proceedings*. Washington, DC: US Department of State, Publication 4392, December 1951, p. 292. By the way, the Vietnam White Paper of 1975 claims that since there was no objection to the Prime Minister's claim at the conference, it was endorsed. This interpretation cannot stand. See also Li Jinming ("Vietnam's Claim on the South China Sea Territory"), (*Window of Southeast Asia*), No. 1, 2005, for an analysis of the issues.

105. A draft was circulated prior to the conference. China also obtained a copy.

106. Statement by Chinese Foreign Minister Zhou En-lai in *Collected Documents on the Foreign Relations of the People's Republic of China,* Beijing, China: World Knowledge Publishing, 1961.

107. See Captain Memoir and Vietnam White Paper.

108. International practice gives more weight to effective control than historical claims. See the Island of Palmas Case ruled by the Permanent Court of Arbitration in 1925 (a dispute between the United States on behalf of its colony the Philippines and the Netherlands on behalf of its colony Indonesia) sets the example of effective exercise of sovereignty taking precedence over the right of discovery and claim of territorial contiguity (see reference Hague Court Reports 2d 83 [1932] [Perm. Ct. 4rb. 1928]). Other cases such as the Clipperton Island, Eastern Greenland, and the Minqulers and Ecrehos Islands all point to the same requirement of effective control over historical claims.

109. The Republic of China (ROC) did station some troops in the Paracel and Spratly islands. However, following its defeat in the Chinese Civil War, it withdrew the troops. The PRC did not replace them with PLA forces, leaving those islands largely unattended.

110. Chinese Government (PRC) Declaration on China's Territorial Waters, September 4, 1958, available from *news3.xinhuanet.com/ ailiao/2003-01/24/content_705061.htm*. "Historically belonging to China" and "China's intrinsic and inseparable territories" are two dogmatic terms in China's claims to its disputed territories. China and Vietnam share borders. China also owned and ruled Vietnam for well over 1,000 years in history. Can China claim its historical ties and inseparable connections with Vietnam and demand its return to China by saying: "Vietnam historically belongs to China; it is an inseparable part of China" International practice (International Court and Arbitration) does not accept congruity as a reason for territorial claim.

111. See Chinese documentation of activities by all relevant parties, including the Europeans, throughout the ages in the South China Sea, available from *www.nansha.org.cn.*

112. Liselotte Odgaard, *Maritime Security between China and Southeast Asia: Conflict and Cooperation in the Making of Regional Order*, Farnham, Surrey, England: Ashgate, 2002, pp. 67-76.

113. Due to definitional differences, the number of islands in the Spratlys is different, so is the number of islands each disputant

holds. See John C. Baker and David G. Wiencek, eds., *Cooperative Monitoring in the South China Sea*, Westport, CT: Praeger Publishers, 2002; Dieter Heinzig, *Disputed Islands in the South China Sea*, Hamburg, Germany: Hamburg Institute of Asian Affairs, 1976, Marwyn S. Samuels, *Contest for the South China Sea*, New York: Metheun, 1982; Li Jinming, ("The Current Status of the South China Sea Disputes"), (*Southeast Asian Studies*), No. 1, 2002, Wikipedia, "Spratly Islands"; Lu Ning, *Flashpoint Spratlys*, Singapore: Dolphin Trade Press, 1995.

114. Deng Xiaoping's first articulation of this policy came in 1978 during his visit to Japan. It was originally proposed to deal with the China-Japan dispute on the Diaoyu/Senkaku Islands (see China Ministry of Foreign Affairs, "Shelving Disputes, Promoting Joint Development," available from *www.mfa.gov.cn/chn/gxh/xsb/wjzs/t8958.htm*). Deng later extended this policy to deal with the South China Sea territorial disputes and to China's other territorial disputes as well. The China-India border dispute is a case in point. Deng Xiaoping's talk about this policy is recorded in the "Speech at the Third Plenary Session of the Central Advisory Commission of the Communist Party of China," *Selected Works of Deng Xiaoping*, Vol. III, October 22, 1984. Chinese leaders advocated this policy at various important occasions. For example, Li Peng, the Chinese Premier, made the following remarks during his visit to Southeast Asia, "Nansha [Spratly] Islands historically belong to China. However, we have patience on this issue. We will wait for the appropriate time to resolve it. At the moment, we can set it aside. It should not affect China improving relations with those disputant nations". Answer to press conference, Manila, The Philippines, (*People's Daily*), December 15, 1990.

115. See Yang Bo (hgâl), ("The Status of Nansha Islands Illegally Occupied by Vietnam"), (*Ordnance Knowledge*), 2010, p. 3A.

116. Zheng Zemin, ("South China Sea Disputes in Asia Pacific"), Dissertation, Central Cadre School of the CCP, May 2004, pp. 111-114; Chen Wei (H–O), ("The Problem and Prospect of the 'Shelving-Dispute-Promoting Joint Development' Approach in Settling the South China Sea Problems"), (*Global Economy*); Lu Xiaowei, ("The Current Situation of South China Sea Disputes,

Reasons and Response"), (*Contemporary Social Science Perspectives*), No. 7-8, 2009; Fang Hui ("Military Intelligence Observation: Half of China's Sovereign Ocean Territory Was Occupied"), *Xinhuanet*, March 3, 2009.

117. See Chinese Foreign Ministry, ("Shelving Dispute, Pursuing Joint Development"): ("The basic components of "Shelving disputes and pursuing joint development" are: first, the sovereign ownership [of the disputed territory] belongs to China; second, with respect to disputed territories that are not ready for complete settlement, China can set aside the discussion of sovereign ownership for the time being and shelve the disputes; shelving the dispute, however, does not mean giving up sovereignty; it only means to set it aside for the time being; third, with respect to the disputed territories, promote joint development; and fourth, the goal of joint development is to promote mutual understanding and create conditions for the eventual settlement of those disputed territories".) Available from the Chinese Foreign Ministry website, *www.mfa.gov.cn/chn/gxh/xsb/wjzs/t8958.htm*.

118. Selected Works of Deng Xiaoping, Vol. III, Beijing, China: People's Publishing. See also Luo Yuan (PLA Major General), ("Deng Xiaoping: South China Sea Sovereignty Not Negotiable"), (*People TV*), July 27, 2010, transcript available from *tv.people.com.cn/GB/14644/135863/12261769.html*; Min Hang ("A Thorough Understanding of Deng Xiaoping's Strategic Thought on Ocean Disputes"), (*Study Times*), January 11, 2011.

119. Zhang Tiegen ("South China Sea Problems: Current Status and Prospects"), (*Asia and Africa Affairs*), No. 5, 2009; Li Hongbo ("PLA General [Zhang Li, who is also a member of the National Committee of the Chinese People's Political Consultative Conference Standing Committee], Suggests Building Airport at the Mischief Reef and Deploying Fighter Jets There"), (*Global Times*), June 19, 2009, available from *war.news.163.com/09/06/19/09/5C5NDU7K00011MTO.html*; Lang Xianping, ("From 'Shelving Dispute, Joint Development' to "China Shelving Dispute, Other Nations' Development'"), (*Financial Forum*), September 25, 2010, available from *www.infivision.cn/bbs redirect.php?tid=104664&goto=newpost*.

120. Lu Minghui ("South China Sea Disputes and Southeast Asian Nations' Military Expansion"), (*Southeast Asian Affairs*), No. 4, 2006.

121. Xi Zhigang, ("New Thinking on China's South China Sea Strategy"), (*Strategy Corner*), February 2010.

122. *China News Net* ("Chinese Foreign Ministry Reaffirms: China Continues the Policy of 'Shelving-Dispute-Joint-Development,' Outsiders Should Not Get Involved in the South China Sea Disputes"), available from *news.sina.com.cn/c/2010-11-04/003121409374.shtml*. Chinese Foreign Ministry's Assistant Minister Hu Zhengyao reiterated China's position on the policy of shelving-disputes-joint-development at an interview with the *China News Agency* on November 4, 2010. "China Reiterates: China Sticking on 'Shelving Dispute and Joint Development'," available from *news.sina.com.cn/c/2010-11-04/003121409374.shtml*.

123. Cai Yanhong ("China's Ocean Monitoring and Administration Covers All of China's Territorial Waters, Sign of Sovereignty Was Placed on the James Shoal"), (*Rule of Law Daily*), February 14, 2011.

124. Cai Penghong ("An Analysis of the US South China Sea Policy"), (*Contemporary International Relations*), No. 9, 2009; Guo Yuan ("US South China Sea Policy in the Post-Cold War Era"), (*Academic Inquiry*), February 2008; He Zhigong and An Xiaoping ("The US Factor in the South China Sea Disputes"), (*Journal of Contemporary Asia-Pacific Studies*), No. 1, 2010; Liu Zhongmin, ("An Analysis of the US-China Relationship and Its Impact on the South China Sea Issues"), (*Northeast Asia Forum*), Vol. 15, No. 5, September 2006; Liu Zhongmin ("South China Sea Issues and Post-Cold War US-China Relations: Conflicting Understanding and Difficult Choices"), (*Foreign Affairs Review*), Issue 85, December 2005; Qiu Danyang ("The US Factor in Sino-Pilipino South China Sea Dispute"), (*Journal of Contemporary Asia-Pacific Studies*), No. 5, 2002.

125. Hu Suping 1950-2004 ("The Evolution of US Policy on the South China Sea, 1950-2004"), (*The New Orient*), No. 5, 2010. Hu mentions in her article that Chinese Foreign Ministry had issued

more than 400 protests against the United States between September 1956 and 1970. But Hu provides no source or reference for this number (a common problem with most Chinese publications).

126. Warren Christopher, quoted in A. James Gregor, "Qualified Engagement: US China Policy and Security Concerns," *Naval War College Review*, Spring 1999. Gregor states in his article that "US Secretary of State Warren Christopher reminded the Chinese foreign minister that the United States had treaty obligations with the Philippines". The reference of this remark is from *Indo-China Digest*, April 21, 1995.

127. An influential piece on the US neutrality on the South China Sea disputes is by Scott Snyder, "The South China Sea Dispute: Prospects for Preventive Diplomacy," *Special Report to the United States Peace Institute*, Washington, DC: United States Peace Institute, 1996.

128. Richard Cronin, "Maritime Territorial Disputes and Sovereignty Issues in Asia," A Testimony before the Senate Subcommittee on East Asian and Pacific Affairs, July 13, 2009; Peter A. Dutton, "China's Views of Sovereignty and Methods of Access Control," Testimony before the US-China Economic and Security Review Commission, February 27, 2008; Dan Blumenthal, "Hearing on Maritime Territorial Disputes in East Asia," Testimony before the Senate Foreign Relations Committee Subcommittee on Asia, July 15, 2009.

129. Gloria Jane Baylon, "US Should Support the Republic of the Philippines' Claim on Spratlys," *Philippines News Agency* (PNA), March 4, 2009; US Senator Jim Webb, "The Implications of China's Naval Modernization for the United States," Testimony before the US-China Economic and Security Review Commission, June 11, 2009; Federal News Service, Hearing of the East Asian and Pacific Affairs Subcommittee of the Senate Foreign Relations Committee Subject: Maritime Disputes and Sovereignty Issues in East Asia, Chaired by Senator Jim Webb (D-VA), July 15, 2009; Federal Information and News Dispatch, Inc., "Senator Webb Completes Landmark Five Nation Visit throughout Asia," August 24, 2009; Greg Torode, "A Classic Display of McCain Resilience," *South China Morning Post*, April 11, 2009; Jason

Folkmanis, "US Vietnam Seek to Limit China, Keep Power Balance," *Bloomberg News*, available from *www.bloomberg.com/apps/news?pid=20601080&sid=aRZ9NTnZ_iml.*

130. Hillary Rodham Clinton, Secretary of State, "Remarks with Thai Deputy Prime Minister Korbsak Sabhavasu," Government House, Bangkok, Thailand, July 21, 2009; Hillary Rodham Clinton, Secretary of State, "Remarks at the ASEAN Regional Forum," National Convention Center, Hanoi, Vietnam, July 23, 2010, available from *www.state.gov/secretary/rm/2010/07/145095.htm.*

131. Robert Gates, "Remarks at the 9th IISS Asia Security Summit, The Shangri-La Dialogue," Singapore, June 5, 2010.

132. Office of the Press Secretary, "Remarks by President Barack Obama at Suntory Hall, Tokyo, Japan," The White House, November 14, 2009.

133. See Assistant Under Secretary of Defense Michelle Finley's statement.

134. Wu Xingtang ("The Fluctuating Nature of US-China Relationship and Its Difficult Journey"), (*The Red Flag Journal*), No. 20, 2010; Zhao Minghao, ("'Return' or 'Repositioning': An Analysis of the US Adjustment of Its Strategy Toward the Asia-Pacific"), (*Contemporary World*), No. 12, 2010.

135. See one interesting reflection from Su Hao, Director of the Center for Strategic and Conflict Management at China Foreign Affairs University in Bejing, "Washington's High Ambition for an East Asian Presence," *China Daily*, August 9, 2010.

136. Edward Wong, "China Hedges over Whether South China Sea Is a 'Core Interest' Worth War," *The New York Times*, March 30, 2010. Steinberg and Bader also shared this new development with the policy circle on various occasions.

137. Bonnie Glaser and David Szerlip, "US-China Relations: The Honeymoon Ends," *Comparative Connections*, April 2010.

138. Remarks by the Secretary of State Clinton, ASEAN Regional Forum, Hanoi, Vietnam.

139. The 27 foreign ministers are from 10 ASEAN nations, namely, Brunei, Cambodia, Indonesia, Laos, Malaysia, Myanmar, the

Philippines, Singapore, Thailand, and Vietnam; 10 ASEAN dialogue partners, namely, Australia, Canada, China, the European Union, India, Japan, New Zealand, South Korea, Russia, and the United States; and seven Asia-Pacific nations, namely, Bangladesh, North Korea, Pakistan, Mongolia, Sri Lanka, Timor-Leste, and Papua New Guinea.

140. The Monroe Doctrine is articulated in a message by President James Monroe to the Congress on December 2, 1823. It asserted that the Western Hemisphere was not to be further colonized by European countries, but that the United States would neither interfere with existing European colonies nor meddle in the internal concerns of European countries. The Carter Doctrine came in the aftermath of the Soviet invasion of Afghanistan in 1980. There was concern that the Soviets might continue their advance down to the Persian Gulf, threatening to take control of the world's oil reserve. President Carter made the volatile Middle East and Central Asia a focal point of his State of the Union address on January 23, 1980. In this speech, Carter stated that "Let our position be absolutely clear: An attempt by any outside force to gain control of the Persian Gulf region will be regarded as an assault on the vital interests of the United States of America, and such an assault will be repelled by any means necessary, including military force". President Carter's message is contained in *Weekly Compilation of President Documents*, Vol. XVI, January 28, 1980, pp. 194-200. See also Cecil V. Crabb, Jr., *The Doctrines of American Foreign Policy*, Baton Rouge, LA: Louisiana State University Press, 1982, for an excellent discussion of US foreign policy doctrines.

141. *Reuters*, "China on the Defensive at ARF over Maritime Rows," Hanoi, Vietnam, July 24, 2010. See the Chinese Foreign Minister's response, "Foreign Minister Yang Jiechi Refutes Fallacies on the South China Sea Issue" at the Chinese Foreign Ministry Website, availabale from *www.mfa.gov.cn/eng/zxxx/t719460.htm*. Also see Andrew Jacobs, "China Warns US to Stay out of Islands Dispute," *The New York Times*, July 26, 2010; and Jay Solomon, "US Takes on Maritime Spats," *The Wall Street Journal*, July 24, 2010.

142. Liu Fengan ("Our Military's Busy Exercises in 2010, Large-scale and Joint Exercises Have Become Regular Practices"), (*Outlook Oriental Weekly*), December 13, 2010.

143. Li Jinming ("South China Sea Problem: The United States Moving from Neutrality to High-Profile Involvement"), (*World Knowledge*), Issue 24, 2010; Cheng hanping ("An Analysis of the Policy and Practice of US Open Involvement on South China Sea Disputes"), [W (*Southeast Asia Forum*), No. 2, 2010.

144. Xie Xiaojun ("What Is the US Intent in the South China Sea Affairs?") (*Current Affairs Analysis*), 2010.

145. Japan, Law on the Exclusive Economic Zone and the Continental Shelf (Law No. 74 of 1996), available from *www.un.org/Depts/los LEGISLATIONANDTREATIES/PDFFILES/JPN_1996_Law74.pdf.*

146. China, Law on the Exclusive Economic Zone and the Continental Shelf, June 26, 1998, available from *www.un.org/Depts/los/LEGISLATIONANDTREATIES/PDFFILES/chn_1998_eez_act.pdf.*

147. See the literature on China-Japan conflict over their efforts to explore fossil resources in the disputed area.

148. See the first UN-sponsored survey and report by KO Emery, Yoshikazu Hayashi, *et al.*, "Geological Structure and Some Water Characteristics of the East China Sea and the Yellow Sea," UNECAFE/CCOP *Technical Bulletin*, No. 2, 1969.

149. Victor Prescott and Clive Schofield, *The Maritime Political Boundaries of the World*, 2nd Ed., Boston, MA: M Nijhoff, 2005.

150. There is a vast literature on the Diaoyu/Senkaku dispute and the disputed maritime delimitation between China and Japan. China's recommended reading is by Zhong Yan ("On the Sovereign Ownership of Diaoyu Dao"), (*People's Daily*), October 18, 1996, available from *news.xinhuanet.com/ziliao/2004-03/26/content_1386025.htm.* Japan's official stand is provided by the Ministry of Foreign Affairs of Japan, "The Basic View on the Sovereignty over the Senkaku Islands," "Q & A on the Senkaku Islands," and "Recent Japan-China Relations (October 2010)," available from *www.mofa.go.jp/region/asia-paci/senkaku/senkaku.html.* The best US public document is the "Okinawa Reversion Treaty," Hearings before the Committee on Foreign Relations, United States Senate, 92 Cong., First Sess., October

27-29, 1971, Washington DC: US Government Printing Office, 1971.

151. The key US document is "Civil Administration Proclamation No. 27" about the geographical boundaries of the Ryukyu Islands by the United States Civil Administration of the Ryukyu Islands, Office of the Deputy Governor, APO 719, December 25, 1953.

152. US Department of State, "Briefing by Secretary Clinton, Japanese Foreign Minister Maehara," Honolulu, HI, October 27, 2010. Secretary of Defense Robert Gates and the Chairman of the Joint Chiefs of Staff Admiral Mike Mullen responding to Japanese NHK News interview questions made the remarks that the United States would support its ally Japan, and "we would fulfill our alliance responsibilities," quoted in Peter Lee, "High Stakes Gamble as Japan, China and the US Spar in the East and South China Seas," *The Asia-Pacific Journal*, 43-1-10, October 25, 2010. Secretary of Defense Robert Gates also echoed the Secretary of State by saying that the United States would honor its military obligation in such a clash.

153. Gao Jianjun ("China-Japan East China Sea Delimitation in the Context of the New International Law of the Sea"), (*Pacific Journal*), No. 8, 2005.

154. China first introduced its policy of "shelving disputes" on these islands in 1972 by the then Chinese Prime Minister Zhou En-lai during the negotiation for resumption of diplomatic relations between China and Japan. China's second take on this policy was by the then Vice Prime Minister Deng Xiaoping during his visit to Japan in 1978. See footnote 199 for the references.

155. Ministry of Foreign Affairs of Japan, "Press Conference by Minister for Foreign Affairs Seiji Maehara," October 15, 2010, available from *mofa.go.jp/announce/fm_press/2010/10/1015_01.html.*

156. Xu Chunliu ("China's Ocean Monitoring Command: Will Strengthen Control and Management on Disputed Maritime Territories"), (*New Capital Daily*), October 18, 2008, available from *military.people.com.cn/GB/8221/51755/141011/141012/8510843.html.*

157. Hai Tao (wm›m), ("Detail Account of China's Maritime Surveillance Vessels to Diaoyu Dao: Japan Attempted to 'Hit' Chinese Vessels"), (*International Herald*), December 12, 2008.

158. *Xinhuanet*, "Ministry of Foreign Affairs Spokesman: China Will Decide When to Send Monitoring Vessels to Diaoyu Dao," Press Conference, December 9, 2008, available from *news.xinhuanet.com/world/2008-12/10/content_1048425.htm*.

159. Qi Lu, "- ("China's Marine Surveillance Fleet Gets World Leading-Edge Vessels and Makes Regular Patrol in All China-Ruled Waters"), (*Ordinance*), February 27, 2009.

160. *China Daily*, "Fishery Patrol Vessel Sets out for East China Sea," November 16, 2010.

161. According to Chinese census 2006, Tibet had a population of 2.81 million. See *Chinese Tibet: Facts and Numbers*, 2008, available from *www.china.com.cn/aboutchina/zhuanti/08xzmx/2008-06/13/content_15782864.htm*. According to *China News Net* report, at year end of 2009, Xinjiang had a population of 21.59 million, information available from *www.chinanews.com/gn/news/2010/01-26/2093001.shtml*.

162. Available from *en.wikipedia.org/wiki/Infrastructure*.

163. Available from *en.wikipedia.org/wiki/Investment*.

164. Available from *en.wikipedia.org/wiki/Reforestation*.

165. Available from *en.wikipedia.org/wiki/Education*.

166. Zhang Chunxian ("Zhang Chunxian emphasizing: Development is the Key of All Keys to Xinjiang's Problems"), *China News Net*, May 25, 2010.

167. CNN.com/Asia, "Hu Calls for Reform in China's Uyghur Region," August 25, 2009; (The CCP Central Committee and the State Council Held the 5th Roundtable Discussion on Tibet in Beijing), Xinhua News Agency, January 22, 2010.

168. China's White Papers on Tibet are *Sixty Years Since Peaceful Liberation of Tibet* (2011), *Fifty Years of Democratic Reform in Tibet* (2009), *Protection and Development of Tibetan Culture* (2008), *Regional Ethnic Autonomy in Tibet* (2004), *Ecosystem Construction and Environmental Protection in Tibet* (2003), *Tibet's*

March Toward Modernization (2001), *Cultural Development in Tibet* (2000), *New Developments in Human Rights in the Tibetan Autonomous Region* (1998), and *Tibet—Its Ownership and Human Rights Situation* (1992). China's key claims on Tibet are from these documents. These white papers are available from *www.china.org.cn*.

169. See also Wangchuk Deden Shakabpa, *Tibet: a Political History*, New Haven, CT: Yale University Press, 1967; Chen Qingying and Gao Shufen (*A Complete History of Tibet*), Zhengzhou, China: (Central China Ancient Books Press), 2003, pp. 17-22.

170. Fei Xiaotong (*The Unity of Multi-Ethnic People of China*), Beijing, China: (Central Chinese Ethnics University Press), 1999, p. 28; Chen Qingying (*History of Tibet*), Beijing, China: (Five Continents Communications Press), 2002, Chap. 1.

171. Inscription source: Wang Yao ("An Analysis of the Tang-Tubo Peace Pledge"), (*History Studies*), No. 4, 1980.

172. Most Western scholars agree with this argument. See Melvin C. Goldstein, *A History of Modern Tibet, Volume I: 1913-1951*, Berkeley, CA: University of California Press, 1989; Melvin C. Goldstein, *The Snow Lion and the Dragon: China, Tibet, and the Dalai Lama*, Berkeley, CA: University of California Press, 1997; Anne-Marie Blondeau and Katia Buffetrille, ed., *Authenticating Tibet: Answers to China's 100 Questions*, Berkeley, CA: University of California Press, 2008; Walt van Praag, *The Status of Tibet: History, Rights, and Prospects in International Law*, Boulder, CO: Westview Press, 1987.

173. The most dramatic admission of the CCP's failure was offered by the CCP's Secretary General Hu Yaobang in the early 1980s. See Chen Weiren ("Hu Yaobang and Tibet—Reflection on My Old Publications at the 90th anniversary of Hu Yaobang's Birthday"), (*DW News*), May 11, 2008; ("Notes on Tibet Inspection"), (*Theory Trends*), No. 217, July 15, 1980; and ("Minutes from Workshop on Xizang [Tibet]"), (*Remembering Yaobang*), Zhang Liqun ed., Hong Kong: Lingtian Chubanshe, 1999. Hu was later ousted by Deng Xiaoping for being too liberal and too tolerant to the Chinese democratic movement. His death in April 1989 triggered the Tiananmen Square movement.

174. The Central Tibetan Administration of the Tibetan Government-in-Exile, information available from *ww.tibet.net.*

175. The PLA fought a decisive battle against the Tibetan military at Qamdo, a town bordering Eastern Tibet and China's Sichuan Province. Chinese leaders subsequently got the Tibetan regime to sign a 17-Point agreement with the Chinese central government, making a "peaceful liberation of Tibet" possible and committing Tibet to the rule of the PRC. When the Dalai Lama defected from Tibet in 1959, he denounced this agreement, arguing that he and his representatives were under pressure to accept the terms in 1951.

176. The Central Tibetan Administration of the Tibetan Government-in-Exile, "the Middle-Way Approach: A Framework for Resolving the Issue of Tibet," available from *tibet.net/en/print.php?id=115&articletype=.*

177. *Ibid.*

178. Ji Shuoming ("Inside Story about Deng Xiaoping's Tibet Policy: an Interview with the Dalai Lama's elder Brother"), (*Asia Week*), 2007. Chinese officials, however, deny the claim. See CCTV (China Central TV), ("Zhu Weiqun Answered Japanese Journalist Question"), November 10, 2008.

179. Address to the US Congressional Human Rights Caucus, September 21, 1987. See Appendix 5.

180. Address to the Members of the European Parliament, Strasbourg, France, June 15, 1988. See the full text at *www.dalailama.com/messages/tibet/strasbourg-proposal-1988.*

181. See the Tibetan Government-in-Exile website for a documented history of the Dalai Lama's representatives meeting with Chinese officials, available from *www.tibet.net* . See also remarks by the Dalai Lama's two special envoys, Lodi Gyari and Kelsang Gyalsten, at various places following their talks with the Chinese officials, especially the most recent one in January 2010. Lodi Gyaltsen Gyari, "The Way Forward on Tibet: The Status of Discussions between His Holiness the Dalai Lama and the Government of the People's Republic of China," Remarks by Lodi Gyaltsen Gyari, Special Envoy of HH the Dalai Lama at the Center

for Strategic and International Studies, Washington DC, March 5, 2010.

182. Lodi Gyaltsen Gyari, remarks at the press conference following the 9th round of dialogue with the Chinese government, February 2, 2010, available from *www.tibetonline.tv/videos/114/press-conference-of-hh-the-dalai-lama's-envoys*.

183. See the Dalai Lama's mentioning of Tibet as an independent nation prior to China's "liberation" in 1950 in Appendix 5.

184. Xiao Ming ("Zhu Weiqun: The 'Middle-Way Approach' in Essence Seeks Fragmentation of Our Motherland and Nations"), (*Chinese Tibet*), No. 1, 2009; Wang Qian ("The Central Leadership of CCP Issued Bottom Line Preparing for the Post-Dalai Lama Era"), (*Phoenix Weekly*), November 25, 2008; -(*China Tibet Information Center*), ("The Dalai Lama Must Change If He Really Wants to Improve Relations with the Central Leadership of the CCP, Remarks by Zhu Weiqun, the Executive Vice Minister of the CCP United Front Work Department to the German Magazine, *Focus*").

185. Department of State, "Report on Tibet Negotiations, March 2009-Feburary 2010". This report is required by the Tibetan Policy Act of 2002 (TPA), enacted as part of the Foreign Relations Authorization ofFY2003 (PL 107-228). See also Kerry Dumbaugh, *Tibet: Problems, Prospects, and US Policy,* Washington, DC: CRS Report for Congress, July 30, 2008.

186. See Li Ye and Wang Zhongchun, ("The Origins of the US Policy on Tibet and the 'Tibet Question'"), (*American Studies*), No. 2, 1999; Hu Yan ("US Policy on Tibet before the Peaceful Liberation of Tibet"), (*Journal of Tibet Nationalities Institute* [*Philosophy and Social Science Edition*]), March 2007; Hu Yan, ("How the United States Obstructed the Peaceful Liberation of Tibet"), (*Journal of Tibet Nationalities Institute* [*Philosophy and Social Science Edition*]), September 2007; Chen Jimin ("The US-China Diplomatic Struggle over the Tibet-Related Motions in the United Nations"), (*Diplomatic Affairs*), No. 2, 2010; Chen Zaojun and Dai Daokun ("US Historical and Current Involvement in the Tibet Problem"), (*Herald of Thought, Theory, and Education*), No. 7, 2010; Guo Yonghu and Li Ye, ("US Policy on Tibet in the 1970s

of the 20th Century"), (*Contemporary China History Studies*), Vol. 16, No. 4, 2009; Yin Xiangyu ("An Analysis of the Post-Cold War US Interference in China's Tibet Affairs"), Master's Thesis, Beijing College of Foreign Affairs, 2006.

187. John Prados, *Safe for Democracy: The Secret Wars of the CIA*, Chicago, IL: Ivan R. Dee, 2006; Kenneth J. Conboy, *The CIA's Secret War in Tibet*, Lawrence, KS: University Press of Kansas, 2002.

188. Guo Yonghu ("US Congress and the 'Tibet Problem' in Sino-American Relations, 1987-2007"), PhD Dissertation, 2007; Guo Yonghu and Li Ye, ("A New Analysis of the US Congress and the 'Tibet Problem' in the US-China Relations"), (*Journal of Tibet Nationalities Institute* [*Philosophy and Social Science Edition*]), January 2008; Wang Fang 1980-2004: ("A Historical Analysis of the US Congress and the Tibet Problem, 1980-2003"), (*International Observation*), No. 2, 2004; Li Li, ("An Analysis of the US Congress Initiation and Voting on the Tibet Problem in the Post-Cold War Era"), (*International Information*), No. 4, 2009.

189. See Chinese analyses.

190. The Central Tibetan Administration, "Note on the Memorandum on Genuine Autonomy for the Tibetan People". A note formally presented to the Chinese officials by the envoys of His Holiness, the Dalai Lama, on February 18, 2010, available from *tibet.net/en/print.php?id=121&articletype=press*.

191. Xiao Ming; Wang Qian ("The Central Leadership of CCP Issued Bottom Line Preparing for the Post-Dalai Lama Era"), (*Phoenix Weekly*), November 25, 2008.

192. Wang Lixiong, ("The Dalai Lama is the Key to the Tibet Question"), available from the author's website, *wlx.sowiki.net*. Wang argues that the Dalai Lama is the only one to settle the Tibet question: He is the only one who has been Tibet's political and religious combined leader, and there is no dispute on the Dalai Lama's legitimacy. The Dalai Lama's reincarnated successor will not have either qualification. For one, if the Dalai Lama passed away outside of China, he would definitely have his reincarnation abroad. The Chinese government, on the other hand, would

definitely find one inside China, thus setting up a fight between possibly two Dalai Lamas in the future.

193. The geographic center point of Asia is located about 25 kilometers (km) from Urumqi, the capital of Xinjiang.

194. Writing about the history of Xinjiang abound. William Mesny, *Mesny's Chinese Miscellany*, Vol. IV, Shanghai, China Gazette, 1905; Christian Tyler, *Wild West China: The Untold Story of a Frontier Land*, London, UK: John Murray, 2004; Frederick S. Starr, *Xinjiang: China's Muslim Borderland*, Armonk, NY: M. E. Sharpe Inc., 2004; James A. Millward, *Eurasian Crossroads: A History of Xinjiang*, London, UK: Hurst and Company, 2007; Colin Mackerras and Michael E. Clarke, ed., *China, Xinjiang and Central Asia: History, Transition and Cross-border Interaction into the 21st Century*, New York: Routledge, 2009.

195. See also Gardner Bovingdon, *The Uyghurs: Strangers in Their Own Land*, New York: Columbia University Press, 2010.

196. There is dispute, however, about the allegations. The United States held 22 Uyghurs in the Guantanamo Bay detainment camp in 2002. Yet 18 of them have since been classed as "No longer enemy combatants (NLECs)" and released in subsequent years. The remaining five are also likely to be released as NLECs as well. Wikipedia's documentation "Uyghur Detainees at Guantanamo Bay" has provided extensive references about the Uyghur detainees and the US treatment of them. See also Wikipedia's documentations of "East Turkestan Islamic Movement" and "East Turkestan Liberation Organization" for extensive references of these two organizations and their alleged connection to the Al Qaeda network.

197. F William Engdahl, "Washington Is Playing a Deeper Game with China," *Global Research*, July 11, 2009, available from *www.globalresearch.ca/index.php?context=va&aid=14327*.

198. Uyghur American Association, "President Bush Praises Rebiya Kadeer as a Human Rights Defender," June 5, 2007, available from *uyghuramerican.org/articles/948/1/President-Bush-praises-Rebiya-Kadeer-as-a-human-rights-defender/index.html*.

199. Engdahl.

200. Liu Weidong ('RkS"N), ("The US Factor in the 'East Turkestan' Problem"), (*Journal of Jiangnan Social University*), Vol. 9, No. 4, 2007; Liu Weidong ("US Non-Governmental Organizations' Interference on China's Xinjiang Problem"), (*International Data and Information*), No. 7, 2010.

201. There is a large literature in China about China's defensive strategic culture. Chinese analysts have stretched their arguments about the so-called Chinese peace-living nature so far that they are suggesting that the Chinese are different human beings. Many of those arguments, however, cannot stand rigorous scrutiny.

202. Organski, p. 371; Steve Chan, *China, the US, and the Power-Transition Theory*, New York: Routledge, 2008.

203. The highest-ranking Chinese official to openly advocate the continuation of this strategy is Chinese Premier Wen Jiabao. He made this call at a meeting with China's ambassadors (who were home to report their duties) in 2004. See Wu Jianmin, a career Chinese diplomatic, former Chinese Ambassador to France, head of the Chinese Foreign Affairs College, and now influential Chinese think-tank, ("Grasping the Theme of the Era and Continuing on the Road of Peaceful Development"), (*Foreign Affairs Review*), No. 84, October 2005.

204. Among the American China watchers, David Lampton probably takes the best note of this special character of the US-China relations. See David M. Lampton, *Same Bed, Different Dreams: Managing US-China Relations, 1989-2000*. Berkeley, CA: University of California Press, 2001.

205. Liu Mingfu. See also President Obama's remark that the United States must not be number two. "Remarks by the President in State of the Union Address," US Capitol, Washington, DC, January 27, 2010. John Mearsheimer calls himself an offensive realist in his book, *The Tragedy of Great Power Politics*, New York: Norton, 2001.

206. There have been many writings about the decline of the United States. However, the United States has shown its power of resilience time and again. There are, therefore, many other writings to warn the world, and China in particular, not to read too much into the

"US decline literature". See Charles Krauthammer, "The Unipolar Moment," *Foreign Affairs*, 1991; Wohlforth, "The Stability of a Unipolar World," *International Security*, Vol. 24, No. 1, Summer 1999; Charles Krauthammer, "An American Foreign Policy for a Unipolar World," Washington, DC: AEI Press, 2004, Robert J. Lieber, "Falling Upwards Declinism, the Box Set," available from *www.worldaffairsjournal.org*; Joseph S. Nye, Jr., "The Future of American Power: Dominance and Decline in Perspective," *Foreign Affairs*, November/December 2010. Nye makes the following observation, "Yet it is unlikely that the United States will decay like ancient Rome, or even that it will be surpassed by another state, including China". See Nye, "China's Rise Doesn't Mean War...," *Foreign Policy*, January/February 2011. For the US relative decline, see Huntington and Toynbee, who were strong advocates. They projected that the United States would be in decline by 2000. Paul Kennedy, *The Rise and Fall of Great Powers: Economic Change and Military Conflict from 1500 to 2000*, New York: Random House, 1988; David Calleo, *Beyond American Hegemony: The Future of the Western Alliance*, New York: Basic Books, 1987; Immanuel Wallerstein, *The Decline of American Power*, New York: New Press, 2007; Charles Kupchin, *The End of the American Era: US Foreign Policy and the Geopolitics of the Twenty-First Century*, New York: A. Knopf, 2002; David Leonhardt, "A Power That May Not Stay So Super," *New York Times*, October 12, 2008; John Gray, "A Shattering Moment in America's Fall from Power," *Guardian*, September 28, 2008; Fareed Zakaria, *The Post American World*, New York: WW Norton & Company, 2008; Fareed Zakaria, "Yes, America Is in Decline," *Time*, March 14, 2011.

207. See for example, Sun Dingli ("Global and Regional Hierarchies in Power Transition: China's Peaceful Rise"), (*Fudan Journal* [*Social Sciences*]), No. 5, 2009.

208. David Lai, "The Coming of Chinese Hawks," Newsletter Op-ed, Strategic Studies Institute, October 2010.

209. Dai Bingguo ("There Are Three Categories in China's Core Interests"), available from the Chinese Foreign Ministry Website, accessed on December 7, 2010.

210. The Preamble of the Constitution of the United States declares the following: "We the People of the United States, in Order to form a more perfect Union, establish Justice, insure domestic Tranquility, provide for the common defense, promote the general Welfare, and secure the Blessings of Liberty to ourselves and our Posterity, do ordain and establish this Constitution for the United States of America".

211. Henry Kissinger, "Avoiding a US-China Cold War," *The Washington Post*, January 14, 2011.

212. The White House, "US-China Joint Statement," January 19, 2011. The subsequent quotes are also from this statement.

213. Henry Kissinger, *On China*, New York: The Penguin Press, 2011.

214. There is a vast literature about these two "consensuses".

215. Yan Feng, ("Dai Bingguo: The United States Reaffirmed its Respect for China's Core Interests; It Had No Intention to Contain China"), Xinhua News Agency, May 10, 2011, Reporting from Washington, DC.

216. See the literature on East and Southeast Asian nations engaging China and the United States and holding a balance between the two big powers.

217. See Sun Xuefeng and Huang Yuxing ("The Rise of China and the Evolution of East Asia Regional Order"), (*Journal of Contemporary Asia Pacific Studies*), No. 1, 2011.

218. Strongly suggested by the Chinese Foreign Ministry note, (Foreign Minister Yang Jiechi Refutes Fallacies on the South China Sea Issue"), July 26, 2010.

219. Sun Hailin ("How to Remove the Time Bomb in China-Japan Relations"), (*China Entrepreneur*), No. 21, 2010.

220. See Wang Lixiong's writings on these problems.

221. See the Australian Government's Review of Australian China Human Rights Technical Cooperation Program.

222. See Pi Mingyong ("Focusing and Surpassing: Perspectives on the History of Military Reform in China"), (*South China Weekend*),

June 12, 2003; and David Lai, "Introduction," Roy Kamphausen, David Lai, and Andrew Scobell, eds., *The PLA at Home and Abroad: Assessing the Operational Capabilities of China's Military*, Carlisle, PA: Strategic Studies Institute, US Army War College, 2010.

223. Deng Xiaoping, "Speech at an Enlarged Meeting of the Military Commission of the Central Committee of the Communist Party of China, June 4, 1985," in *Selected Works of Deng Xiaoping*, Vol. III, Beijing, China: *The People's Daily Online* available from *english.peopledaily.com.cn/dengxp/contents3.html.*

224. See David Lai's discussion of China's embracement of this concept and strategy in the introduction to the studies in: *The PLA at Home and Abroad.*

225. Office of the Secretary of Defense, *Annual Report to Congress on the Military Power of the People's Republic of China*, 2009.

226. "China Aircraft Carrier Confirmed by General," *BBC News Asia-Pacific*, June 8, 2011.

227. See Strategic Studies Institute PLA conference series: *Other People's Wars: PLA Lessons from Foreign Conflicts* (2011), *The PLA at Home and Abroad: Assessing the Operational Capabilities of China's Military* (2010), *Beyond the Strait: PLA Missions Other Than Taiwan* (2009), *The "People" in the PLA: Recruitment, Training, and Education in China's Military* (2008), *Right-sizing the People's Liberation Army: Exploring the Contours of China's Military* (2007). All are available on line at *www.strategicstudiesinstitute.army.mil/.*

228. See David Lai, "Introduction," *The PLA at Home and Abroad*, for a discussion of China's revolution in military affairs (RMA) and the PLA's new mission in the new century.

229. Chinese PLA Senior Colonel Zhao Xiaozhuo's interview with *South China Weekend* correspondent in Liu Bin 0R ("US-China Military Relations: From 'Best Times' to 'Low-level Exchanges'"), November 18, 2009.

230. Secretary of Defense William H. Perry, "US Strategy: Engage China, Not Contain It," Remarks delivered to the Washington State China Relations Council, Seattle, Washington, October 30, 1995.

231. See Dianne E. Rennack, *China: Economic Sanctions*, Washington, DC: CRS Report for Congress, May 18, 2005.

232. See Shirley Kan, "US-China Military Contacts: Issues for Congress," Washington, DC: CRS Report for Congress, May 10, 2011, for a comprehensive discussion of the US positions.

233. There are numerous Chinese writings on this issue. The following are from a few of the better-written ones, unless otherwise referenced. ("Why Is It Difficult to Establish US-China Military Mutual Trust?") (*Foreign Affairs Review*), No. 2, 2010; Wang Baofu ("A Review of 30 Years US-China Military Relations and an Outlook for the Future"), (*International Issues Studies*), No. 1, 2009; Luo Yuan, ("US-China Military Relations Warm Up Again"), (*Outlook*), January 17, 2011.

234. See Chinese Senior Colonel Dai Xu's new book, "C" (*A "C" Shape Encirclement: China's Way Out of Its Internal and External Troubles*), Shanghai: Wenhui Chubanshe, 2010. See also Chinese Major General Luo Yuan's (Wnôc) echo to Dai's observations at ("PLA Major General Asserts that the United States Has Completed a 'Full Moon' Shape of Encirclement around China"), (*People's Net*, Military Affairs), July 18, 2010, available from *military.people.com.cn/GB/12174174.html.*

235. Xu Yongling ("China Showed Unprecedented Openness in US-China Military-to-Military Exchanges"), (*People's Net*, Military Affairs), available from *military.people.com.cn/GB/15160155.html.*

236. PLA National Defense University Center for the Study of CCP History and Construction, ("Why Must We Vehemently Reject the 'Nationalization of the PLA'?") *PLA Daily*, May 7, 2009.

237. Luo Yuan (Wnôc), ("The Four Major Obstacles in US-China Mil-to-Mil Exchanges"), (*International Herald*), December 15, 2009. See Kan, "US-China Military Contacts," for a comprehensive discussion of the restrictions and Congressional oversight on the US-China mil-to-mil exchanges.

238. "US Blocks Taiwan's F-16 Request Again," *Defense News*, June 27, 2011; and "Taiwan Expects US to Help with F-16 Upgrades," *Defense News*, March 29, 2011.

239. "What Is Egyptian Military's Role Going Forward?" Robert Siegel of *National Public Radio*, interview with former Army War College Commandant Major General Robert Scales, February 10, 2011.

240. Organski, p. 371.

241. Barry Buzan, "China in International Society: Is 'Peaceful Rise' Possible?" *The Chinese Journal of International Politics*, Vol. 3, 2010, pp. 5-36.

Appendix - 1

Selected Articles from the United Nations Convention on the Law of the Sea signed in 1982, came into effect in 1994

Article 19: Meaning of Innocent Passage

Passage is innocent so long as it is not prejudicial to the peace, good order or security of the coastal State. Such passage shall take place in conformity with this Convention and with other rules of international law.

Passage is innocent so long as it is not prejudicial to the peace, good order or security of the coastal State. Such passage shall take place in conformity with this Convention and with other rules of international law.

- any threat or use of force against the sovereignty, territorial integrity or political independence of the coastal State, or in any other manner in violation of the principles of international law embodied in the Charter of the United Nations;
- any exercise or practice with weapons of any kind;
- any act aimed at collecting information to the prejudice of the defence or security of the coastal State;
- any act of propaganda aimed at affecting the defence or security of the coastal State;

- the launching, landing, or taking on board of any aircraft;
- the launching, landing, or taking on board of any military device;
- the loading or unloading of any commodity, currency, or person contrary to the customs, fiscal, immigration or sanitary laws and regulations of the coastal State;
- any act of willful and serious pollution contrary to this Convention;
- any fishing activities;
- the carrying out of research or survey activities;
- any act aimed at interfering with any systems of communication or any other facilities or installations of the coastal State;
- any other activity not having a direct bearing on passage.

Part V: Exclusive Economic Zone

Article 55: Specific Legal Regime of the Exclusive Economic Zone

The exclusive economic zone is an area beyond and adjacent to the territorial sea, subject to the specific legal regime established in this Part, under which the rights and jurisdiction of the coastal State and the rights and freedoms of other States are governed by the relevant provisions of this Convention.

Article 56: Rights, Jurisdiction and Duties of the Coastal State in the Exclusive Economic Zone

In the exclusive economic zone, the coastal State has:

- sovereign rights for the purpose of exploring and exploiting, conserving and managing the natural resources, whether living or non-living, of the waters superjacent to the seabed and of the seabed and its subsoil, and with regard to other activities for the economic exploitation and exploration of the zone, such as the production of energy from the water, currents and winds;
- jurisdiction as provided for in the relevant provisions of this Convention with regard to:

- the establishment and use of artificial islands, installations and structures;
- marine scientific research;
- the protection and preservation of the marine environment;
- other rights and duties provided for in this Convention. In exercising its rights and performing its duties under this Convention in the exclusive economic zone, the coastal State shall have due regard to the rights and duties of other States and shall act in a manner compatible with the provisions of this Convention. The rights set out in this article with respect to the seabed and subsoil shall be exercised in accordance with Part VI.

Article 57: Breadth of the Exclusive Economic Zone

The exclusive economic zone shall not extend beyond 200 nautical miles from the baselines from which the breadth of the territorial sea is measured.

Article 58: Rights and Duties of Other States in the Exclusive Economic Zone

In the exclusive economic zone, all States, whether coastal or land-locked, enjoy, subject to the relevant provisions of this Convention, the freedoms referred to in article 87 of navigation and over flight and of the laying of submarine cables and pipelines, and other internationally lawful uses of the sea related to these freedoms, such as those associated with the operation of ships, aircraft and submarine cables and pipelines, and compatible with the other provisions of this Convention.

Articles 88 to 115 and other pertinent rules of international law apply to the exclusive economic zone insofar as they are not incompatible with this Part.

In exercising their rights and performing their duties under this Convention in the exclusive economic zone, States shall have due regard to the rights and duties of the coastal State and shall comply with the laws and regulations adopted by the coastal State in accordance with the provisions of this Convention and other rules of international law insofar as they are not incompatible with this Part.

Part VI: Continental Shelf

Article 76: Definition of the Continental Shelf

The continental shelf of a coastal State comprises the seabed and subsoil of the submarine areas that extend beyond its territorial sea throughout the natural prolongation of its land territory to the outer edge of the continental margin, or to a distance of 200 nautical miles from the baselines from which the breadth of the territorial sea is measured where the outer edge of the continental margin does not extend up to that distance.

The continental shelf of a coastal State shall not extend beyond the limits provided for in paragraphs 4 to 6.

The continental margin comprises the submerged prolongation of the land mass of the coastal State, and consists of the seabed and subsoil of the shelf, the slope and the rise. It does not include the deep ocean floor with its oceanic ridges or the subsoil thereof.

(a) For the purposes of this Convention, the coastal State shall establish the outer edge of the continental margin wherever the margin extends beyond 200 nautical miles from the baselines from which the breadth of the territorial sea is measured, by either:

- a line delineated in accordance with paragraph 7 by reference to the outermost fixed points at each of which the thickness of sedimentary rocks is at least 1 per cent of the shortest distance from such point to the foot of the continental slope; or
- a line delineated in accordance with paragraph 7 by reference to fixed points not more than 60 nautical miles from the foot of the continental slope.

(b) In the absence of evidence to the contrary, the foot of the continental slope shall be determined as the point of maximum change in the gradient at its base.

The fixed points comprising the line of the outer limits of the continental shelf on the seabed, drawn in accordance with paragraph 4 (a)(i) and (ii), either shall not exceed 350 nautical miles from the baselines from which the breadth of the territorial sea is measured or shall not exceed 100 nautical miles from the 2,500 meter isobath, which is a line connecting the depth of 2,500 meters.

Notwithstanding the provisions of paragraph 5, on submarine ridges, the outer limit of the continental shelf shall not exceed 350 nautical miles from the baselines from which the breadth of the territorial sea is measured. This paragraph does not apply to sub-marine elevations that are natural components of the continental margin, such as its plateaux, rises, caps, banks, and spurs.

The coastal State shall delineate the outer limits of its continental shelf, where that shelf extends beyond 200 nautical miles from the baselines from which the breadth of the territorial sea is measured, by straight lines not exceeding 60 nautical miles in length, connecting fixed points, defined by coordinates of latitude and longitude.

Information on the limits of the continental shelf beyond 200 nautical miles from the baselines from which the breadth of the territorial sea is measured shall be submitted by the coastal State to the Commission on the Limits of the Continental Shelf set up under Annex II on the basis of equitable geographical representation. The Commission shall make recommendations to coastal States on matters related to the establishment of the outer limits of their continental shelf. The limits of the shelf-established by a coastal State on the basis of these recommendations shall be final and binding.

The coastal State shall deposit with the Secretary-General of the United Nations charts and relevant information, including geodetic data, permanently describing the outer limits of its continental shelf. The Secretary-General shall give due publicity thereto.

The provisions of this article are without prejudice to the question of delimitation of the continental shelf between States with opposite or adjacent coasts.

Article 77: Rights of the Coastal State over the Continental Shelf

The coastal State exercises over the continental shelf sovereign rights for the purpose of exploring it and exploiting its natural resources.

The rights referred to in paragraph 1 are exclusive in the sense that if the coastal State does not explore the continental shelf or exploit its natural resources, no one may undertake these activities without the express consent of the coastal State.

The rights of the coastal State over the continental shelf do not depend on occupation, effective or notional, or on any express proclamation.

The natural resources referred to in this Part consist of the mineral and other non-living resources of the seabed and subsoil together with living organisms belonging to sedentary species, that is to say, organisms which, at the harvestable stage, either are immobile on or under the seabed or are unable to move except in constant physical contact with the seabed or the subsoil.

Article 78: Legal Status of the Superjacent Waters and Air Space and the Rights and Freedoms of Other States

The rights of the coastal State over the continental shelf do not affect the legal status of the superjacent waters or of the air space above those waters.

The exercise of the rights of the coastal State over the continental shelf must not infringe or result in any unjustifiable interference with navigation and other rights and freedoms of other States as provided for in this Convention.

Article 79: Submarine Cables and Pipelines on the Continental Shelf

All States are entitled to lay submarine cables and pipelines on the continental shelf, in accordance with the provisions of this article.

Subject to its right to take reasonable measures for the exploration of the continental shelf, the exploitation of its natural resources and the prevention, reduction and control of pollution from pipelines, the coastal State may not impede the laying or maintenance of such cables or pipelines.

The delineation of the course for the laying of such pipelines on the continental shelf is subject to the consent of the coastal State.

Nothing in this Part affects the right of the coastal State to establish conditions for cables or pipelines entering its territory or territorial sea, or its jurisdiction over cables and pipelines constructed or used in connection with the exploration of its continental shelf or exploitation of its resources or the operations of artificial islands, installations and structures under its jurisdiction.

When laying submarine cables or pipelines, States shall have due regard to cables or pipelines already in position. In particular, possibilities of repairing existing cables or pipelines shall not be prejudiced.

Article 80: Artificial Islands, Installations and Structures on the Continental Shelf

Article 60 applies *mutatis mutandis* to artificial islands, installations, and structures on the continental shelf.

Article 81: Drilling on the Continental Shelf

The coastal State shall have the exclusive right to authorize and regulate drilling on the continental shelf for all purposes.

Article 82: Payments and Contributions with Respect to the Exploitation of the Continental Shelf Beyond 200 Nautical Miles

The coastal State shall make payments or contributions in kind in respect of the exploitation of the non-living resources of the continental shelf beyond 200 nautical miles from the baselines from which the breadth of the territorial sea is measured.

The payments and contributions shall be made annually with respect to all production at a site after the first five years of production at that site. For the sixth year, the rate of payment or contribution shall be 1 percent of the value or volume of production at the site. The rate shall increase by 1 per cent for each subsequent year until the twelfth year and shall remain at 7 percent thereafter. Production does not include resources used in connection with exploitation.

A developing State which is a net importer of a mineral resource produced from its continental shelf is exempt from making such payments or contributions in respect of that mineral resource.

The payments or contributions shall be made through the Authority, which shall distribute them to States Parties to this Convention, on the basis of equitable sharing criteria, taking into account the interests and needs of developing States, particularly the least developed and the land-locked among them.

Article 83: Delimitation of the Continental Shelf Between States with Opposite or Adjacent Coasts

The delimitation of the continental shelf between States with opposite or adjacent coasts shall be effected by agreement on the basis of international law, as referred to in Article 38 of the Statute of the International Court of Justice, in order to achieve an equitable solution.

If no agreement can be reached within a reasonable period of time, the States concerned shall resort to the procedures provided for in Part XV.

Pending agreement as provided for in paragraph 1, the States concerned, in a spirit of understanding and cooperation, shall make every effort to enter into provisional arrangements of a practical nature and, during this transitional period, not to jeopardize or hamper the reaching of the final agreement. Such arrangements shall be without prejudice to the final delimitation.

Where there is an agreement in force between the States concerned, questions relating to the delimitation of the continental shelf shall be determined in accordance with the provisions of that agreement.

Part VII: High Seas

Section 1. General Provisions

Article 86: Application of the Provisions of this Part

The provisions of this Part apply to all parts of the sea that are not included in the exclusive economic zone, in the territorial sea or in the internal waters of a State, or in the archipelagic waters of an archipelagic State. This article does not entail any abridgement of the freedoms enjoyed by all States in the exclusive economic zone in accordance with article 58.

Article 87: Freedom of the High Seas

The high seas are open to all States, whether coastal or land-locked. Freedom of the high seas is exercised under the conditions laid down by this Convention and by other rules of international law. It comprises, *inter alia*, both for coastal and land-locked States:

- freedom of navigation;
- freedom of over flight;
- freedom to lay submarine cables and pipelines, subject to Part VI;
- freedom to construct artificial islands and other installations permitted under international law, subject to Part VI;
- freedom of fishing, subject to the conditions laid down in section 2;
- freedom of scientific research, subject to Parts VI and XIII.

These freedoms shall be exercised by all States with due regard for the interests of other States in their exercise of the freedom of the high seas, and also with due regard for the rights under this Convention with respect to activities in the Area.

Article 88: Reservation of the High Seas for Peaceful Purposes

The high seas shall be reserved for peaceful purposes.

Article 89: Invalidity of Claims of Sovereignty Over the High Seas

No State may validly purport to subject any part of the high seas to its sovereignty.

Article 90: Right of Navigation

Every State, whether coastal or land-locked, has the right to sail ships flying its flag on the high seas.

Article 301: Peaceful Uses of the Seas

In exercising their rights and performing their duties under this Convention, States Parties shall refrain from any threat or use of force against the territorial integrity or political independence of any State, or in any other manner inconsistent with the principles of international law embodied in the Charter of the United Nations.

Endnotes

1. The United Nations, Oceans and Law of the Sea, Division for Ocean Affairs and the Law of the Sea. Available at *http://www.un.org/Depts/los/index.htm.*

Appendix -2

Cairo Declaration

Conference of President Roosevelt, Generalissimo Chiang Kai-shek, and Prime Minister Churchill in North Africa.

President Roosevelt, Generalissimo Chiang Kai-shek and Prime Minister Churchill, together with their respective military and diplomatic advisers, have completed a conference in North Africa.

The following general statement was issued:

The several military missions have agreed upon future military operations against Japan. The Three Great Allies expressed their resolve to bring unrelenting pressure against their brutal enemies by sea, land, and air. This pressure is already rising.

The Three Great Allies are fighting this war to restrain and punish the aggression of Japan. They covet no gain for themselves and have no thought of territorial expansion. It is their purpose that Japan shall be stripped of all the islands in the Pacific which she has seized or occupied since the beginning of the First World War in 1914, and that all the territories Japan has stolen from the

Chinese, such as Manchuria, Formosa, and the Pescadores, shall be restored to the Republic of China. Japan will also be expelled from all other territories which she has taken by violence and greed. The aforesaid three great powers, mindful of the enslavement of the people of Korea, are determined that in due course Korea shall become free and independent.

With these objects in view that three Allies, in harmony with those of the United Nations at war with Japan, will continue to persevere in the serious and prolonged operations necessary to procure the unconditional surrender of Japan.

Endnotes

1. Released to the press by the White House on December 1, 1943. Source: The Department of State Bulletin, Vol. IX, No. 232, Washington DC, December 4, 1943.

Appendix -3

Potsdam Proclamation

Defining Terms for Japanese Surrender

We—the President of the United States, the President of the National Government of the Republic of China, and the Prime Minister of Great Britain, representing the hundreds of millions of our countrymen, have conferred and agree that Japan shall be given an opportunity to end this war.

The prodigious land, sea, and air forces of the United States, the British Empire and of China, many times reinforced by their armies and air fleets from the west, are poised to strike the final blows upon Japan. This military power is sustained and inspired by the determination of all the Allied Nations to prosecute the war against Japan until she ceases to resist.

The result of the futile and senseless German resistance to the might of the aroused free peoples of the world stands forth in awful clarity as an example to the people of Japan. The might that now converges on Japan is immeasurably greater than that which, when applied to the resisting Nazis, necessarily laid waste to the lands, the industry and the method of life of the whole German people. The full application of our military power, backed by our resolve, will mean the inevitable and complete destruction of the Japanese armed forces and just as inevitably the utter devastation of the Japanese homeland.

The time has come for Japan to decide whether she will continue to be controlled by those self-willed militaristic advisers whose unintelligent calculations have brought the Empire of Japan to the threshold of annihilation, or whether she will follow the path of reason.

Following are our terms. We will not deviate from them. There are no alternatives. We shall brook no delay.

There must be eliminated for all time the authority and influence of those who have deceived and misled the people of Japan into embarking on world conquest, for we insist that a new order of peace, security and justice will be impossible until irresponsible militarism is driven from the world.

Until such a new order is established and until there is convincing proof that Japan's war-making power is destroyed, points in Japanese territory to be designated by the Allies shall be occupied to secure the achievement of the basic objectives we are here setting forth.

The terms of the Cairo Declaration shall be carried out and Japanese sovereignty shall be limited to the islands of Honshu, Hokkaido, Kyushu, Shikoku and such minor islands as we determine.

The Japanese military forces, after being completely disarmed, shall be permitted to return to their homes with the opportunity to lead peaceful and productive lines.

We do not intend that the Japanese shall be enslaved as a race or destroyed as a nation, but stern justice shall be meted out to all war criminals, including those who have visited cruelties upon our prisoners. The Japanese Government shall remove all obstacles to the revival and strengthening of democratic tendencies among the Japanese people. Freedom of speech, of religion, and of thought, as well as respect for the fundamental human rights shall be established.

Japan shall be permitted to maintain such industries as will sustain her economy and permit the exaction of just reparations in kind, but not those which would enable her to re-arm for war. To this end, access to, as distinguished from control of, raw materials shall be permitted. Eventual Japanese participation in world trade relations shall be permitted.

The occupying forces of the Allies shall be withdrawn from Japan as soon as these objectives have been accomplished and these has been established in accordance with the freely expressed will of the Japanese people a peacefully inclined and responsible government.

We call upon the government of Japan to proclaim now the unconditional surrender of all Japanese armed forces, and to provide proper an adequate assurance of their good faith in such action. The alternative for Japan is prompt and utter destruction.

Endnotes

1. This proclamation, issued on July 26, 1945, by the heads of the governments of the United States, the United Kingdom, and China, was signed by the President of the United States and the Prime Minister of the United Kingdom at Potsdam and concurred with by the President of the National Government of China, who communicated with President Truman by dispatch. Source: The Department of State Bulletin, Vol. XIII, No. 318, Washington DC, July 29, 1945.

Appendix - 4

Treaty of Peace with Japan

Article 2

Japan, recognizing the independence of Korea, renounces all right, title and claim to Korea, including the islands of Quelpart, Port Hamilton, and Dagelet.

- Japan renounces all right, title and claim to Formosa and the Pescadores.
- Japan renounces all right, title and claim to the Kurile Islands, and to that portion of Sakhalin and the islands adjacent to it over which Japan acquired sovereignty as a consequence of the Treaty of Portsmouth of September 5, 1905.
- Japan renounces all right, title and claim in connection with the League of Nations Mandate System, and the accepts the action of the United Nations Security Council of 2 April 1947, extending the trusteeship system to the Pacific Islands formerly under mandate to Japan.
- Japan renounces all claims to any right or title to or interest in connection with any part of the Antarctic area, whether deriving from the activities of Japanese national or otherwise.

- Japan renounces all right, title and claim to the Spratly Islands and to the Paracel Islands.

Article 3

Japan will concur in any proposal of the United States to the United Nations to place under its trusteeship system, with the United States as the sole administering authority, Nansei Shoto south of 29 deg. North latitude (including the Ryukyu Islands and the Daito Islands), Nanpo Shoto south of Sofu Gan (including the Bonin Islands, Rosario Island and the Volcano Islands) and Parece Vela and Marcus Island. Pending the making of such a proposal and affirmative action thereon, the United States will have the right to exercise all and any powers of administration, legislation and jurisdiction over the territory and inhabitants of these islands, including their territorial waters.

Endnotes

1. Neither the Republic of China in Taiwan nor the People's Republic of China in mainland China were invited because of the Chinese Civil War and the controversy over which government was the legitimate representative of China. Fifty-one nations attended the conference, but 48 nations signed the treaty at San Francisco on September 8, 1951, the Soviet Union, Czechoslovakia, and Poland refused to do so. Source: United Nations Treaty Series 1952 (reg. no. 1832), Vol. 136, pp. 45-164.

Appendix - 5

Treaty of Peace between the Republic of China and Japan, signed at Taipei, 28 April 1952

Article 2

It is recognized that under Article 2 of the Treaty of Peace which Japan signed at the city of San Francisco on 8 September 1951 (hereinafter referred to as the San Francisco Treaty), Japan has renounced all right, title, and claim to Taiwan (Formosa) and Penghu (the Pescadores) as well as the Spratly Islands and the Paracel Islands.

Endnotes

1. United Nations Treaty Series 1952 (reg. no. 1858), Vol. 138, pp. 38-44.

Index